THIRD IN LINE

Written and Illustrated by
PETE MELBY

Third in Line

Print ISBN: 978-1-66783-518-1

eBook ISBN: 978-1-66783-519-8

Printed in the United States of America

DEDICATION

This story is dedicated to my family, Cindy, Hannah, Caroline, Brent, and Wren, whose love, example, and support helped me through its creation.

ACKNOWLEDGMENTS

The nurture of a southern mother, along with a lifelong interest in Mississippi and South Louisiana, enabled Third in Line to evolve. Southern mothers are family peace keepers, nourishment providers, and activity planners which empowered the father to focus on being a successful breadwinner. The result was the growth of a stable and upwardly mobile family. Penny Chatham, the story protagonist, has those same skills for her family, and for her country.

Experiencing the Deep South taught me how to enjoy new places different from where I grew up. In this land of cotton, where old friends are not forgotten, rivers are abundant, as are many creeks and bayous. I have swum in the Pearl River, waded in the Mississippi Sound, and jumped into Gulf of Mexico breakers on the Horn Island beachfront.

Huge natural lakes with brackish water are filled with speckled trout, redfish, mullet, and blue crabs. Pine savannahs have understory grasses and flowering forbs that are among the prettiest natural plant combinations. Longleaf pine forests abound, as do swamps of bald cypress and tupelo gum trees. Thanks to the Great Maker for the diversity of people and landscapes artfully crammed into such a small, luxuriant region.

My friends at LSU proved that all settings could have a sense of adventure. Whether it was sitting and visiting on our large, west facing porch, or trekking in swimsuits, or less, down Little Bayou Sara with the lead explorer carrying the flagpole with the stars and stripes. It was fun and adventurous. Thank you, John, Lake, Steve, Jakk, Carl, Joe, Norman, and Roberto.

I thank my family for being eager team members ready for new ventures. All three girls are able cast net throwers; my wife taught me how to throw one. Two of the three can back a trailer down a boat ramp and not miss the water. From the rivers and marshes, to softball fields, and to the performance stages in Bogalusa, Gulfport, New Orleans, Starkville, Kosciusko, Huntsville, Mobile, and the Ryman Auditorium in Nashville, you have been the adventure.

Thank you to Ann Bonner who edited this story. As an LSU graduate, I think she felt compelled to do it; for that I am grateful. The story has a wonderful Ann Bonner influence!

Thanks, as well, to Pauline Brunt, Cindy Melby, Caroline Melby, John Tomlinson, Clay Herring, and Don Hall for reviewing and making suggestions on this one- and one-half yearlong effort.

Those who provided fisheries and landscape knowledge, and who created opportunity in the region, were Tommy Munro, Franklin Kyle, Judy Steckler, Chuck Loftis, Scott Gordon, John Byrd, David Nagel, John Lopez, Tom Cathcart, Connie Rockco, Robin David, and Victor Mavar. Thank you all. I hope this story will please you and increase the health and enjoyment of these remarkable and yet fragile landscapes which are endearing to all of us.

Pete Melby

TABLE OF CONTENTS

Cat Boat on the Mississippi Sound

CHAPTER 1

The Mississippi Sound Expedition

Totally distracted from the daily challenges of her job, Penelope Chatham browsed through family pictures in a photo album on her enormous desk. To her creative mind lost in thought, the overly large size of the desk could actually have been part of the original raft that accommodated Tom and Huck on their Mississippi River adventures. While she knew those irreverent boys never really did all that Samuel Clemons wrote about, adventure was in her blood and her way of thinking was boundless like that of past political leaders that had sat at the time-honored walnut desk.

The lady politician from South Mississippi who now resided in Washington, D.C., had often been called a modern-day Tom Sawyer but with education, class, and connections. That comparison was okay with her; just like Tom she was a traveler. Experiencing aboriginal culture and untouched natural environments with her family was what she enjoyed the most!

The up-and-coming Representative from Mississippi's Third Congressional District was high spirited and bubbling with energy nearly all of the time. Her smile was endearing, and her shoulder length blonde hair, naturally blond of course, was often pulled back in a high pony, signaling she was deeply involved working with some issue. Mississippi's emerging political leader was the only lady among the state's four congressmen which included a lawyer, an accountant, and an educator. She was a teacher and graduate of Mississippi State University and LSU. Together with her good looks and inquisitiveness, Congresswoman Chatham could have easily won the most popular House member contest, if such a competition was ever held.

Musings of her husband and three children were interrupted by her cellphone, "Madam Speaker, it is fifteen minutes until the roll call vote on your Sustainability Bill. You will soon need to walk over to the House Chambers." She was anxious as anything could happen at the last minute.

Senator Long of Louisiana and Speaker Chatham had worked unceasingly to convince their colleagues to establish a national effort that would restore damaged coastal ecosystems. The legislation would also promote methods for conserving energy and reduce carbon emissions in housing.

All of the hard work creating the landmark bill for coastal marsh and estuary restoration, and carbon emission reduction should be an easy sell to congressional colleagues. It was legislation that was beneficial to the individual taxpayer and popular with outdoor enthusiasts. For home owners, becoming sustainable would put individuals in charge of a never-ending supply of free electricity and water.

"Ok, Jake, I'm about ready. Can you walk over with me?" Now, she wanted a friendly accomplice to walk over the House Chamber. Sharing the experiences of her position with her staff was important for their careers and helped build allegiance on her team.

"Of course, Madam Speaker. I'll meet you in the front office." Jake, a Coast Guard Fellow and one of her twenty-eight staff members had proven himself dependable in every challenge. Experiences in the military had molded him into a capable liaison between the Speaker and the many requests made by Third Congressional District constituents. His athletic build was concealed by his usual attire of heavily starched pants with stiff creases in the front and back. His long-sleeved dress shirts were uniformly white and blue, and had buttoned down collars. Rounding out his traditional look were shiny, Oxford shoes which were probably spit-shined, a technique he, no doubt, learned while a Coast Guard Cadet.

One last flip before closing the album, she paused at an outstanding family group shot in front of a Sitka Spruce tree in Washington State. The monster patriarch of the forest was thirty-feet across at its base and over 1000 years old. A feeling of awe while in the presence of one of nature's most remarkable trees came back every time she reflected on the picture. Memories such as this one got her through the days and weeks of meetings and wealthy constituents who occasionally felt they deserved special treatment.

As she checked her hair and makeup, her security detail provided by the Capitol Police was gathering in the hallway for the walk to the House Chamber. While making a funny smirk in the mirror, she slapped her hands together making a loud pop. Confidently, she spoke to the face staring back, "Ok, you dazzling, charming mother of three, and one of Mother Nature's best friends, let's get this show on the road!"

Breezing through her spacious office in the historic Longworth House Office Building, the energetic Penny Chatham greeted staff member Jake Ingram who was holding the door open for her. "Thank you, Sir," she said with a big smile and did a little hop going out the door and into the marbled floored hallway. As a mother of three children and one who bore the daily burden of political leadership, she always looked like she was enjoying what she was doing, and indeed she was. Changing her friendly and folksy ways to fit the formality of the prestigious position of Speaker of the House of Representatives was not going to happen. For one who was likened to the courageous style of gritty Tom Sawyer, she was not going to give up what it takes to gather friends and foe together and solve major problems that improve people's lives and productivity in the nation!

Leading her entourage of Capitol Police, the Speaker and staff member Ingram briskly walked, snaking back and forth through the Longworth House hallways, and rapidly moving toward the Chamber of the House of Representatives. Here in the center of the U.S. Capitol's south wing in a large, plush assembly room grass roots Americans had their say in how their country was managed.

The legislative chamber which held representatives of the country's people was the most symbolic place in America to hear and feel the heartbeat of the nation. To see law making going on in the chamber was awe-inspiring.

She and Jake animatedly chatted about pretty much nothing important as her entourage worked its way down the cavernous corridor. Nodding to her colleagues and smiling confidently to everyone that looked her way, the Speaker was proud of her fellow legislators and their staff members who worked together to create a great vision for the country that would benefit both people and the environment.

Penny Chatham had become a pretty-big deal on Capitol Hill. She had worked hard on behalf of Mississippi as a representative, and now, as Speaker of the House of Representatives, she championed larger issues that would make her state and country better socially, financially, and environmentally. House members elected her to the Speaker position because of her genteel ways of doing business, and their belief that she would lead justly and be generous to her colleagues.

As expected, the vote to support the Sustainability Bill was overwhelmingly in favor of the restoration of coastal edges and estuaries, and the conversion of the built environment to be in harmony with nature through reliance on its reoccurring natural cycles. People believing the prevailing view of scientists that planet earth was in trouble wanted their country to work with others to fix that situation. Recognition of the adverse impacts man's developments were having on the nation's coastal edges and offshore estuaries was apparent and frequently covered in evening newscasts. Voters had become unified nationwide in being a part of a movement to reduce carbon emissions and return coastal waters to their once healthy condition.

Once the bill was passed in the House, it would go to the Senate for final approval. With Mississippi's Senator Knox and his close alliance with Louisiana's Senator Long, it was only a matter of time before there would be a national emphasis on working toward the restoration of coastal estuaries and adopting sustainable ways to reduce mankind's impact on the environment.

Predictably, with the creative leadership of Penelope Chatham and her manner of networking with her peers to construct smart and useful legislation, her favorability ratings grew. She was doggedly committed on issues and had a great capacity and zeal for making meaningful accomplishments. Going into politics had been an easy choice for her. Either she was going to be able to sell others on changes that were good for the country such as using regenerative designs to create healthful and economically beneficial sustainable environments, or she was going to get out of the political business and return to teaching to promote her ideas. Once her peers understood the value to the nation of what she was seeking to achieve, they were convinced of its merits and confident it would be advantageous to their constituents and to the country.

However, the burden of creating positive changes and networking with senators and representatives was beginning to slow her energetic way of doing things. She was becoming exhausted and needed a breather. With the demands of being Speaker of the House and one of Mississippi's four Representatives, taking a break had to be in her future. She fantasized adding another picture of her exceptional family in a genuinely natural setting to the picture album on her Tom Sawyer's Raft-sized desk. Thinking of family and travel experiences with her kids and supportive husband was the stimulant that would sustain Speaker Chatham as she prepared to oversee implementation of the restoration of coastal waters and reduction of carbon emissions bill.

Walking back from the House Chamber, Penny Chatham had a faint grin on her face. Jake Ingram assumed she might be reflecting on the positive vote which would have a dramatic impact on enhancing life in the United States. He was proud to know this warm and public-spirited personality who was momentarily in her own world enjoying a moment of personal contemplation. While taking fast strides alongside this blooming political celebrity, he was respectful of her solitude and did not want to interrupt her moment of reflection on her latest accomplishment. He presumed she did not have much of the usual down-time like most people had, but that was understandable because she was also a mom with a family.

Penny broke the silence, "Jake, now that it is very probable the Senate will also approve the Sustainability Bill, a great burden will be on me and my office to lead its implementation. I need to get away from Washington and clear my mind before that time comes. I need to go home to Mississippi.

"I was elected to bring back the health of the Mississippi Sound, and of Lakes Pontchartrain and Borgne in Louisiana, and three years ago we did just that. It was an outstanding accomplishment by vocal citizens on both sides of the Honey Island Swamp. Even though it was a tough sell, through working closely with families and businesses in Louisiana and Mississippi, and learning exactly why seafood harvests along the coast were in a serious decline, we solved the problem! That experience was led by the Hand of God and we now know what will have to happen along our nation's other coastlines to effectively implement changes to our shorelines and estuaries."

Speaker of the House Penny Chatham from Mississippi had become the poster child for creating positive environmental changes that boosted productivity from land and water. Now that positive results were coming in from her three years of work, it was a good time to take a break from hectic Washington, D.C., and make an inspection trip back to her political roots. It would be beneficial to see those improvements that were going to be the model for estuaries up and down the east and west coasts, and in other areas along the nation's third coast, the Southern Gulf Coast.

Honey Island Swamp

CHAPTER 2

Battle Over the Pearl

The needed break from Washington work would be a return trip to the Pearl River Basin where both sides were in conflict with one another and ultimately each had won the battle. Penny Chatham envisioned her inspection of changes could be an adventure for her and her family. Important modifications to water quality and reestablishment of salt marshes had evolved since she and Senator Long had rolled up their sleeves and put on their rubber knee boots to enter into the battle between those entrenched on both sides of the swamp.

Because Jake Ingram had played such a big part in the water sharing project three years ago through keeping the settlers clearly informed and building a consensus among all the participants, he would be the logical one to be in charge of setting up the week-long travel itinerary. The locals knew him and his smooth-talking ways by name only. His Yankee accent and proper northeast manner of speaking were unforgettable and totally different from anything the Honey Island Swamp dwellers had ever experienced. That in itself, left a lasting impression. Just like Speaker Chatham was thought of as a celebrity, the name Jake Ingram was also thought of in a positive way and would be received with gratitude by the swamp rats because of the positive changes in the Louisiana and Mississippi estuaries in which he had played a part.

Traveling with her husband Jim and their family to the Louisiana and Mississippi Coast would be an opportunity to see and experience, up close, the successes in the region in which she had been intimately involved. Achievements in the three years since changes were made were so exceptional that they were being regularly featured on regional news programs. The Speaker had been hearing and reading about the increase in seafood production and the respect of participants from both sides of the Honey Island Swamp toward one another.

On a recent national evening news program, positive changes in the natural environment featured Louisiana and Mississippi families who had once sparred over plans to divert additional freshwater from the Pearl River into the Mississippi Sound, now coming together to support the restoration of oyster reefs that benefitted both states. The two sides also came together for a wedding between a Louisiana boy and a Mississippi girl who fell in love and got married on a Shrimp boat out among the once again productive oyster reefs in the Biloxi Marsh. Guests showed up in their shrimp boats, oyster dredges, and skiffs for the Bayou Wedding. News commentator, Lester Holt, quoted Mississippi Magazine, the popular Southern society periodical which featured the event, calling it the "Southern Wedding of the Decade."

In other coverage, writer Danny Brunt explained how major increases in oyster and shrimp production had evolved for two significant reasons. Seasonal Mississippi River flood water was now being diverted through the Atchafalaya River basin instead of through the delicately balanced brackish waters in the Mississippi Sound, and additional freshwater from the Pearl River helped to restore salinity cycles in the Mississippi Sound. The resulting brackish water cycles fluctuated between eight and thirteen parts salt per 1000 parts of freshwater. This ideal range of saltiness required by oysters discourages a pathogen called Dermo, or Perkinsus marinus, which moves in and kills oysters when water salinity falls below eight parts salt per 1000 parts freshwater. Similarly, the oyster drill, a carnivorous snail, can move into a reef when the salinity increases above fourteen parts salt per 1000 parts freshwater and consume all of its oysters.

Unnatural extreme swings in salinity had been caused by too much flood water in the spring and not enough fresh water from the Pearl River in the summer and fall. Without the right saltiness in the estuary's brackish water, the ecosystem lost its balance causing the loss of all of its wild oysters, and the decline of shrimp and blue crab harvests.

Once back at the Speaker's Office, Penny Chatham turned to the always prepared Mr. Jake Ingram and said, "Ok, Hot Shot, you are going to make the travel plans for our return to the Mississippi and Louisiana Gulf Coasts since you already know all the key players and they know you." In his recollection, he had never before been called Hot Shot. As a clean cut, Coast Guard Fellow on his way to moving up the ladder in the military, working for the Speaker was a calculated part of the climb. He took the comment personally, but in a positive way. Being recognized by someone as influential as the Speaker of the House of Representatives made him feel like he was a dependable staff member. If she felt that way, she could call him Hot Shot any time she wanted to and that would be fine with him.

"Make sure you make it a real adventure," she admonished, "I want it to be thrilling to me and my family, and especially for my children who will be a big part of the adventure. Rubbing elbows with grass roots Mississippi and Louisiana natives has to be part of it. You can do it Jake, I know you can, or at least I hope you can. If you can't, then you are fired!" She smiled at the distinguished coast guard fellow as she explained his employment fate.

"You've got it, Madam Speaker," Jake said with a slightly worried look on his face, along with a little bit of a shy smile. He got the point. All stops would be pulled out to complete this task successfully. He would put together an agenda that would meet and exceed her dreams! Jake Ingram was the right man to do this trip planning. He never provided anyone just what was asked for, instead, he always went beyond. That was his nature and would likely be part of why, one day, he would surpass his lofty military career dreams.

Coast Guard Officer Ingram also knew he had been asked in desperation to make her adventure plans. He fully understood Penny Chatham's level of exhaustion. It was similar to what happens to many hard-working people. She had had enough of her daily routine and needed a break. Call it a vacation, call it a sabbatical, or call it whatever you want. The need for people to take time off from work to restore their senses was even Biblical! This had to be a family experience of which even ornery old Samuel Clemons would be proud. Staffer Jake Ingram would go beyond expectations. With the shove from Speaker Chatham, the coast guard fellow was sure he could arrange a sequence of experiences that would rival any living soul's abilities to plan an adventure!

And he did. Jake Ingram planned an adventure trip of a lifetime that was full of diverse and authentic Gulf Coast activities and surprises. It even included a public presentation about the Sustainability Legislation to the Bay St. Louis Historical Society. That would surprise her. She would never be expecting to include a little work in her family vacation adventure!

Once the trip was arranged, he offered to take her step-by-step through the week-long itinerary he had planned. However, she said as long as it had the stuff of which memories were made, she would be fine with it. As he insisted on explaining all the details and stops, she put her finger to his lips and shushed him. "It will not be an adventure if you tell me all the details! I prefer you reveal the experiences on an as needed basis!"

"Ok, Speaker Chatham," he smiled. "As your trip planner, I am here at the very last minute before we get on the road to at least tell you what kind of outfits you will be needing to pack appropriately on this extraordinary getaway. Firstly, you will be getting dirty as well as rubbing elbows with nicely dressed townspeople. You will be venturing through historical urban conditions and through the marshes, forests, and swamps, and along the beaches of the Gulf of Mexico and Mississippi Sound. Your modes of transportation will be boat, kayak, rail and foot on this quest through Louisiana and Mississippi."

"Your journey through the richest part of the Deep South will begin as your plane lands at the Louis Armstrong Greater New Orleans Airport. You will be met by......no one. You will be traveling anonymously as the Chatham family from the northeast. Only your staff and security detail will know where you are, and when you are going on to the next experience. They will keep a low profile. After an afternoon and night in New Orleans, you will board the Gulf Coast Comet at the New Orleans Union Passenger train station and travel east, out of the city, along the edge of Lake Pontchartrain, through the Rigolets, and then along the border of the Honey Island Swamp and open waters of the Gulf of Mexico as you make your way to Bay St. Louis, Mississippi. That, Madam Speaker, is it. That is all I'm going to tell you at this time. The rest will be revealed as it happens."

He stared at the Speaker in case she had any questions, after all, she was the boss. Quietly, she stared back but with a startled look, like she was going somewhere but had no clue where she was being taken. After a few more uncomfortable seconds of silence, he concluded, "Ok, let the good times roll Madam Speaker. Your detail will pick you up at your home tomorrow morning at 7:30 am and I will meet you at Ronald Reagan National Airport. Because of the number in your party, Chief of Staff Craig Gill has arranged military transportation for all of us. I will assure you," he said as he looked her in the eyes with a devious smile, "your family and you will have an outstanding experience." He turned confidently with his shoulders pulled back and head held high, and departed the office.

Calling after him with watery eyes she shouted, "Thank you Mr. Ingram." Ecstatic about getting her travel adventure wish, she was looking forward to being gone from Washington, D.C., for one, whole, glorious week.

New Orleans – Land of Dreams

CHAPTER 3

Hot as Africa

Chief of Staff Craig Gill was the bottom-line regarding communication with the Speaker. With twenty-eight staff members and the myriad of projects constituents were seeking to have Representative Chatham help them with, telephone calls with her had to be strictly limited. The process for including the Speaker's support for a particular project that was beneficial to people and the environment was for citizens to initially communicate with a member of her staff who then shares the subject of the call with team members. The most appropriate projects were then evaluated with staff administrator Craig Gill and other senior staff members depending on the scope and size of the project needing attention at the federal government level. It was an effective way of getting large scale projects in the que for receiving support by government agencies.

In addition to being the central conduit to Speaker of the House Chatham, Craig Gill was always aware of any travel plans in which she would be a part. It was essential that he knew her whereabouts even though in this particular case she did not and that was because she elected to be purposely unaware of any details on her upcoming travel to the Mississippi and Louisiana Gulf Coasts. His knowledge of her travel plans was protocol.

If something happened to the president and vice president, the Speaker of the House of Representatives would succeed to the presidency of the United States. For safety's sake, travel for her trip to the Mississippi and Louisiana Coasts was made using military aircraft. Additionally, during the week-long trip a capitol police security detail would accompany Speaker Chatham and her family wherever they went. Travel by the Speaker was always afforded a high level of protection.

In accordance with trip plans made by Jake Ingram, the family adventure beginning in New Orleans would move by rail across lakes Pontchartrain, along the edge of the Gulf of Mexico and pass through the southernmost part of the Honey Island Swamp. Once they arrived at the seaside hamlet of Bay St. Louis, the Speaker would deliver a public presentation on the recently passed Sustainability

Bill. Since staff member Jake Ingram had been sternly admonished to include plenty of outstanding experiences, speaking to a large public gathering would be something that was not on Penny Chatham's radar. She would be very surprised, to say the least.

Traveling from Washington, D. C., to the Deep South and the region in which Penny Chatham was raised was always exciting to the Chatham family. Flying into New Orleans was a destination the children had never experienced so there was guarded enthusiasm about being in a city that had been around more than a hundred years before most cities in the United States were even founded. New Orleans was 120 years older than both Chicago, Illinois and Dallas, Texas! The earliest settled part of the city is called the Vieux Carre and boasts elaborate 240-year-old Spanish style masonry buildings with iron balconies forged by slaves, and quaint wooden French-style buildings 300 years old. The Vieux Carre, whose name in French means the Old Quarter was settled in 1718.

Emerging from the plane onto the scorching hot tarmac, the oldest daughter, Sarah who was in the seventh grade and already taller than her mother, wiped her brow and said, "Wow, this place is hot as Africa!" At ten in the morning, South Louisiana was already 92 degrees Fahrenheit and 94% humidity. The humidity made the air thick and hard to breath. It was as hot as Africa. The children had recently traveled to equatorial Tanzania, Africa with their mom.

Once the family disembarked from their military jet, they boarded an airport shuttle bus to take them to the French Quarter like most tourists would do. They did this so as to not attract attention, as well as to keep their travel experience surprising. This was another aspect of Jake Ingram's planning for authentic trip experiences. The kids enjoyed crowding into the packed bus and preferred to stand and hold the sway straps on the twenty minute ride to the Quarter. Three of the Speaker's security detail stood nearby, and others followed in nondescript Ford SUV's. The packed shuttle was transformed into a tour bus due to Jake Ingram's efforts. As they drove down Canal Street so passengers could enjoy the high-rise American section of the city, the driver gave a running narrative on the sights they were seeing and the significant historical events that had occurred along the way.

Following behind one of the St. Charles Avenue Streetcars rolling toward the Aquarium of the Americas and the Mississippi River, the shuttle turned east on a tree-lined boulevard called Rampart Street. It and Esplanade Boulevard were the northern and eastern edges of the old Vieux Carre. After a few blocks, the packed shuttle turned south on St. Ann Street into the heart of the Vieux Carre, dropping off passengers at different hotels. Narrow roadways in the Quarter were lined with one to three story buildings that abutted the sidewalks, or banquets as the French locals called them.

The driver announced the family's arrival at the Place d'Armes Hotel which was flying the French, Spanish, Louisiana, and American flags. He explained, "The site of this hotel was originally used for the first school in French Colonial Louisiana in 1725. Girls and boys were taught reading, writing, music, French, and Latin. Napoleon gave the Louisiana colony to Spain in 1762 and in 1788 most of the old wooden buildings were destroyed by fire. They were replaced by fine, masonry buildings built in a Spanish Style around enclosed courtyards."

"You will be experiencing this Spanish style of building at the Place d'Armes Hotel. The hotel's name literally means an assembly point for weapons and troops. It was taken from the original name of the parade field less than a block away that had been used for marching military troops and public gatherings. Formal gardens surrounded by a cast iron fence in that location now honor General Andrew Jackson who led a mixed group of Americans, Frenchmen and pirates to defeat an invasion by the British in 1814." Passengers on the bus were in awe of the diverse history of the place but were also impressed with how many years ago the area had been settled in the wilderness and thrived as a small town on the edge of a mighty river. The airport shuttle driver's history lesson had heightened expectations for those checking into the Place d'Armes.

He continued, "The Spanish style masonry buildings were built to be comfortable in Louisiana's hot-humid climate. Contributing to comfortable interior temperatures were the building's thick walls of brick and plaster, high ceilings, shuttered windows, and broad overhangs over windows that kept hot sun out of living spaces. Courtyards were enclosed by the main residences, servant's quarters, and high walls and were planted with tropical trees and vines and provided cool, damp, and secure places for outdoor living which in those days included washing and hanging out clothes. Many also had a small fountain that was dripping water for the sight and sound of its cooling effect. The pressurized water flowed from elevated cisterns that captured rainfall from the rooftops. "

"As the French Quarter became dilapidated in the 1920's, many of the fine old homes became tenement houses and quarters for roustabouts working on the busy Mississippi River port. Recognition of the character and historical significance of the old part of the city began in the 1950's as area artists made a concerted effort to stave off demolition of the French Quarter by painting street scenes and the character of its buildings and courtyards to draw attention to this attractive and yet neglected part of the city." The Chatham children who enjoyed painting and drawing, liked that local artists led the revival of the old city by producing and displaying their art!

Stopping in front of the Place d'Armes, the Speaker's entourage was excited finally to get off the cramped and steamy shuttle. Three smiling uniformed attendants were lined up to welcome them. The lead bellhop, a short and very slim black man greeted, "Well lookie-lookie here, Washington has come to town, and in a big way! Yessir, in a really big way!" Jake Ingram did not plan for that kind of recognition and salutation, and his face showed it.

"The City of New Orleans and Place d'Armes Hotel in the smack dab middle of the world-famous Vieux Carrie welcomes you and your family Mrs. Chatham, the Honorable Speaker of the House of Representatives for these blessed United States!"

After that salutation, staffer and Coast Guard Fellow Ingram, standing straight as an arrow with his shoulders drawn back, barked, "These humble travelers are hot and tired and would like to be shown to their rooms please."

"Of course, of course sir," now looking back at Penny Chatham and smiling broadly the lead bellhop said, "Madam Speaker let me just say we has a wonderful swimming pool that's just waiting for your sweaty and tired looking children to splash around in. It is surrounded by big ole tropical banana trees hanging heavy with fruit. For the grownups in the crowd, the world-famous Café du Monde coffee house is located only a short block away. They has just finished brewing up some of the finest café au lait in the world, just for you and your party!"

As they were led through the lobby without checking in, they entered into the 1800's courtyard brushing past several members of the security detail that came in the day before and were dressed like tourists. Their dark colored suits had been abandoned for more casual wear like you might see on mannequins in a J.C. Penny store window. Grinning and humming a happy tune all the way, the bell hops took the luggage to their various rooms. Jake, feeling bad about being so curt, tipped them generously, thanking them for their kindness and friendly welcome.

The lush tropical plantings in the patio were overwhelmingly beautiful, as were the inviting pool and a raised fountain nearby dripping water from an old cast iron urn. The entire courtyard was bordered either by the old home and servant's quarters, or with tall brick walls covered with cat's claw vines giving the area a protected and yet welcoming feeling. It was very exotic. The air felt cool, probably because of the sight and sound of the dripping fountain. Jake Ingram felt good about the authentic historical experience that his first night's accommodations were providing.

The Chatham family would be staying in a two-story brick servant's house from the 1820's with a slanted slate tile roof covering a narrow balcony extending across the front of the building. Jake Ingram and the security detail were in the downstairs rooms as well as elsewhere on the property.

Long ago the servant's quarters were inhabited by the family's cooks, housekeepers, and nannies. They had seen pictures of these quaint buildings with second story balconies but had never been in one. It was also the first time the kids had ever been in such a storybook courtyard with a dripping fountain and a swimming pool surrounded by lush tropical foliage including banana trees hanging heavy with spikes of little green bananas.

Jim, the father whom the children grew up calling Pop, and Penny Chatham were on one side of the two-story building, and the children were on the other side with adjoining balconies overlooking the tropical plants and courtyard. Having taught geography at LSU for twenty years, Jim was tall and had a healthy-looking build for a man in his 40's. His manner of dress was casual and neat. He was always clean and detailed looking, and yet he loved to shoot baskets and play Whiffle ball with his kids and wife. Involving the kids in sporting activities was a favorite pastime for college professor Jim Chatham.

For their first night in New Orleans, all of the family put on their swimsuits and headed to the pool. They did things together. Penny Chatham never asked her staff to look after her children. After a refreshing swim, where the kids expended pent-up energy from the flight and cramped shuttle ride, they all put on their best vacation outfits and struck out to explore the French Quarter.

Walking down St. Ann Street just outside of their hotel toward the Mississippi River, they window- shopped in the stores on the ground floors of early red brick apartment buildings that bordered the east and west side of Jackson Square. The elaborate looking buildings were embellished with cast iron posts holding up ornate iron balconies and are the oldest apartment buildings in the United States. A tarnished brass plaque on the corner of the building read:

"The Pontalba Apartments were built in the 1840's by Baroness Micaela Almonester Pontalba, a wealthy Creole aristocrat born in New Orleans."

Sister Leah asked, "Momma, what's a Creole?"

"Creoles in South Louisiana refers to people of French and Spanish ancestry. A very fine writer named Grace King, wrote about life in New Orleans and refers to the French and Spanish characters in her novels as Creoles." That explanation momentarily satisfied her most inquisitive child.

After visiting the shops on the ground floor of the Pontalba Apartments, the Chatham family strolled toward the Café du Monde coffee house on Decatur Street. Excitement was building in Andrew Reardon because the hotel bellhop said it was a "must-see attraction and don't miss it!" Seeing the crowd of hungry patrons from across Decatur Street, he announced, "That place is as busy as bees around a beehive. All those people crammed together reminds me of going to the lunchroom cafeteria at my school." The confident ten-year-old was beginning to speak out confidently on nearly any situation or subject.

Pop, who was a voracious reader, gave his sightseers a little background on the oldest and largest coffeeshop in the country they were about to experience. "Café du Monde, was established in 1852 and serves café au lait coffee and beignets which attracts both tourists and locals. On Sunday mornings, there would always be a large crowd of parishioners from St. Louis Cathedral enjoying their morning café au lait before and after church. "

As the largest coffee bar in the country, the sight of so many café au lait coffees being poured with the steamed milk into simple signature mugs was astounding. The family could also watch the beignets being rolled out and fried, and then smothered in powder sugar. Sarah Jane was so fascinated with watching fifty orders of steamed milk being poured into coffee mugs at one time her mother had to grab her shoulders and push her mesmerized self out onto the patio.

After merging into the crowd, the family found a table in the adjacent outdoor room. It was covered with a green tailored-looking canvas awning to protect its customers from the afternoon rains which in south Louisiana occur around 4:00 during the summer. Ceiling fans stirred the air to keep patrons cool and to shoo the flies away from the abundance of powdered sugar which seemed to be everywhere.

Tables were so jam packed together under the big green awning you had to smile and speak to your neighbors when you sat down. Smiling, Penny Chatham said to the older couple sitting next to an open adjacent table, "Do you think the five of us could squeeze into this table for four?"

"Why sure," replied the dapper looking man with light colored trousers and an open collared linen shirt. "Could you use an extra chair?" Sarah Jane, who looked like she was going to be the one without a chair said, "Thank you, Sir, it's always a little challenging for our family of five to fit into most restaurants which have plenty of tables for four and none for five." Both tables laughed and the Chathams from Washington, D.C. nestled around the table of four under the crowded canopy.

The Formica tabletops were sticky from all the powdered sugar that fell off the beignets somewhere between the serving platter and patrons' mouths. The Chatham family could not wait to add a little sprinkled sugar on their table as well. Their children were allowed to drink the café au lait coffee with chicory and steamed milk which was a special experience for them because coffee was usually reserved just for adults. Breathing in as he put a beignet to his lips, the overly confident Andrew Reardon accidently inhaled a large dose of powdered sugar. Immediately he coughed and exhaled the sweet powder all over the table and on his shirt and shorts. The surprised powdered sugar explosion also ended up on noses, chins, and on shirts and blouses of everyone around the table! The whole family laughed and laughed at his anything but timid mannerisms.

With the assistance of the energetic surge from the powdered sugar-coated beignets and the caffeine in the coffee, the Chathams next enjoyed walking through the tropical looking formal gardens in Jackson Square. Pop was in his element and was proud to provide more background of what they were experiencing. "A good friend of mine, a local landscape architect Luis Gueverra, told me the square was dedicated to Andrew Jackson who led the battle against the invasion of the British in 1814 to save the city. Jackson pulled together prisoners and pirates as well as Americans from up the Mississippi River to join well-heeled gentlemen from New Orleans to defeat the invading British in the Battle of New Orleans. This open area is now called Jackson Square, but it was first named the Place d'Armes and used for troop marching drills as well as an outdoor city forum for gatherings. In 1803 the square played a part in the signing of the Louisiana Purchase."

The family enjoyed the brief history of the square and mentioned the subtropical plantings looked like what was in the courtyard where they were staying. Pop, again interjected, "The tall, cast-iron fence erected in the 1850's that surrounded the formal gardens served a second purpose which enabled graphic artists to hang their artwork on the street side of the gardens, thereby creating a very large outdoor art gallery."

Seeing the art outside Jackson Square was what the Chatham kids really enjoyed. They were particularly attracted to one artist who painted wilderness scenes with muskrats, great blue herons, and alligators. Andrew Reardon and his younger sister, almost in unison and interrupting one another saying, "Momma, that is what we hope to see on the part of our vacation where we explore the swamps and marshes."

Andrew Reardon followed solo with, "Mom, I have dreamed about seeing these wild animals and it has just got to be part of our experience! Can you and Pop make that happen?"

"You bet, Big Guy and Sweet Princess, we will make that happen."

That clear affirmation calmed the two youngest Chathams and peace was restored, for a while. After enjoying the outdoor art and talking with the quirky artists, the family walked westward down Royal Street to look in the fine art galleries and antique shops. It took about forty-five minutes for the coffee and sugar high to wear off as the Chatham kids began to lag behind and express boredom from the repetition of objects in the antique shops. Sister Leah, the perky fourth grader told her mother, "If you've seen one crystal glass chandelier, you've seen them all."

Her fifth-grade brother aggressively agreed and proclaimed, "I'm ready to go swimming again with the banana trees!"

Sister Leah's real name was just Leah, but when she was born and thereafter, her brother had called her his sister and the "Sister" part of Sister Leah stuck. She was a doll. Her precocious attitude added a great deal to the young child that you just wanted to pick up and hug her and also because what she would say was so endearing. Sister Leah was gifted in many ways and that was probably because her family did so much together and her not-so-timid brother was always challenging her both athletically and mentally. Like her brother, she would often speak for her mother and father.

Upon hearing a long, deep drone from a nearby ship's horn on the Mississippi River, the family was drawn with others to walk up the levee to the River Walk, a park built on top of the river levee where you can sit and watch people and ocean liners. The French Quarter was built in the bend of the river and became a busy river-port in the early days of steamboat traffic.

At the River Walk, Jake Ingram joined Speaker Chatham and her husband on a bench watching the enormous ocean-going vessels carefully making sharp turns in the swiftly flowing river. They were relying on the aid of multiple, struggling tugboats who all seemed to be barely able to prevent their ocean liners from ramming into the river levees. Pop Chatham was also keeping an eye on their kids as they walked down broad wooden timber steps leading to the edge and even into the muddy Mississippi River.

Since it was toward the end of their New Orleans adventure, Jake came to explain what was planned for the next day. Speaker Chatham noticed he didn't have the usual button-down shirt, pressed pants, and shined Oxford dress shoes appearance like when they were riding on the airport shuttle. His manner of dress had changed from that of an east coast Washington urbanite, to a Gulf Coast ecotourist! Along with pressed Khaki shorts, he was wearing a short-sleeved open collared shirt with a pelican themed pattern. His socks had images of little blue crabs on them, and he wore a pair of leather open-toed sandals with white socks.

Penny Chatham complimented his regional outfit less the socks and sandal combination. He thanked her for her approval and replied he was trying to live up to his new "Hot Shot" nickname. Having grown up in a puritanical east coast family, he found dressing in thematic clothing featuring wildlife and marine creatures not a normal part of his life. Smiling at the Speaker's comment, he got down to the next day's expedition plans.

Competing for the big boss's attention from cruise ships, tugboats and swirling muddy river, Jake explained the next day's experiences while Pop was busy monitoring his kids at the bottom of the wooden steps on the river levee which were temporarily disappearing from waves from passing boats on the Mississippi River.

Trip planner Ingram explained, "For you Deep South travelers, I have plans to work in a little rest tomorrow when we travel to Bay St. Louis, Mississippi, by Amtrak Train. The Gulf Coast Comet will depart from the New Orleans Union Passenger Terminal eight blocks from here at 8:30 am. The tickets will be under Professor Chatham's name and you will need to be there thirty minutes or more before departure to pick them up. Try to get seats looking north from the windows for the best views of Lake Pontchartrain and the Honey Island Swamp. All of those aboard will be able to take part in a rolling hands-on class about the coastal ecosystems through which we will be traveling."

The Speaker looked bright eyed at her trip planner and smiled big. Jake Ingram returned the gesture with a wide grin as he could tell he had scored some points with the eco rail trip surprise. He continued, "Charles Delgado, an oyster specialist and water quality scientist, will be traveling with us along with his assistant Tasha Truxillo. They work with the Lake Pontchartrain Basin in New Orleans and are the scientists who are in charge of evaluating water conditions and monitoring seafood catches on Louisiana's Lake Pontchartrain and Lake Borgne. Now, they are also working with Mississippi's Department of Marine Resources monitoring water quality and seafood catches in Mississippi Sound waters. The Pearl River Keeper position you created depends on that scientific data to regulate the correct amount of freshwater released into the Mississippi Sound. The guest ecologists will share information on plant and aquatic ecosystems as well as the marine life in the marshes and brackish water bayous you will be seeing from the north side of the train."

Speaker Chatham looked pleased, in fact, she appeared carried away with her emotions. It was all about the trip and the wonder filled experiences that her family was having. It began in one of the country's oldest cities and was about to take her and her family of adventurers across a huge natural lake and along the edge of a freshwater swamp that faced the open waters of the Gulf of Mexico. Jake could see her eyes squinting behind her dark sun glasses as she turned and stared over the broad waters of the Mississippi River; the Father of Waters and one of the country's greatest treasures. Pulling a tissue from the pocket of her blouse, she said, "Thank you Jake, we will see you tomorrow at Union Station." As he got up to leave, she pulled her sunglasses away from her face and wiped a few tears from her eyes.

Oyster Drill in the Mississippi Sound

CHAPTER 4

Gulf Coast Comet

Looking forward to traveling along the Gulf of Mexico by train, the Chatham family and their capitol police security detail made it to the New Orleans train terminal with plenty of time to see the many platforms and tracks leading into New Orleans's center city from all over the country. Walking toward Train Platform Number nine where they would climb aboard the Gulf Coast Comet, the kids began to talk about Harry Potter and his train travel to Hogwarts School of Witchcraft and Wizardry that always departed from Platform Nine and Three Quarters. "This is just too coincidental," said Sister Leah! "We've got to check around for Harry Potter's platform."

Looking carefully around the nearby steel columns under the train shed, Andrew Reardon and Sister Leah were disappointed in not seeing the platform, but instead, were caught up in all the attention from their mom and Pop about a train called the City of New Orleans. The iconic passenger train was preparing to depart on an overnight trip to Chicago. The area was busy with attendants servicing the Pullman, passenger, and dining cars, preparing for departure. Penny was awe-struck seeing one of the best-known icons of passenger rail travel in the country. She asked Pop, "Do you remember Arlo Guthrie's song the City of New Orleans?"

He responded to his bride by looking into her blue eyes and softly singing, "Good morning, America, how are you? Say, you don't know me? I'm your native son, I'm the train they call the City of New Orleans, I'll be gone five hundred miles when the day is done."

Penny smiled and grabbed his arm, holding it tight. The pair got a couple of forgiving stares from their children who were used to the occasional bouts of public display of affection from their parents. It was not that big of a big deal to see them singing to one another and even giving each other a tight hug in public.

Once on the train, Jake met up with the family and asked Pop to pull everyone together for a brief orientation of the day's activities. Settling into big padded seats facing out the north side of the passenger car as it began pulling out of Union Station, the Chathams huddled close to Jake Ingram across the aisle as he shared details about the trip, "Charles Delgado, an oyster specialist and water quality scientist, will be traveling with us along with Tasha Truxillo. They are with the Lake Pontchartrain Basin Institute in New Orleans who are in charge of evaluating water conditions and monitoring seafood catches on Louisiana's Lake Pontchartrain and Lake Borgne. Both are really big natural lakes. We will soon be traveling on thirteen miles of elevated tracks across Lake Pontchartrain.

"Our guest ecologists are also working with Mississippi's Department of Marine Resources monitoring water quality and seafood catches in Mississippi Sound waters. Mississippians can thank Senator Long of Louisiana, and you, Speaker Chatham, for engaging the Lake Pontchartrain Basin Institute to include monthly coastal information on the Mississippi Sound estuary and the suitability for marine life along the Mississippi coast.

"Dr. Tasha Truxillo, a thirty-year-old PhD, is an expert on shellfish including blue crabs and oysters. Lake Pontchartrain has a large blue crab population and numerous processing facilities which send the product all over the Midwest and Deep South. Dr. Charles Delgado is a well-known ecologist. You will enjoy him. He is a low key, native New Orleanian whose family settled in the city in the 1840's. They will conduct activities with those aboard, including the young folks, about the ecosystems through which you will be traveling. Dr. Delgado will be in direct contact with the train engineer who at times, will slow down and even stop for them to collect water samples and maybe even throw a cast net from a levee or bridge to examine aquatic life along the route. Those experiences will depend on what conditions our ecological experts are noticing along the way." This was sounding very exciting for Penny and Pop Chatham. They couldn't wait for their kids to take part in the activities.

Departing from Union Station, the train swayed back and forth on the steel rails that creaked and screeched as it carefully moved through the American section of the city which was composed of high-rise buildings. Passing by Canal Street, one of the most notable urban boulevards in the country, they saw the long rows of forty-foot-tall Canary Island Date Palm Trees with their arching feather-like frons. Skyscraper buildings were located on its west side and two- and three-story masonry buildings lined the boulevard's east side. The east side buildings were part of the Old French Quarter whose history and culture began in 1716. As one of the oldest cities in the United States, the old Vieux Carre was cherished by city inhabitants whose decision, in the 1950's, was to preserve the origins of their 300-year-old city.

Traveling on tracks adjacent to the Mississippi River and along the edge of Faubourg Marigny, passengers saw ocean liners in the river and the small, tightly packed cottages which, two hundred years ago, were the first suburb beyond the old Vieux Carre. Jake explained, "You will notice that the oldest part of the city is mostly two-and three-story Spanish style masonry buildings with iron balconies, and Faubourg Marigny is its "suburbs." It is composed of predominately one and two-story wooden, Creole-style cottages. "

Riders were fascinated by the diverse character of the city passing by the broad windows of the Amtrack passenger cars. As they moved southeast, in the direction of Lake Pontchartrain and the Honey Island Swamp, they saw canals whose water level was fifteen feet higher than the residential development at the base of the levees. Half of the city was below sea level and depended on pumps to remove rainfall out into Lake Pontchartrain. The trip across the lake was overwhelming in that the passenger cars were sixteen feet above the water level and on a single track for thirteen miles!

Now slowing to a speed of 30 miles per hour, Dr.'s Delgado and Truxillo pulled together those who wanted to be part of the environmental study experience and they began to talk about the interrelationships between plants, animals, and water they were seeing outside of the passenger car windows.

Approaching the arched, single-track, bridge over the Rigolets Pass, Dr. Delgado explained the importance of the Pass to water quality in Lake Pontchartrain. "The Rigolets Trench is 40 – 100 feet deep and connects Lake Pontchartrain with the Gulf of Mexico. Through this Pass, salty water from the Gulf of Mexico moves into the Lake during high tide to mix with its fresh water from runoff and bayous. What we call brackish water is created with a salinity of 1-10%. Blue crabs enjoy brackish water with low salinities up to fifteen parts salt per 1000 parts of fresh water. Salty water from the trench mixed with the lake's freshwater creates ideal brackish water for blue crabs and nurtures a major industry for the sale of crab meat."

A small hand of a boy who appeared to be a third grader shot up, "Mr. Dr. Delgado, what is brackish water? Is it dirty water?"

"No, Son, the word comes from the Dutch word "brac," which means salty. We scientists use it to mean salty water, like from the Gulf of Mexico, that is mixed with fresh water and becomes just a little bit salty."

That answer seemed to please the boy who told Andrew Reardon standing next to him, "I guess we can speak Dutch now!" Andrew only smiled shyly at his new acquaintance.

Sister Leah, in her usual bold manner asked, "If you dragged a net in the water near the train tracks, would you be able to catch some blue crabs?"

"Absolutely, we would. In fact, let's give it a try." Dr. Delgado lifted his cell phone out of his front shirt pocket and called the train engineer, asking him to stop so they could throw a cast net. Slowly, the diesel engine came to a halt with brakes squeaking and cars gently bumping into one another. Tasha Truxillo pulled a cast net out of a canvas bag and moved to the north facing exit of the passenger car where she threw her net. The cast net hit the water in a perfect circle making a quiet splash. Gathered tightly behind the scientist, the group peered around her to see if anything would be alive the dark, brackish water. While pulling the net slowly back, the weights around its perimeter gathered together closing the net and trapping what was inside. Lifting it up and out of the water, Tasha emptied the net on the steel landing where they were standing and an impressive cache of marine creatures spilled out. There was a large variety of small fish and crabs no larger than a quarter, and there were three big blue crabs.

Dr. Delgado, interrupting the excitement inspired by nature's bounty, explained, "This is, no doubt, ideal brackish water for our blue crabs, and perfect, as well, for juvenile fishes and even shrimp. A healthy and productive estuary discourages predator fish species that cannot tolerate low salinity water. If y'all don't remember anything else, I want you to know that estuaries are the safe sanctuary and nursery providing fish, crabs and shrimp for coastal waters.

As Tasha returned the captive critters to the marsh pool, Dr. Delgado said, "Now let's look and see if we really have brackish water. We will put a drop of water from the marsh on our salt refractometer instrument, and then look through the scope to see what the reading is on the salt gauge." Dr. Delgado looked, and said nothing. He smiled and asked, "Speaker Penny Chatham would you take a look and announce to the group the salinity of the marsh water?"

Eagerly, with the unbridled quest of one of the children, Speaker Chatham moved close to the ecologist and looked through the lens of the refractometer. Squinting, with one eye closed, she slowly announced, "We have brackish water that is eight parts salt per 1000 parts freshwater." As she lowered the refractometer and looked around the room smiling, the group grinned back and clapped vigorously!

The sporty looking Dr. Tasha Truxillo shared, "When salinity levels rise above fourteen parts of salt per 1000 parts of freshwater for an extended time, oyster drills, which are carnivorous snails, will move into a reef and feed on the oysters. This is precisely the reason for the loss of all of the wild oysters in the Mississippi Sound."

Another hand shot up, "How does a snail feed on an oyster?"

Tasha explained, "They drill a hole in its shell and eat the oyster meat." Faces looked both sad for the oyster and disgusted about eating an oyster through a small hole in its shell.

Dr. Delgado added, "Before the wild and extreme fluctuations of freshwater flowing into the Mississippi Sound caused by the construction of river levees and channeling flood waters through the Bonnet Carre Spillway northeast of New Orleans, salinities regularly fluctuated between eight and fourteen parts salt per 1000 parts of freshwater. This range of brackish water created conditions oyster drill predators could not tolerate but were ideal for oysters to flourish. The Mississippi Sound Estuary became one of the most productive areas in the world for harvesting wild oysters."

Delgado had a strong New Orleans accent and was very self-assured in all of the descriptions and scientific statements he made. The short New Orleanian of Spanish descent was quite a storyteller, providing those enjoying the ecology lessons a continuous stream of interesting facts and illustrations, including disturbing impacts to wildlife and shellfish, courtesy of mankind. "To illustrate how salinity can change so quickly in our estuary's brackish water, I've asked the train engineer to take us down to where the Rigolets flows into the Gulf of Mexico. We are at a rising tide so water from the Gulf will be flowing into the Pass and on into Lake Pontchartrain." Once there, Tasha cast a small tube on a string into the water and brought it back up to test the water sample for its salinity level. The reading was twenty-three parts of salt per 1000 parts of freshwater.

Dr. Delgado asked, "All right my eager marine scientists, the question we now need answered is, do you think the higher salinity will make a difference in the marine life we might catch? Let's throw our net again and see if there is a difference."

Dr. Delgado threw the cast net with great precision as the onlookers watched the net land on the water in a perfect circle. Emptying the net of its marine life contents, Dr. Delgado identified a catch of fingerling speckled trout, redfish, and mullet along with an oyster drill snail with its pretty shell as part of the catch. The oyster drill and the more mature fish were able to tolerate the saltier water. Penny Chatham reached out and asked to hold the oyster predator in her hand. It had a pretty shell but a terrible impact on oysters. It was almost unbelievable that such a ravenous creature in a shell small enough to easily fit into the palm of your hand could devastate the oyster population in a reef!

As Jake Ingram expected, the novel eco-trip was turning out to be an exceptional experience. The children on the train were thoroughly engrossed with hands-on learning about native plants like the pond cypress trees and emergent salt marsh grasses. They saw animals like the blue herons and schools of mullet jumping and swirling all along the way. It was enjoyable learning about how the quality of the water played such a big part in the health and productivity of the estuaries and freshwater swamp landscapes. Penny Chatham was like a child on a nature field trip. Hearing from local ecologists and seeing examples of untouched natural landscapes was thrilling.

As the Gulf Coast Comet progressed through the picturesque south Louisiana and Mississippi marshes and swamps, passengers enjoyed panoramic views to the Gulf of Mexico from the south side of the train, and the Honey Island swamp from the north windows. Broad expanses of salt marshes merged into placid pools of open brackish water beyond the edge of the riverine swamp. Sarah Jane, the inquisitive oldest sibling commented to her mother, "The views from the train are like being in an IMAX 3D movie complete with the sights and sounds of surprised flocks of gulls being flushed upward from their remote nesting places and by the squeaks and groans of the slow-moving train." Penny Chatham, after her hands-on learning experience with the devastating oyster drills that brought down an entire seafood industry, was now settled into a relaxed mode.

There was so much to learn about the interdependence of plants and animals on one another and their physical environments. She realized people in America could not fully support environmental issues unless they had hands-on experiences with nature that would convince them of how God and Mother Nature meant for the landscapes to be and how they were so reliant on one another. It was useful to read about an ecological subject, but to touch the plants and animals and know first-hand why high salinity levels caused the decline of oysters in the Mississippi Sound was convincing beyond a doubt.

Easing upward through the ecologically diverse Pearl River Wetland Basin, the eco tour moved from swamps densely packed with tupelo gum and bald cypress trees to higher and dryer land thick with tall longleaf and slash pine trees planted in rows. At one time, trees in the longleaf and slash pine plantations were tapped to collect sap for making turpentine. In this still and monotonous culture of tree plantations, the landscape became still with no animal sightings or sounds.

The transition from natural salt marshes and swamps to the monoculture of the pine plantation forests announced to the train full of ecology enthusiasts that change was occurring and that created a sense of anticipation. As the tourists slithered through the towering coastal plain pine tree farms and into Bay St. Louis, Mississippi, they eased into the deep, quiet shade of a maritime forest of evergreen live oak trees. The change in landscapes from the swamp to pine forests and finally into a gulf coast maritime forest was dramatic. The town of Bay St. Louis's historic tree cover is the predominant image and pride of the community. The family was to be immersed for two days in small town experiences in this coastal treasure. The magnificent and revered oaks, some 300 and 400 years old, provided a setting with a strong sense of enclosure and security for the 320-year-old seaside village.

Jake Ingram shared with the Chatham family as they gathered to disembark the train, "This historic French settlement which became Bay St. Louis was founded in 1699 by French colonists Pierre Le Moyne d'Iberville and Jean-Baptiste Le Moyne de Bienville. New Orleans was founded eighteen years later on the banks of the Mississippi River by Pierre Le Moyne d'Iberville. The soil you will be stepping on in just a few minutes has been part of the stomping grounds for French and Spanish explorers and an occasional Gulf Coast pirate for over 300 years!" While the family appeared impressed, Sister Leah and Andrew Reardon looked awe struck. In their minds, they were imagining going to a place that existed further back in time than anyplace they had ever been!

Before departing the train, Jake shared the next leg of experiences to his boss, "Part of your first day in Bay St. Louis, you will be making a forty-five-minute presentation on the practical applications of your Sustainability Bill to the Historical Society at an auditorium adjacent to the Bay St. Louis Train Station." The volume and confidence level in Jake's voice dropped at the inclusion of the speaking engagement. He was not so sure how the Speaker would react to having to give a public speech right after two full days of adventure with her family. However, she smiled and appeared ok with integrating a little work with the sensational touring experiences that had been arranged for her benefit.

Bay St. Louis Live Oak Tree

CHAPTER 5

Mother Nature a Benevolent Overseer

As the Gulf Coast Comet pulled into the Bay St. Louis Train Station, Jake Ingram said to the Speaker, "You will like the Bay St. Louis Historical Society folks. They are the movers and shakers of the western side of Mississippi's coast and for all of Hancock County which includes the 13,800-acre Stennis Space Center where they test the rocket motors for the space shuttles. The locals are really looking forward to your talk on conversion of their homes and businesses to be sustainable so they can save money on their utility bills. The national reaction on the bill is that people are interested in becoming reliant on Mother Nature's natural cycles, but they want to know just what do they have to do to make all of that happen."

Switching subjects he continued, "I have also set up a photo opportunity with Dr. Hamilton Byrd who is finishing a book on Jean Laffite, the Gulf Coast pirate who had a fine beachfront home in Bay St. Louis and hid his contraband there. Your image is a little too squeaky-clean, Madam Speaker," he said as he fidgeted and shifted the weight from one foot to another, "In order to have a broader appeal to others besides coastal Louisiana and Mississippi people, I think Penny Chatham needs a little grit to go along with her shiny public image. Showing interest in a renowned Gulf Coast Pirate might be what you need to create some enticing press."

Jake realized what he had just said and his face turned red. He was really pushing it with the Speaker but knew she needed to broaden her public appeal if she were going to be considered for a higher office one day. She was surprised by his boldness and wondered if her seemingly no-nonsense conservative staffer from the northeast had been to the train's club car to sample their Margaritas, or worse yet, their new drink called the Blazing Comet which has as profound an impact on the drinker as the Hurricanes served at Pat O'Brian's on St. Peter Street in the French Quarter. After letting him squirm a bit, she responded, "Ok," and simply smiled at his boldness but did not comment on his evaluation of her image. Nevertheless, he had struck a nerve with her; maybe she did need to rub shoulders with a few rowdy characters to go along with her honest, all-American girl image, especially if she was considering running for a higher office one day.

The reaction of her kids was immediate and in support of Jake Ingram's need of more grit for their mother comment. They also clamored to be in the photo with the professor who was a pirate expert and was even writing a book about the notorious Jean Laffite. "Ok, my educated and darling squeaky-clean sophisticates, yes, you can be in the picture with the man who is intimately familiar with the pirate that plundered and sank Spanish ships all along the Mississippi and Louisiana Gulf Coasts."

Six-year-old Sister Leah asked, "Momma, is that phrase Andrew Reardon likes to use ok to ask Dr. Professor Byrd?"

"Do you mean the saying 'it takes one to know one' we've been hearing lately? I don't think your brother would have any problem with that. You may borrow it just this once," replied her mother. "When we meet the famous Dr. Hamilton Byrd, you can ask him if there is some truth in the saying as it applies to him and the pirate Jean Lafitte. Make sure the reporter and photographer hear you ask him that question, and then be sure to smile broadly. That could make a really good photograph and might help the good Mr. Dr. Byrd sell some books. Besides that, he will think you are really something else, Girl!"

Everyone laughed, including the trip planner who had regained his composure and said, "Yes, Sister Leah, I will make sure the reporter that is covering your mother's talk hears your question to the eminent writer about our local Gulf Coast pirate."

She replied like a grown up but with her own spin, "Thank you, congressional staffer J. Ingram. By the way, you really know how to plan a super trip." He smiled at Sister Leah but said nothing further. Time for visiting was short and he knew this conversation could go on for a while.

As they pulled into the Bay St. Louis Train Depot, there were three local police cars with officers standing outside their vehicles pulled up very close to the passenger arrival platform. As Speaker Chatham stepped down the heavy steel grate steps from the huge silvery-gray passenger train, she took the hand of Brent head of her capitol police detail, instead of the waiting porter. The local police snapped to attention and saluted. This was too much for Penny Chatham who waved and said, "Thanks for coming! My family and I are glad to be here." The officers stood at attention beside their black and white marked Bay St. Louis police sedans until the plain clothes capitol police walked the Speaker and her family the short distance to the auditorium where she was to speak.

Since there was such broad support on the sustainability bill, there would be plenty of opportunities for telling the story of why living sustainably will be good for the country and for individuals as well. This would be her first opportunity for sharing specifically what the bill would do now that it had been passed by the Senate and was law. Of course, the gathering at the auditorium was interested in learning about the benefits of becoming sustainable, but they were also interested in seeing Speaker of the House of Representatives Penny Chatham who was becoming a well-known political celebrity.

To the dedicated members of the Historical Society, and to those who came to see and hear a nationally recognized personality from their home state, the Speaker jumped right into the heart of the Sustainability Bill. She confidently and yet endearingly implored, "Walk with me Mississippi as we begin to recognize, and be thankful for what is available daily from the natural world we call planet earth."

Pausing, as she looked over the dead silent audience, and then with the confidence of an Indian Chief talking to the tribal council, she began, "We must learn to live in harmony with the earth's natural systems that provide water for drinking, bathing, cooking, and irrigating, and sunlight and fertile fields for the production of our food. Sunlight gives us warmth in the wintertime and can heat water for use in our homes and businesses. You probably do not know this, but one-third of the yearly cost of your residential power bill is for heating water! Solar hot water panels that face south can heat nearly all of the hot water you need."

"Senator Long of Louisiana, along with our own Senator Knox and I have created environmental legislation that would restore damaged coastal ecosystems and create a movement to integrate sustainable technologies in housing and other buildings to reduce carbon emissions and diminish global warming." Senators John Long and Micah Knox were respected legislators in the U.S. Senate and each was regularly interviewed about environmental issues on the national evening news.

"Your Sustainability Bill, which is now law, will build back lost salt marshes and restore those that are degraded. Water quality in coastal estuaries will be restored to its original, highly productive condition. Those changes will result in a dramatic increase in marine life and that will create a revival of struggling seafood industries. The coastal waters part of the bill is going to be modeled after a successful project led by Senator Long and me in the Mississippi Sound three years ago. From working with local Louisiana and Mississippi fishermen and seafood processors, we began to understand the problems our nation's coastal waters are facing and we know what it will take to restore healthy saltmarsh and estuarine water conditions.

"At your local home and neighborhood level," the Speaker of the House paused to let that sink in as she stared across the podium and pointed her finger for emphasis at those in the auditorium, "we will thoroughly explain how to implement energy efficient building techniques that will reduce your home and business utility bills. You might not believe it, but this is true. The combination of making your building more energy efficient and equipping it with regenerative technologies will decrease personal home utility bills by 70 -100%!" There was clapping and a few amens shouted from the audience.

Penny Chatham peered over the top of the podium like a teacher emphasizing what the student would need to review for the upcoming exam. "That remarkable feat is going to take the pressure off of rebuilding out-of-date electric grids, crumbling potable water systems, and aging sewer lines. Instead, federal government incentives will help you install the regenerative technologies at your home and businesses. We are serious about reducing the impact to our environment and your congressional delegates decided it would be best to provide changes at the home level rather than provide cities and towns with the money to rebuild aging city utility systems."

A roar of applause and shouts of support erupted. This was popular and made sense to those in the audience. They liked the idea of being in charge of making their own electricity and collecting their own water. They weren't so sure about treating their own sewage, but since making the sustainable changes were optional, they would wait and see how the biologically based sewage treatment gardens would work.

Continuing, she said, "Considering the larger and more critical picture of our damaged environment, those local improvements you can make will slash the production of carbon emissions and reduce the hazards of global warming. Humankind, that's you and me, baby," she said scanning the audience with a wide grin, "has evolved to the point where the health of our environment is being damaged by our ignorance on how to live in harmony with the limitations of planet earth.

"Simply, people in this beautiful world of ours are ignoring the impact of additional carbon dioxide that is rising into the atmosphere and keeping heat from the earth from radiating into space like it used to do. Earth's atmosphere is delicately balanced and additional carbon dioxide is making the planet warmer.

"Before the industrial revolution in 1880, the naturally occurring gases in our atmosphere were balanced. Now, because of worldwide reliance on electricity and transportation, too much carbon dioxide from burning ancient reserves of fossil fuels along with other gases is rising into the atmosphere surrounding planet earth. The greenhouse gases which are carbon dioxide, methane, and nitrous oxide, are holding on to heat from the earth that used to be radiated into space, with the result being that the earth is getting hotter.

"Just like Atlanta and Los Angeles require additional electrical energy made from fossil fuels for cooling because they have so many concrete and masonry structures, those of us in Bogalusa, Pascagoula, Pearlington, and even Itta Bena, Mississippi, using coal, oil, and natural gas are also producing carbon dioxide from burning fossil fuels. The heat naturally emitted from the earth used to be dissipated into outer space, but now the buildup of carbon dioxide and other gases in the atmosphere holds onto that heat with the result of warmer and changing climates.

All around the world, people are affecting the climate with this enormous increase in heat being detained in the atmosphere! We are at seven billion people in the world now and that will increase to thirteen billion by 2050. It is not something that's coming y'all, we are there. We are at a disaster level and we need to get a handle on our problem!" Again, there was enthusiastic applause because of the truth in what the Speaker was saying, but also because of the powerful way she was explaining the crises.

Speaking in a more reserved tone she said, "Now, I'm going to get personal with you. One result of having too much carbon dioxide and other gases holding onto heat in the atmosphere is the increase in storms. The people in this auditorium, more than most in this magnificent country of ours, have experienced the worst of what global warming can bring to our culture. I'm sorry you and your family members in South Mississippi and Louisiana had to experience Hurricane Katrina." Penny Chatham slowed the pace and tenor of her talk and slowly declared, "The storm was the most destructive natural disaster ever in the United States!"

The auditorium was dead silent as she continued, "It occurred because of global warming; too much carbon dioxide from burning fossil fuels that rises up into the atmosphere and holds onto heat that used to be emitted into space. You people, more than most, realize there is an immediate need to change our ways and keep our planet clean and healthy. Rely on the abundant sunshine, water and other resources provided by our natural world. We have got to change our ways."

Winding down her talk, the Speaker reiterated, "Federal incentives are now provided to educate and help you install the regenerative technologies. While our government calls these incentives, I like to think of them as enticements that will give you the opportunity to experience the success of using regenerative technologies. Financial and professional help will be on the table. It is up to you to consider and to take advantage."

"Regenerative technologies will provide you light, heating, cooling, water to drink, food, and electricity, and it treat your waste. These technologies are based on reoccurring phenomena provided by nature that will enable existing and new homes and businesses to become more comfortable throughout daily and seasonal fluctuations of temperatures. The shape of your building and the direction it faces makes a major difference in maintaining comfortable conditions inside your home. Residences and businesses can produce all of the electricity they need through the use of solar panels that make electricity from sunshine. In some cases, like along our coastline, small wind turbines can also produce power. Rainwater can be harvested, treated, and stored for on-site use. Sewage waste can be treated by the combination of sunshine, plants and microbes. Plantings that assist in treating sewage can be arranged to be attractive garden features. For those of us who have sunny areas around our homes and businesses, a large amount of the food we need can be grown in raised bed gardens!"

There was another applause. The audience liked the idea of becoming sustainable and having regenerative technologies to replace or at least reduce their city utility bills. It all sounded logical and desirable! As the clapping continued, many started holding up their car and house keys to make a jingle noise which meant they were looking forward to improving their home and business environments and increasing the 'jingle' in their pockets. They trusted Speaker Penny Chatham. Smiling and taking out a cowbell from under her podium, she joined in the ringing of the impending jingle in people's pockets.

At the conclusion of each speech, when selling the need and value for becoming sustainable, Senators Long and Knox, and Speaker Chatham would step back from the podium microphone, pause, and then walk back up and say as she did that early afternoon in Bay St. Louis, "One day, through the use of regenerative technologies, your family home and businesses will be as considerate to the environment as a self-sustaining forest, meadow, or marsh which takes care of itself through relying on nature's cycles."

At this point, Penny Chatham leaned forward again and in a low resonating voice said, "We will finally respect Mother Nature and become a partner in the use of her natural cycles and processes. Becoming sustainable will enhance our health, and increase our wealth!"

With the drama of those closing words, the audience was stirred. The Bay St. Louis Mississippi crowd stood and vigorously clapped. There was also sporadic Mississippi-style hooting and hollering in support of the high-spirited diminutive Miss from Mississippi.

People were genuinely interested in being a part of these optimistic ideas coming from a highly placed politician. But it was more than that, it was Penny Chatham talking to them. She was an iced tea drinker who enjoyed her cornbread and black-eyed peas just like the rest of the audience. She probably had a pickup truck and for sure her family went to church and Sunday School every Sunday that they could! Penny Chatham had an intense level of public commitment going for her. It was not something she planned, but instead, it was who she was! She could not help it. She was just like her supporters and they knew and liked that.

After the ovation died down, Penny Chatham thanked the people for supporting her and said she hoped that she had done them right. "If you have ideas, share them with us. Write a letter, send it to my staff including Jake Ingram, he is the slim and fit Coast Guard Fellow that you see around here today. Let him know your good ideas and what you are thinking. We will discuss it and get back to you. Network with those who believe like you do in order to support the improvements we are proposing. This is the USA and we work together to get things done!"

The crowd appreciated the opportunity to suggest ideas and once again, vigorously clapped for the substance of her presentation and for her obvious willingness to work with others.

Nevertheless, with all of her good works and support growing for her ideas everywhere she made a presentation, wariness by those that had a completely different viewpoint about the direction in which the country should progress was emerging.

Rabbiteye Blueberries

CHAPTER 6

Jean Lafitte the Pirate

There was no question-and-answer time because the audience was too big and besides, the Speaker and her family were on a vacation, sort of. Going backstage for the photo op with the local writer, Sister Leah pulled on her mother's dress, "Is this the time where I can visit with Dr. Professor Byrd?"

Looking down at her anything but shy six-year-old Penny said, "Of course, darling. Have you thought through what you are going to say to him? You don't want to stumble with your words. Be sure of yourself, Sweetie."

Dr. Byrd was a tall man and looked even taller because his plaid sports coat was obviously too short, making his legs look really long. His jet-black hair was combed straight back and he wore gold, wire rimmed glasses.

After introductions were made to the professor and before photos were taken, Speaker Chatham told the research professor that her children were intrigued about meeting someone who was so knowledgeable about a real Gulf Coast pirate who had lived in Bay St. Louis, Mississippi. Dr. Byrd smiled at the kids and as he bent to shake hands he said in French, the native tongue of Jean Lafitte:

"Cest si bon de te voir mes petits chéris. Mous avez l'air si intelligent et fiable. Est-ce que l'un de vous serait intéressé à faire partie de mes adeptes de pirates ?" [1]

Looking at the ten-year-old boy he said: *"Vous me semblez être quelqu'un qui pourrait aimer naviguer avec nous."* [2]

He asked him, *"Que pensez-vous du pillage d'un navire espagnol? Nous nous attendons à ce que la Calle de Oro soit juste à côté de la baie de Barataria ce soir sur son chemin vers la Nouvelle-Orléans."* [3]

After a brief pause when there was no response, he demanded in English, "Are you in or are you out?" Unbuttoning and pulling his blue plaid sports coat slightly back he revealed a long Spanish Dagger. The kids were stunned. As he reached across his torso, and wrapped his hand around its ornate handle and began to pull it out, a member of the Speaker's security team shouted "Knife!" and quickly stepped between her and the professor while two others grabbed both of her arms and rushed toward the rear door.

Ernest Goldman, the historical society director who arranged for the photo op quickly intervened, stumbling with his words trying

---

1 "It is so good to see you my little darlings. My you look so smart and reliable. Would any of you be interested in becoming part of my pirate followers?"
2 "You strike me as being one who might enjoy sailing with us."
3 "What do you think about plundering a Spanish ship? We are expecting the Calle de Oro to be just off Barataria Bay this evening on its way up to New Orleans."

to diffuse the situation. "I believe everything is all right. It's not what you think! Dr. Byrd probably has no idea even to how to use a dagger. He only carries it for show!"

At any rate, the photo op was over. There was not even a picture taken. Sister Leah, in the midst of the chaos, stepped forward quickly to ask a question of the professor who was now pinned down by two additional capitol police security agents on the backstage wooden floor with his right arm pulled tightly behind his back. "Dr. Professor Byrd, does it take one to know one?" In the turmoil of the minute, her question was ignored. Had this been a normal interview and photo-op, that comment would have evoked some smiles and laughs, and no telling what kind of answer, but this time, the Speaker had already been rushed out to a waiting SUV with the rest of her security detail. She protested but in matters of security, a strict protocol is followed.

After a few short minutes, her family was also rushed out to join her as she sat between two security police in the back of the big SUV with two other agents on either side of the vehicle with automatic weapons drawn across their torso. Penny asked, "Well Sister, did you get to ask your question?"

A little flustered and disheveled looking after all of the maneuvering by the bodyguards, Sister Leah loudly responded, "Well I sure did!"

"And what did the expert on pirate Jean Laffite say?" asked the caring mom.

"Well Momma, I think I heard him say, *C'est si bon*." The entire car laughed. Sister Leah sat smugly with her arms crossed. At least, she felt pretty good about getting a good laugh out of her family!

The not-so-subtle caravan of three SUV's quickly left the auditorium and moved on to the Bay St. Louis historic district, about six blocks away from the Bay St. Louis Historic L & N Amtrak Train Depot. They stopped in front of the First Baptist Church located in the historic district and the family was allowed to get out where they gathered on a large, round wooden elevated platform built around an ancient live oak tree. Penny, Pop, and Jake Ingram sat along the edge and the kids played "You're It," running around on the raised area and jumping off when they were close to being tagged. Even Sarah Jane, the reserved thirteen-year-old, joined in on the fun, while three security agents kept watch around the perimeter of the Chatham family gathering.

The incident with the pirate authority complete with an authentic Spanish dagger tucked under his sports coat was on everyone's mind, and a good laugh over the crazy occurrence had been enjoyed by the group. Word of the incident quickly made it to Washington. Craig Gill excitedly called Jake Ingram while the family and security detail were decompressing on the raised platform around the old live oak tree. He was very concerned and had been busy most of the day pouring cold water on stories coming out of Mississippi about the "knife incident with the Speaker of the House of Representatives." Even President Harrison's personal secretary had called on behalf of the President.

Poor Professor Byrd and the photo opportunity that turned so distressing. If it had not been for the Spanish dagger, his book would have gotten outstanding press with Speaker Chatham and her family!

Instead, the next day there was a brief article at the bottom of the front page in the Wall Street Journal about a college professor who was wrestled to the floor after brandishing a pirate's Spanish dagger while meeting with Speaker of the House of Representatives. After Speaker Chatham's being rushed away from the convention hall by her security detail unharmed, the professor was arrested for threatening a government official. The write up went on to talk about the professor's new book and Mississippi Pirate Jean Lafitte.

After the group calmed down from the morning's exciting events, Jake Ingram continued with options for the continuing adventure, "Madam Speaker, you and your party are about to be taken to three adjacent bed and breakfast homes located a block from the beach and three blocks from the historic downtown shopping village. You will have the rest of the afternoon to rest, go to the beach, or walk to nearby shops.

"Dinner will be at a restaurant of your choice, but I have selected one in particular if it sounds good to you. The North Shore Seafood House overlooks the boat harbor Marina and St. Louis Bay, and specializes in shrimp, crab, oyster, and speckled trout dishes. All of the seafood is harvested locally from the Mississippi Sound. Three years ago, when the water quality was so out of balance, much of the seafood had to be brought in from South Louisiana and the Florida Panhandle. Your and Senator Long's efforts have created changes that enables "beau coups" of seafood to be harvested from our own Mississippi Sound."

Seeing that the family seemed pleased with his dining choice, he continued. "What you do after dinner is on your own. Of course, I will be with you and can make any arrangements you want. Tentatively though, we have an event at 8:30 this evening on the beach for your kids to meet with the local Methodist Church youth group. There will be a small bonfire and the youth, who are your kid's ages, along with their leaders will be playing acoustic instruments and singing. You and Professor Chatham will be welcome as well."

Feeling a tug on her wrap around skirt she bent down as her youngest daughter Sister Leah quietly asked to also be part of the bonfire and music on the beach. She replied, "Of course you can, Baby." Turning to face her astute staffer Penny Chatham breathed deeply and said, "Thank you, Jake Ingram. This sounds wonderful and will be a great way to end the day and have something else to think about besides meeting the local author. Please be sure to tell the Methodist Church folks we would all like to come to the bonfire and music. That was sweet of them to invite us."

The Chathams took Jake Ingram's recommendation to dine at the North Shore and were seated around tables outside, in the front of the restaurant, with a view to the boat harbor as the sun was going down. It was a perfect place for enjoying dinner and seeing people walking by. From their table, they watched the colors of the boats in the harbor changing from bright white to subtle shades of yellow and orange as they reflected the setting sun.

For dinner, Penny and her husband shared a platter of grilled oysters with slices of French bread, and then split a grilled redfish dinner with a shrimp and crawfish sauce over the fish and wild rice. Both were outstanding. Penny Chatham had gone to Mississippi State University and was no teetotaler. With dinner she had a Pem and ginger ale on ice, and Pop had a Margarita on the rocks with salt around the rim. The kids all had to have a little taste of the salty rim. Sarah Jane also took a very small taste of the potent liquid and scrunched up her face and shivered at its tangy flavor!

Boiled shrimp was the unanimous entre choice of the three kids. They liked the hands-on experience of peeling the large, locally caught shrimp and making their own cocktail sauce. They loved mixing the ketchup with straight horseradish and lemon juice. Sniffing the horseradish up close and momentarily losing their breath was part of the test to see if they had gotten it too spicy! After several tries, all three usually got their cocktail sauce to the preferred mix of mostly catchup with a little lemon juice and not very much horseradish at all!

After dinner, Jake and one of the Methodist youth counselors named Aubrey stopped by the restaurant to meet the family. The counselor was a spirited high school junior. Smiling as he talked about their beach bonfire gatherings and speaking directly to each of the Chatham children with only occasional glances toward their parents. The children were excited about the experience and Penny Chatham said they could go on with Jake and Aubrey leaving their parents to catch up later. That pleased them to no end.

As they briskly walked across the street toward a concrete seawall to where they would descend thirty feet down oversized steps to the sand beach, their mom yelled out to Sister Leah to hold either her brother or sister's hand, which she did immediately. They were followed at a close distance by two casually dressed guys in their early thirties who were part of Speaker Chatham's Capitol Police Security detail.

Stepping down twenty huge concrete seawall steps they finally reached the sand beach. Aubrey sat down on the last eighteen-inch-high step and took his shoes off and the Chatham kids did the same. Sarah Jane exclaimed, "Wow, the sand is so soft and cold! "The change from wearing shoes to going bare feet on the sand was a game changer. It was almost as though the new freedom without shoes or parents created a greater sense of excitement. Approaching the youth group gathered near the shoreline, the Chatham's were introduced and each was hugged by those in the gathering and told their names. Immediately the newcomers from Washington, D. C., felt good and enjoyed being part of the group.

After a brief overview of ground rules for being around the bonfire, they drew straws to see who got to light the pine firewood that would set ablaze the larger stack of dry driftwood. Out of the eighteen kids that were there, the one who got the short straw was Sarah Jane! There was clapping and some southern style whooping and yelling on her being selected. Aubrey gave instructions on lighting the fire. Most of the wood was sun bleached driftwood that had washed up on the east facing sand beach. The prevailing wind along the coast was from the southeast so there was always an abundance of washed-up wood along with parts of boats, plants from distant islands, beach towels and articles of beach clothing.

The wood pile was six feet across and four feet high. As Sarah Jane was preparing to light the bonfire with a long match, the leader of their security detail came up and stood beside her. He was a large man in his early forties. With a short haircut and pleasant but quiet manner, he clearly was not trying to attract any attention but his job was the safety of the Chatham children. She was not startled in any way, but instead was calm and very used to her safety being a priority wherever she went. So that the others would realize who the fit, forty-year-old guy was right beside her, she said in a matter-of-fact manner, "Hey y'all, this is Brent, one of my and my mom's caretakers.

Besides being armed and dangerous, he is a pretty cool guy." The group laughed and welcomed Brent with vigorous clapping. They had no idea what she meant about Brent being her family's caregiver but figured the armed and dangerous part was probably a joke of some kind. His presence was not a big deal to the Methodist youth. For the most part, all of the kids gathered there had parents who kept a pretty close eye on them and knew who all of their friends were. They also made a point to know where they were most of the time. The youth group probably assumed Brent was a close family friend or a relative of some sort.

As the fire was lighted, the group stepped back to a comfortable distance from the heat. The confident and easy-going youth began to nestle into the sand much like a sea turtle preparing to lay her eggs. They were getting comfortable for an evening of stories, singing, and just soaking up the atmosphere of a really dark beach, the sound of waves gently lapping along the shoreline, and the absolutely spectacular flames of the bonfire! It was magical.

The Chatham children sat next to each other with their new friends on either side, as well as in front and behind. They felt absorbed by this group of peers who probably had similar values as they had. "It's such a great feeling making friends so quickly," thought Sarah Jane, looking around the happy bonfire group. Turning to a longhaired brunette girl her same age who sat next to her named Christine, she said, "What a cool place to meet! If we had a beach like this, we would come out here all the time!"

Christine grinned and said, "We do, Sarah Jane, almost every week. I even have my birthday parties out here. When I was younger, we had a kite flying party! It was great and it is almost always windy enough for kites. My brothers and their friends walk their dogs every day along the beach and usually bring home some pretty cool stuff that washes up." Sarah Jane could not relate to that as she was not a collector, however, she said her brother would fit in well with that group!

Penny and Pop Chatham walked up about twenty feet behind the bonfire gathering and nestled into the deep, white-as-snow sand. There they eavesdropped and enjoyed their first beach bonfire, which they later learned was a Mississippi Gulf Coast Tradition. At 10:30 pm, as they were leaving, they asked their security supervisor Brent if he would see to it that the kids stayed together and got home safely, whatever that time might be. Speaker Chatham was given an assurance that would happen and everything would be all right.

She and Pop took their time returning to their beach cottage, all the while enjoying the sea breeze and seeing others strolling along the dark beach watching the moon lit waves washing onto the shoreline. Like the Methodist youth group, there were others quietly playing acoustical guitars and singing. One small group facing the rising moon in the east was doing yoga repeats of Downward Facing Dog and Warrior poses. A young family was using their cell phones and an App called SkyView to identify stars, constellations, and even spot orbiting satellites.

The next morning Penny Chatham looked at her texts and saw that the family got home and was in bed by 12:30 am. Sister Leah had fallen asleep and been carried home by Brent. Sarah Jane had brushed the sand off of her legs and clothes and put her in her bed. Penny recalled Sarah Jane stopping by her bed to say good night and that all were fine and asleep or on the way to being asleep. What a great first child she was! In fact, all three were good kids. They were kind, thoughtful, and had big hearts for others. Andrew Reardon was the only one she worried about, but he was ten and easing into activities boys like to be a part of and which often cause them to stumble. He had not tripped yet, but he was pushing it and would have to have some discipline measures soon. Penny was glad she had two girls and only one boy, as with more boys she might not have had the mind or energy to be Speaker of the House.

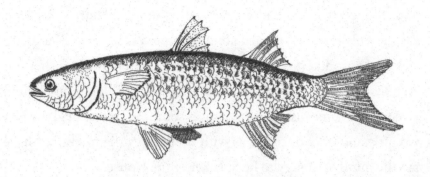

Mullet Schools in Shallow Marsh Waters

CHAPTER 7

Cast Net Bonanza

Jake Ingram showed up for coffee with the Chatham's early the next morning. He shared the itinerary for the day, just as his boss had asked, "Reveal what we are going to be doing as it develops." Since they had traveled to New Orleans, and then rode the eco rails through the Rigolets and Honey Island Swamp, they deserved a travel break. "Today, Madam Speaker, I hope you are set to go on a self-guided bicycling tour of historic Bay St. Louis after breakfast. We have reserved some of those fat tire bikes which will be fun especially if you have never ridden one. Four will have baskets for your family members and Sarah Jane's new friend, Christine, since I know you all like to stop and collect mementoes along the way. About midday, sack lunches will be delivered to a pontoon boat at the marina for a fishing and boating experience up the Jourdan River. The professor will be given a map and you will be depending on his abilities while exploring the river and marshes. You can also bring up the Jourdan River on your cell phones using Google Earth which provides a real time satellite image to see where you are and where you might want to go."

"About 2:30 pm, we hope to see y'all at Mr. Pat's bait shop. It is highlighted with a red dot on your map. There you will pick up some fishing gear and live shrimp for bait and Pat will demonstrate how to throw a cast net." After just a few days of being in the Deep South, Jake was getting pretty good with his ways of speaking Southern and always put extra emphasis on the word "y'all" to make sure others noticed his improvements. "Each of you will be given a cast net and instructions on how it is thrown. For Sister Leah and Andrew Reardon, there will even be a couple of six-foot diameter nets which they will be able to throw. The rest of y'all will be using twelve-foot diameter nets. Learning to throw a cast net and line fishing with live shrimp are important skills to learn because what you catch this afternoon will be what you will have for dinner tonight."

That comment drew some smiles and evoked a few teasing comments like the one from Andrew Reardon who quipped, "Looks like Pop is going to have bait shrimp for dinner tonight!"

Sister Leah added, "Don't worry, Momma, I will share my fish dinner with you." Self-confidence and a sense of humor was not in short supply for any of the Chatham children.

Jake continued, "A talented seafood chef who also fishes the local area will meet you when you return to the marina and if you have caught fish, he will demonstrate how to clean them and will put them on ice to take to your beach cottage."

Andrew Reardon quickly injected, "And don't forget the shrimp too! Be sure he explains to Pop how to clean the left-over bait shrimp!" Andrew had a thing for dogging his dad that would probably backfire on him sometime during the next day or two.

The trip planner continued talking about the seafood chef, "He will take the fish back to the beach cottage and prepare the evening meal. If there are those who are interested in assisting the chef in either cleaning fish or in dinner preparation, he would welcome the help. It would be a good experience for you because Brandon Boudreaux, besides being a native Louisiana Frenchman, is one of the finest seafood chefs on the coast. Keep in mind y'all, no luck fishing, no seafood for tonight's dinner. The alternative dinner will be Vienna Sausages, saltine crackers, Beanie Weenies, and a Moon Pie for dessert."

"Hmmm," said the Speaker, "I'm not sure I would have told the kids about the alternative dinner as it has some components that are their favorites! Maybe drop the Moon Pie for dessert unless you want them to throw the competition!"

After their bike ride and while they were changing into their fishing outfits to go to the marina, Sarah Jane asked if her new friend Christine could go. Penny said, "She sure can if there is room on the boat. Let me call Jake and see." At the Bay St. Louis Marina, the pontoon boat was waiting for the Chatham expedition and was plenty big enough for six passengers. The back half of the boat had a canopy providing shade and the front half was open and suitable for throwing cast nets and line fishing.

That afternoon's challenge was to explore the Jourdan River marshes and not get lost, and secondly, to catch dinner! The fishing experience was going to be in the brackish water salt marshes which had an occasional cabin located all along the shoreline where land met marsh. Getting lost was probably not going to be a problem with the fishing camps located nearby. Besides, skiffs from the Department of Marine Resources with capitol police security agents would always be in sight from the pontoon boat. Getting out of sight of the Speaker's armed security detail was not going to be a probability. After a brief orientation on driving the pontoon boat, the group was off.

Sarah Jane and her friend Christine from the beach bonfire sat in the front chairs facing forward for the best views of the spectacular marsh landscape. Pop drove the boat at a pretty fast clip, which on a hot, sunny afternoon, created a strong breeze that blew back hair and evaporated sweat from arms, faces, and legs. Sister Leah and her brother were standing on the open deck of the boat balancing themselves with arms in the air, calling to the frequent pelicans they saw and even the occasional osprey. The pelicans were shaped just as they were in the prehistoric era; when they dropped from the sky at an acute angle, zeroing in on an unsuspecting mullet or speckled trout, they were precision avian carnivores. When a pelican hit the water from a sixty-foot-high dive, Sister Leah and Andrew would slap their hands together and call out a loud boom. The osprey, or fish eagles as the locals called them, by contrast were elegantly shaped and displayed beautiful form as they dove for their seafood dinners. Both birds appeared to be successful hunters.

At 2:30 pm, the family pulled up to the bait and tackle shop along the edge of the Jourdan River marsh. Pat Kalucik was there to meet them and provide tackle for line fishing and casting nets. Pat demonstrated how to throw the big nets so that they opened like a Frisbee. The group became moderately proficient after eight or more tries. The Croatian owner of the bait shop loaded the nets and a Styrofoam bucket with live shrimp in the boat and wished them luck. Fishing with live shrimp was a successful technique for making sure there was going to be fish for dinner that evening. The shrimp were especially good for catching speckled trout, redfish, and flounder which were common in the nearshore marshes.

The Jourdan River narrowed as they traveled up the marsh. Pop, slowed the motor and when the area looked like it would hold fish, he then cut it off and switched to the ultra-quiet trolling motor mounted on the front right side of the boat. The hand-held controls for the mini boat motor that looked very much like a video game controller enabled him to guide the wide pontoon boat with precision. "All right" he said, "it's time to get those cast nets ready. I'm seeing a school of mullet over near the edges of the marsh grasses. We will ease the boat over that way and let y'all try your luck."

Sarah Jane and Christine were the first to get ready to cast their nets toward the school of mullet which were swirling and jumping out of the water. You never had to guess if mullet are concentrated in an area because of all of the disturbance they create. Once the girls had their nets in position, Sarah Jane said, "You throw first Christine. I need to see how it's done again."

While Christine was tall and slim and ran track at her middle school, she looked like she would also be skilled at net throwing. With a quick glance at Sarah Jane, she whispered under her breath, "Ok, here goes." She had already drawn a bead on the swirling school of fish and was watching intently to see what direction it was moving.

Taking the final step with the large diameter net, the experienced fisherman reached down, grabbed a section of the net bottom with the weights on it, and placed it between her teeth so when she launched the net that portion would be released last causing it to open in a big circle. She then reared back with a slightly arched back and cast just beyond where the swirling school of mullet was headed. Her form was beautiful, much like the graceful moves of a ballet or modern dancer! The sound of the lead weights along the bottom ring of the large diameter cast net all hitting the water surface at the same time made a subtle and hopefully lethal splash. Sarah Jane watched closely. As the net left Christine's hands, it looked as though it morphed from a mass of confused and mixed-up looking netting into a perfectly opened circle. It became a magical looking flying disk hurtling toward its target, hopefully, tonight's dinner!

The Chatham family stared as if in a frozen trance, watching with anticipation. Once the net hit the water, Christine's instinct was to give the weights two seconds to fall to the shallow bottom, she counted out loud, "One Mississippi, two Mississippi," and then quickly pulled the rope attached to her wrist so that the bottom ring of weights pulled together and enclosed what was trapped inside. Staring intently at the water, Christine, quietly said to Sarah Jane, "We got 'em, Church Sister."

Everyone was mesmerized, staring at the spectacle of a big cast net jerking and splashing, full of fighting and yanking fish being dragged toward the boat. Andrew Reardon Chatham could hardly contain his ten-year-old self and excitedly hollered, "Should we get the net? Where's the net? Get the net!"

Christine passively replied, "They are already in a net. Get ready to grab some unhappy flopping fish when we lift the net into the boat. These are good sized fish, and they are crazy heavy!"

Andrew was beside himself. This was one of those boy dreams. A big net full of no telling what kind of fish about to be lifted from the water and onto the boat deck! As Christine struggled to lift the cast net packed with fish, she anxiously barked an order to her new friend, "Sarah, help me lift this. Grab the rope right above the net and let's pick it up together. It's going to take the two of us to get them out of the water!"

As the bonfire friends lifted the wiggling and splashing net full of big mullet into the boat, the Chatham family watched in amazement at the size and energy of the captive fish. Normally never one to let a combative encounter go by without being a part, brainy little Sister Leah quickly separated herself from the landing experience of aggressive family members on the front deck grabbing and holding down the flopping and squirming aquatic captives. "Count me out! I'm not going to be part of attempting to subdue those aquatic herbivores."

For a six-year-old, she was pretty smart and enjoyed learning about subjects new to her. When she found out they were going fishing, she did a web search on her phone to see what types of fish they might catch in the coast salt marshes and what type of bait was best to catch them. Mullet were common around marsh edges and being herbivores that ate algae and plant parts, they had to be caught with a cast net. The locals considered them to be really good eating primarily because of their plant diet.

Like her momma, the petite, blonde first grader had an insatiable need to learn new things and be able to speak with authority on a subject. Because Andrew Reardon was outspoken, she assumed that was the norm and would jump right into a topic with her new found knowledge.

Andrew Reardon, who was still as hyper as any ten-year-old boy could be in this crisis situation, shouted, "Get a bucket, get a bucket y'all, we can't let any of them get away!"

Penny who had been a frequent visitor to the coast when she was growing up excitedly agreed and chimed in, "I'm with you Andrew, looks like a better dinner than Vienna Sausages and Beanie Weenies."

Sister Leah replied, "Hey, I didn't know we had a choice. I might prefer the Vienna Sausages and baked beans. Are those the ones that come in the little cans and have hot dogs in them?" That comment was ignored in the chaos of eight large mullet flopping around the front of the boat. Once the broad-shouldered fish were transferred to a five-gallon bucket and then poured into the boat's aerated live well, the group regained their composure. Pop extended a selfie stick and called for a group photo with Christine in the middle holding up her successful cast net. Everyone was smiling and talking about Sarah Jane's friend and her prowess with the cast net. They were thanking her because, thus far, she was the only one that had provided dinner for the group.

Andrew Reardon wanted another picture, this time of just him and Christine. He carefully grabbed two of the smaller mullet from the live well and held them up for his group photo. He was a lot like his mom as he declared, "This is the kind of photo I will cherish for the rest of my life!" It was also one of the photos that Penny Chatham would add to her family album once she was back at her desk in Washington, D.C..

With all the excitement generated by just that one net cast, the group decided to let the boat drift while they had lunch. Penny was the mom on this trip and looked in the gourmet paper bags from the Sycamore House, an upscale restaurant located in an old house in Bay St. Louis. Jake had delivered the two big sacks personally to the pontoon boat before they departed for their marsh trip. Expecting fine gourmet sandwiches, there were ten small cans of Vienna Sausages, eight cans of Beanie Weenies, eight plastic forks and spoons, and plenty of napkins. Individually wrapped packages of saltine crackers were in the other bag along with a dozen Moon Pies and a can opener! Penny laughed out loud. The adventure was still unfolding. Who would have ever guessed such gourmet fare would be provided on the pontoon boat fishing trip on Mississippi's Jourdan River salt marshes? A small ice chest nearby was filled with bottled waters and bottles of Barq's Root Beer drinks! Nestled down in the ice was a Mississippi State Bulldog bottle opener. The opener apparatus was inside the bulldog's mouth. To make it work you had to pull his mouth open with your thumb and stick the bottle in to remove its cap. Laughing out loud Penny thought, "That creative soul thought of everything!" Andrew Reardon was also impressed and volunteered to open all of the Barq's with the novel bulldog bottle opener. With kids, it's never the final achievement that is important, it is how you get there!

There was a good bit of jawing over lunch and about lunch. Sister Leah said she was not going to eat one of those pale-looking hot dogs, but she would try the baked beans but only if they were heated up. The root beer sounded good, but she wanted hers poured in a cup over ice (no cups were enclosed) and she told Andrew she wanted to open her own bottle. The rest of the group was too hungry to discuss the meal or referee any sibling conflict. They were ready to dig in. Christine had no problem with the meal and shared, "Vienna Sausages and Beanie Weenies are pretty standard on a fishing trip where eating is secondary, and fishing is the main reason you're out on the water."

Pop set the ground rules, "You get to have a Moon Pie when you finish the main courses of your South Mississippi gourmet lunch." No one had a problem with that except Leah, who again was ready to debate the issue of the need for ground rules when taking a lunch break.

Skiff with Sculling Oar

CHAPTER 8

Stalker from the Tchoutacabouffa

After the lunch break, which was pretty brief, Pop challenged the group to add to the variety of what they caught for dinner that night. "Ok, y'all, we have enough mullet for each of us. It would be nice to catch some redfish or speckled trout so we can have more to eat and different fish to enjoy tasting." Nobody objected to that and all were ready for the next fishing encounter. He handed out the fishing poles which were seven-foot-long graphite rods with open faced reels. They had all fished with open faced reels and were ready to bait their rigs with live shrimp provided by Mr. Pat at the bait shop.

Andrew Reardon was the first to hook his shrimp. Mr. Pat had shown them all how to thread the hook through its horn along the top of its head. He cautioned them not to hook it too deep as that could get into its brain and then you would be fishing with dead shrimp instead of live shrimp. After baiting his rod, Andrew did the same for Sister Leah and his mother. Christine showed Sarah Jane who was glad because she was not going to hook a live shrimp if she could avoid it. As Pop began to ease the pontoon boat within casting distance of the edge of the marsh, she and Christine positioned themselves along the side rail and cast their shrimp with a ¼ ounce weight toward the edge of the salt marsh grasses.

Sister Leah explained to the group in the fashion of a YouTube tutorial that they had a pretty good chance of catching a bottom feeder redfish, or a speckled trout which both enjoy a meal of live shrimp! "Sometimes you can hook a flounder which is a great tasting flat-shaped fish with both of its eyes on its top side and mouth on the bottom. I'm hoping to catch a flounder because it is prehistoric looking, and I've never seen a real live one." She and Andrew Reardon had consulted their cell phones to get acquainted with the challenges they would meet in this afternoon's fishing trip. Both kids loved to learn about upcoming experiences the family was about to have so they could become knowledgeable and share it.

After casting toward the edge of the marsh, Penny and Andrew both got good tugs on their line and immediately pulled back hard to set their hooks, with no luck. This happened several times to the others as well. As they continued fishing along the edge of the salt marsh, a rusty looking fisherman in a small john boat quietly eased up on the river side of their pontoon boat. His skinny and weather worn appearance matched the dented and discolored aluminum skiff, as he checked out who and what was in the uptown looking pontoon boat.

Noticing movement with his peripheral vision, Pop turned to see the man standing in his boat just feet away. In a raspy voice, he said with a thick Cajun accent, "Hey, Mon, I see you ah fishin fo dem redfishes. Dey take da shrimps in da mouth whitch is on de bottom of der body. Dey are plenty feedin long the edge of de marsh grasses where you is fishin, but I see you is not givin dem babies enough time to get da shrimps an hook in dey mouth. You be jerkin dem fish poles too soon, soon as dey bite. When dey pull on da line, I'm tellin ya, count, three – two - one, and den ra back to set dat hook. Do ya read me?"

The whole family, now facing the Frenchman, was surprised by how quickly he eased up on them, but they were also listening to his advice spoken in his thick Cajun accent. Just as the fisherman was about to reach over and grab the pontoon boat to better communicate with the novice fishing party, Department of Marine Patrol boats pulled up along either side of the fisherman. Two capitol police agents stood facing the intruder who grabbed hold of the pontoon boat to keep his balance in the wakes made by the patrol boats. The larger of the two agents boarded the pontoon boat and got between the fisherman and Speaker Chatham. The other one asked the intruder to sit down in his boat, put his hands-on top of his head, and keep them there. Boarding his rickety boat, the other agent sat down to interrogate him.

The agent on the pontoon boat maintained his position shielding Penny Chatham as a third DMR patrol arrived and towed the surprise fisherman and agent away from the pontoon boat and back toward Mr. Pat's Bait Shop. When conditions were calm again, the capitol police bodyguards thanked Speaker Chatham for her patience and told the group to continue their fishing trip. They explained it was standard procedure to engage anyone who would approach the Speaker's party unannounced, especially in a rural setting like along the Jourdan River marshes.

Christine was totally unprepared for what had just occurred and looked stunned. It was common for fishermen who did not know one another to visit about whether or not the fish were biting, and what lure or bait they were using. Sarah Jane said, "Come on Christine, let's see if we can make those redfish take our bait by giving them a little more wiggling time like the man said."

Christine looked at her new friend face to face, and quietly said, "What was that all about?"

Sarah responded, "I'm sorry if that scared you. My mom is pretty high up in Congress and has to have that level of protection. She does not like all of that attention; nor do we, but it comes with the job."

Seeing that Christine was disturbed by what happened, Penny Chatham came over and said, "I guess Sarah Jane told you why we have security officers that come with us wherever we go."

Christine said, "Yes, Ma'am, she told me, and I understand."

Penny put her arm around Christine and said, "Ok, Girls, let's get back to catching dinner tonight!"

The rest of the afternoon eased back into the simple life of a family and friends on a fishing trip, and a successful one too. The marsh fishermen applied the Frenchman's wait-and-see to set the hook technique. That change resulted in adding five redfish in the three to five-pound range to the live well, and that was plenty for the fish dinner they were all hoping for!

Jerry Fotenot, the fisherman with the Cajun accent was taken to Biloxi where he was photographed, questioned, and detained to be further interviewed by FBI agents. His appearance in the proximity of the Chatham group's pontoon boat was surprising, especially since there were security agents in DMR Marine Patrol boats located up and down river from the fishing party, blocking any access by a floating vehicle heading toward the Chatham pontoon boat. All boaters would have been intercepted, interviewed, and accompanied away from Speaker Chatham's fishing party, but somehow Fotenot's boat had eluded them.

There was concern about the fisherman that seemingly appeared out of nowhere. While his interaction with the Chatham's was not unusual, it was odd that he did not have any fishing gear in his boat and the aluminum skiff did not have a registration sticker or numbers on either side of its bow. During the interviews, he was compliant and appeared not to have any sinister motive toward the Speaker's party. Nevertheless, agents were dispatched to the address of his home further to verify the intruder that suddenly appeared and interacted with the Chatham party.

They found that Jerry Fotenot lived in a boathouse on the Tchoutacabouffa River north of Biloxi. The river flowed into Biloxi Back Bay and his boathouse was twenty-three miles from the Jourdan River Marshes. Local marine patrol officers did not know Mr. Fotenot and said they doubted he drove his small boat with a twenty HP Evinrude motor that far against strong headwinds out of the southwest and choppy water conditions. However, he could have trailered his skiff that far. With that information police were checking boat launches and parking lots with access to the Jourdan River. They found no vehicle with an empty trailer that would accommodate his sixteen-foot flat-bottomed skiff.

Seeking to find out where the boat came from, law enforcement officers focused on the local area. Pictures of the boat and of Jerry Fotenot were circulated by DMR Marine Patrol Officers who inquired with local bait shops and boat launches. It was becoming an important priority to find out how the skiff and its stealthy intruder got to the Chatham pontoon boat. Mr. Fotenot said it was his boat and he drove it over to the Jourdan River marshes that morning. Officers said that was unlikely because they never found his truck or trailer and he wasn't sure where he launched the skiff.

For reasons greater than the encounter with the man from the Tchoutacabouffa River, an FBI regional Task Force had been hastily assembled in Gulfport, Mississippi, to make other law enforcement officers aware the Congressional Speaker of the House of Representatives was visiting the region. This was increasingly important because the President of the United States was now hospitalized at the Walter Reed Hospital in Washington with a sickness his physicians were trying to learn more about. Reports were that he was in stable condition but was not improving.

Back on the Jourdan River, the fishing party landed three eighteen-inch-long speckled trout to go with the redfish and mullet. Andrew and his mother brought two to the boat and Sister Leah hooked the third one and just about lost it as she was lifting it into the boat. It was a nice one. Leah insisted on releasing her fish because it really did not want to be caught and be crowded in the live well with the other captive fish. Pop complied with her request. Shortly after Pop's liberating Leah's fish, Sarah Jane hooked another speckled trout and brought it to the boat. She said to the group, "Looks like this big guy is ok with being a keeper. He told me on the sly that he wanted to be in the live well because he had heard the water quality was wonderful and was being managed by a very smart young lady from Washington, D.C."

The youngest member of the Chatham family looked and smiled at her big sister who was also one her best friends, if not her best friend. "Thanks, Big Sister," she snapped. "I figured you for the compassionate kind when it came to Speckled Trout." Trout were also called Specs in southern waters and were known as one of the finest eating of the fishes commonly found in the coastal marshes of Mississippi and Louisiana.

Sister Leah was given the responsibility of regularly checking on the catch in the live well. If the water became cloudy or the fish were coming to the surface to breath, she was to sound the alarm and Pop would show her how to manually turn on the aerator and pump new water and oxygen into the live well. She made a mental note to go online when they got home and read more about live well aerators and just how efficient they were for injecting oxygen into the water.

After Sarah Jane's speckled trout, Pop called the security team on his cellphone and told them they had caught their dinner and were ready to return to the marina. He turned the pontoon boat around to go south and head back home. The morning winds from the south-west had moved to their usual prevailing southeast direction and were blowing hard enough for a light flag to be fully extended. That eight-twelve mile an hour light breeze along with the speed of the boat caused dip net man Andrew Reardon and live well supervisor Sister Leah to fall asleep on either side of their mother. One of the DMR security launches stayed a couple of hundred feet behind the Chatham's and the other the same distance ahead as they accompanied the successful but very worn-out fishing party on the twenty five-minute pontoon boat ride back to the Bay St. Louis Marina.

As Pop pushed the speed control lever forward and the motors revved up, Andrew Reardon briefly woke up and mumbled, "There is something about the movement of a boat on the water, or some chemical in the air while on the water that is so relaxing it always makes me want to take a nap. But don't worry." he declared to his mother, "That is not going to happen on the ride going back to the marina because Pop needs my boating expertise and cunning ability to go the right direction."

It wasn't long before he was again asleep on his mother's soft shoulder.

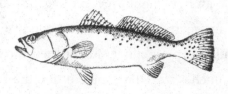

Speckled Trout from the Jourdan Marshes

CHAPTER 9

Bayou Chef

As they pulled up to the pier, Jake Ingram was there to meet them along with a tall, olive-skinned man in his early thirties. Jake hollered out, "I sure hope you caught some fish because I wiped out all of the available Vienna Sausages this morning at the store, and they are also out of cans of Beanie Weenies!"

Sister Leah hollered back, "Lunch was great Mr. Jake! I sure hope we can have the same thing again real soon. Everyone ate his Moon Pie and I got to bring the two-extra ones back for dessert after dinner tonight. I also have a bag with our glass containers and plastic bottles for recycling." Jake, looking comfortably casual in his khaki Columbia shorts and a pale blue long sleeved fishing shirt with the sleeves rolled up, reached his tanned muscular arm down into the boat grabbing her small hand and hoisting her up to the pier.

"What a cutie…!" he said softly to himself as he took her paper bag with the recyclables.

Leah gave him a sweet smile and said, "Thank you Mr. Jake Ingram, trip planner extraordinaire." Jake was not surprised at anything she said nor how she said it. He was not even sure he could spell the word extraordinaire.

The handsome, smiling guest accompanying Jake also offered his big, soft hand to help the other fishermen get from the edge of the pontoon boat up to the big wooden pier. When it came time for Penny Chatham to get out, two of the security guys who met the party at the dock boldly moved in front of Jake to assist her out of the pontoon boat and onto the wide wooden planked marina pier. Jake introduced the Speaker and her husband to Emile. He had already told the chef he was not to offer his hand or touch the Speaker or her husband. That was a security protocol that had recently been established on this trip since they had arrived in Bay St. Louis.

Every so often, security was tighter around Speaker Chatham and this was one of those times. Jake had privately shared with the Speaker when they met this morning that increased security restrictions were in place because of the hospitalization of the president. A potential reason being investigated was that he was potentially poisoned in some manner.

Emile Laurent was the chef that would prepare the seafood dinner for the Chatham family that night. Trim and clean cut, he grew up among French descent people from the Bayou Manchac area near Baton Rouge where he learned all about fishing and cooking New Orleans French style. Now living in Mississippi and working along the Gulf Coast, he prepared fine meals for private dinner parties and distinguished visitors who came in to visit the Maritime and Seafood Industry Museum in Biloxi. After introductions were made to the family and their guest, he asked Sarah Jane, who appeared to be the one who could take a little ribbing, about the afternoon fishing trip. "Miss Sarah, tell me what y'all bought at Mr. Pat's Bait Shop for dinner tonight?"

Firstly, Sarah Jane was surprised that a handsome guy in his thirties spoke to her about fishing, and secondly, did he really think they looked like such inexperienced fishermen that they didn't know how to catch their own dinner? The idea that they would buy somebody's fish so they would not have to have Vienna Sausages and saltine crackers for dinner was not even worth addressing!

In a somewhat cocky manner, she replied to the handsome chef, "Mr. Emile, you are so perceptive, how did you know we bought bait shrimp at Mr. Pats for dinner tonight instead of wasting them fishing for redfish and speckled trout along the edges of the salt marshes?"

Emile was taken aback and laughed, "Ok, Missy, I got cha. Sounds like a shrimp and grits dinner tonight. I thought you looked like such talented and experienced fisher-ladies that I would pull your leg a little bit. The locals have been catching plenty of redfish next to the marsh grasses, and specks two to four feet deep in the same area. Bait Shrimp will do though, but I was sure hoping to tease your taste buds at dinner tonight with some redfish, speckled trout, and maybe mullet since I heard Mr. Pat was giving lessons on how to throw a cast net."

Sarah Jane and Christine were grinning at one another, enjoying teasing with this regionally renown Gulf Coast chef. Sarah responded, "You must be living right, Emile, we actually caught what you hoped for. With one throw of her cast net my friend Christine caught eight really big mullet. It was bedlam on the deck of the pontoon boat when she opened her net, but we will not dwell on that." The kids all grinned at each other reliving the complete chaos that lasted for a full two minutes after Christine opened her cast net! "When we switched to fishing with our graphite rods and open-faced Penn Reels with live shrimp, we brought in a five-pound Redfish and two more that weighed two pounds. Andrew Reardon, my sister Leah, and my mom caught a total of four eighteen-twenty-inch speckled trout, of which we kept three. For humanitarian reasons, one trout communicated to my sister Leah that it preferred to not be tossed into the aerated live well with the others, so it was released."

Emile grinned at the lively Junior High girls, "That's great, ladies, I see there is no lack of confidence and articulacy among the Chatham family sisters and girlfriends. I can do a lot with that kind of seafood you coaxed out of the Jourdan River marshes. Do you want me to tell you what I'm going to prepare for dinner, or would you rather be surprised?"

As all the kids shouted, "Surprise us!" Penny and Pop smiled and agreed. Lunch was a surprise, so why not dinner too.

Pop and Emile along with Andrew Reardon boarded the pontoon boat and netted the frisky salt marsh fish out of the live well. Andrew had cleaned fish before, but they were mostly bream and crappie, freshwater fish that made great table fare, but were not nearly as big as the saltwater redfish and speckled trout. The meaty redfish were filleted by Emile with precision, creating perfect white slabs of coarse textured, but outstanding tasting fish. Renowned New Orleans Chef Paul Prudhomme, for whom Emile worked, created his blackened fish spice for the redfish, one of the most flavorful saltwater fishes along the Gulf Coast.

As Andrew Reardon and Pop were watching the expert prepare the freshly caught fish at the fish cleaning table on the pier, Emile asked, "Andrew, have you ever filleted fish with an electric knife?"

"No, Sir, he eagerly responded, hoping he would be asked to give it a try. After waiting patiently for an invitation to give it a shot, he cautiously asked, "Do you think I could try it?"

"If your dad gives the ok, we can give it a go," said Emile. With Pop nodding his permission to taking a turn at cutting the fillets away from the bone and separating it from the scales of the big fish, Emile explained how to hold the electric knife and where to cut to avoid bones in the ribcage and along the backbone. Andrew Reardon took the celebrated chef's electric knife, and holding it like he was told, pushed the on button and looked to see how the two stainless steel blades would slide back and forth. He then gripped the front side of the fish with his left hand and created two slabs of boneless fish meat. It was a perfect job. His daddy was complimentary, but not at all surprised. For a ten-year-old boy, he was precise in following directions and very respectful of power tools.

Complimenting the boy, Emile declared, "What a great job, Andrew Reardon. That was perfect. You took your time and didn't get in a hurry. Just what are your plans for the rest of the summer? I'm looking for an apprentice to help with seafood preparation at special parties for which I am booked. You would work six or seven days a week and get to eat all the seafood you want."

Andrew looked inquisitively at his daddy who smiled and said, "It's ok; take him if you really want him, Emile. He will miss going to explore Cat Island on kayaks and fishing the grass beds, but it's ok with me if he wants to go. You will have to take good care of him, nurse his colds and if he gets the flu, he's usually down for three or four days. At the end of the summer, you will have to buy him a ticket and send him back to Washington on a Greyhound Bus."

Both men looked at Andrew Reardon who had a very blank look on his face. Finally, the boy responded, "Well, Mr. Emile, I might need some time to think about it."

Pop smiled big and Emile said, "Ok, Hot Stuff, you think about it and have your daddy call me when you are ready to start your summer job."

It was time to go back to the beach house and begin preparing the evening meal for the Chatham family. Emile loaded the iced down fish in his extended cab truck that was equipped with a stove and refrigerator built in the covered truck bed. Pop and Andrew decided to walk back. They enjoyed being with one another just walking together and talking about whatever came up. For a father and son, they had a strong friendship and really enjoyed each other's company.

The distance from the Marina to the beach cottage was only four blocks so they made a slight detour through downtown to pass by the interesting shops, restaurants, and antique stores. In a junky-looking resell-it-shop, Andrew Reardon found some old boy scout patches his daddy bought for him. He was always on the lookout for things to sew onto his blue jean jacket to go along with his prized patches he got on trips with his mother to Tanzania and Ecuador.

Back at the cottage, Penny Chatham and Jake visited briefly while the others changed out of their fishing clothes and into more comfortable outfits. Sarah Jane had asked her mother if Christine could have dinner with them and was told of course she could. Since the girls were close to the same size, Sarah loaned Christine some clean shorts and a favorite T-shirt.

Jake told the Speaker that her chief of staff needed to visit with him on the satellite phone. Penny asked "Do you know what's up?"

"No," he said, "That's probably above my pay grade." The satellite connected phone was completely secure and only used when matters of public importance were being discussed.

The Speaker smiled and said, "Well Jake, after this trip, I think you will have earned an increase in your income and I will visit with our chief of staff about that when we return. Let me call Mr. Gill while there is a break in our activities and see if everything is holding together or if the office is fixin' to come apart at the seams!"

Her staffer smiled and said, "Let me know if there is anything for which you will need me. Emile will serve dinner at 6:30 pm. I told him Sarah Jane's friend Christine will be joining your family. From what I hear, you are in for a real fine meal. The fresh fish you caught were just right for your celebrity chef to create an outstanding dinner."

"Let's visit again after dinner this evening." She then went into her back bedroom and closed the door to make her call to Washington.

Crow in a Longleaf Pine Tree

CHAPTER 10

Craig Gill

Connecting with the office of the Speaker of the House of Representatives, Penny replied, "Craig Gill, Chief of Staff for Penny Chatham?"

He responded slowly and deliberately, "Yes."

"This is Penny Chatham."

It was apparent his boss was calling but he was a little baffled by her question.

Craig was a no-nonsense guy who managed her Congressional staff of twenty-eight people and scrutinized the many requests that would be presented to the Speaker. He preferred a business-like appearance where he did not stand out but rather appear as a background kind of guy. As the manager of the Speaker of the House of Representative's staff, he was too busy to be concerned about fashion. He probably did not own one of those colorful Christmas sweaters and his colorful winter scarf was gray.

"What news do you have to share with me?" The Speaker was in a great mood and it was reflected in her clear voice and playful salutation. The work load on her mind was obviously lifted and Craig was glad to hear that in her voice.

"Madam Speaker, those of us in hot and very muggy Washington, D.C., are glad to hear your voice. I have been keeping up with you through your security detail and hear you have been having a nonstop series of exceptional experiences that are adding up to a marvelous adventure!"

"You are right, Craig. Jake Ingram has planned a wonderful trip and it ain't over yet! What's up on the home front?"

Craig slipped into his business mode and spoke clearly, precisely, and directly. "Madam Speaker, the president is very sick. His physicians think he might have picked up a virus or was given one, or he might have been poisoned. No one around President Harrison has contracted the sickness and that fact has the security team concerned about the type and source of the illness. As a precautionary measure, Vice President Steve Hardy and his staff have been relocated to Camp David where his safety can be guaranteed if anything happens to the President." After a pause with no comment from the Speaker, he continued.

"Camille Latady, the Director of the Secret Service called and inquired about your whereabouts. They were aware of your trip by Amtrak train from New Orleans to Bay St. Louis, and I told her you and your family were still there but were preparing to go to an island twenty-five miles off the Mississippi coastline."

The Speaker interrupted Craig, "Well, you know more than I do. So, we are going to one of the Mississippi Sound's barrier islands?"

Craig responded, "Yes, you will be traveling there tomorrow morning and will stay four days. Jake will fill you in on all the details. Director Latady has directed the Capitol Police to increase your protective detail by six agents as a matter of proactive security. She said to emphasize that you nor your family is to have physical contact with anyone except one another and your security detail. When you depart for the island, your daughter's friend Christine cannot go with you. Brent with the Capitol Police who is down there with you has already briefed the other agents about this precautionary measure. Additional security agents are flying into the Stennis Space Center Airport located about an hour away and will be in Bay St. Louis by 11:00 pm. They will be under the direction of Brent Parker, just like the other members of your security detail. Madam Speaker, this is all standard protocol and not meant to alarm you or encourage you to change your travel plans in any way."

There was more dead silence on the line as the Speaker Chatham took it all in. She did not want anything to change her travel plans. Every day had been a different surprise, just like she had requested! Her family and she were having wonderful experiences and would be looking forward to the island trip that Jake Ingram had not yet sprung on them yet. That was going to be a fantastic experience!

"Craig, I appreciate all of the extra precaution, but tell me what is your gut feeling about this situation with the president?"

"Madam Speaker, he is not doing well. No one in the media is aware of his condition. He has not been labeled critically ill, but he is. He's pretty sick and the big question is, why? I can see the need to isolate the Vice President to ensure he remains healthy. I would say, Madam Speaker, be careful, don't hold back from taking any chances like you would normally do when you travel on your adventures. You will be provided with enough security to make sure you and your family are protected from any situation that may arise, although none is expected. The Secret Service thinks your moving offshore to an island that is deserted and has only one home in which you and your party will be residing is a good thing."

Penny Chatham took it all in. Of course, it was a daunting situation for the president. He and his wife were nice people, and Penny hated to see them going through this situation. "Thanks for the update, Craig. I will tell Jake you already let the cat out of the bag on the Cat Island adventure! Seriously though, send a note today to Connie Harrison from me saying, 'We are thinking about y'all and praying for Jim's speedy recovery. Love, Penny Chatham.'

"I will do that," her astute chief of staff responded matter of factly.

"Jake can always quickly get in touch with me when we need to talk again. By the way, he arranged for a seafood dinner cooked in our beach cabin by a local chef with the fish we caught in the Jourdan Marshes today. We haven't had it yet but the whole local chef thing was a real surprise, and the family is looking forward to it. Pop and

Andrew Reardon helped with the dinner preparation. Thanks for the report on the president. Keep me informed, Craig, goodbye."

Andrew Reardon blasted opened the door to the bedroom as she was finishing her call to Washington. "Momma, it's time to meet on the porch for drinks and 'oara-de-oors', or whatever you call them," he said almost too fast to understand. "Anyway, there are little baked apples with a crust around them and miniature forks. There is also a bowl of hot cheese with a little fire under it, bubbling like lava in the cone of a volcano. It is for dipping homemade chips in. Emile says he made them. I never heard of making your own chips! They are kind of a green color. Emile won't tell me what they are made of, but they sure smell good! He and Sarah Jane are ringing the dinner bell right now, so come on! We are all so famished there might not be anything left when you and I get there!"

The little things to eat before dinner prepared by Chef Emile with a little help from his apprentice Andrew Reardon were unusual, fun, and just right to stir their hunger senses. That was a term Sister Leah always likes to use when talking about the predinner appetizers. It was apparent that a lot of preparation had gone into this special Gulf Coast meal. As the young folks were sipping on fruit flavored iced drinks with slices of strawberries and kiwi in small clear glasses, the grownups were enjoying Pem with ginger ale on the rocks. Speaker Chatham had enjoyed the English before-dinner-drink on a recent trip to Scotland to meet with members of the European Union. Jake Ingram had informed the chef it was one of her favorite predinner drinks.

During a momentary lull in the conversation where dinner party goers were working on reducing their famish level, (a hunger term created by Andrew Reardon), Penny revealed the next phase of the Gulf Coast adventure. All were spellbound to hear about boating to a deserted island that was so far out it was only infrequently visible from the mainland, and that was on a very clear and calm day! The deserted part of the island trip intrigued Andrew Reardon and Sister Leah the most, and probably had the same effect on Sarah Jane but she was almost a teenager and was beginning to be careful about being exuberant on any subject her parents had a hand in arranging. She did ask, "Can Christine go with us?" They had become best buds since the bonfire on the beach.

Penny responded, "We all love Christine and enjoy her company very much, but she will not be able to join us on this trip. There is some danger exploring a deserted island. Besides snakes and alligators, it is rumored there is a family of mountain lions or cougars on the island. This might be the last remaining pair of large cats existing in Mississippi! I think y'all ought to plan to get together when we return to the mainland. I'm sure you will have lots to visit about." That was good enough for Sarah Jane. While all of the kids were very social and really enjoyed their old friends and making new friends, they were disciplined enough not to whine or beg. That kind of attitude would not work in the Chatham family and the kids had learned that early in life.

While the hors d'oeuvres that stirred the hunger-senses were very popular and enjoyable, the seafood dishes from the fish they had harvested from the Jourdan River marshes were outstanding! The three choices of entrees were mullet, redfish, and speckled trout, all fish they had caught. The portions were small so the diner could enjoy the flavor of each type of fish.

On top of the baked mullet was a row of lemon slices and the fish was stuffed with thyme and bay leaves. It was a visual work of art. The juices remaining after baking were collected and butter was added to pour across the top of the fillet which was then sprinkled with fresh, cut up parsley leaves. Because of its exotic appearance, everyone wanted to try it! It was also popular because their dinner guest, Christine, had caught it. No one in that family would ever forget the chaos on the deck of the pontoon boat that followed when Christine had opened her cast net and eight large mullet poured out and flopped around everywhere!

The larger redfish fillets were visually simpler as compared to the preparation of the mullet. Emile had worked for Chef Prudhomme in New Orleans at his world-famous restaurant K-Pauls Louisiana Kitchen on Royal Street in the French Quarter. From Opelousas in Saint Landry Parish, the Louisiana French chef originally developed his blackening spice for Crappie, a freshwater fish called Sac au Lait which means white as milk in French. Because the fresh water fish is classified as a game fish, it was not commercially available for the application of the blackened fish spice so Chef Paul began serving it with redfish, a more plentiful, course textured fish caught in the salt marshes and commercially available. The dry spice is sprinkled on both sides of the fillet which is then cooked in a red-hot black iron skillet. The flavor and simplicity of the dish makes it a coast favorite. Everyone enjoyed trying the coarse texture of the redfish blackened in the iron skillet. Penny Chatham stated, "This has got to be the best flavored fish I have ever eaten anywhere!"

As all eyes turned toward Emile, who was standing nearby in his chef's hat and coat, he bowed toward the Speaker, and expressed his appreciation of her approval in French.

"*Ma chère Madame Penny Chatham, je suis ravie que vous appréciiez le sébaste noirci. J'ai appris à le préparer auprès du maître lui-même, le chef Prudhomme de la Nouvelle-Orléans, qui serait ravi d'apprendre que vous appréciez un plat aussi spécial. Il serait également impressionné que vous et votre famille ayez fait l'effort d'aller là où vit le sébaste et de les récolter pour votre dîner de ce soir. Je vous suis redevable Madame Penny. Puisse Dieu vous bénir vous et votre famille.*" [4]

The family members and Christine looked at each other. Penny Chatham who made numerous trips to France on business returned the compliment in French as best she could.

"*Le plaisir de votre présence est le mien et que la jouissance de vos créations culinaires fasse plaisir à beaucoup d'autres, comme nous l'avons fait, Chef Emile.*" [5] She returned his kind thoughts with a smile and slightly exaggerated nod when she finished.

The Chatham children looked at their mom with awe and knew from her expression she was complimenting the creator of their dinner in his native language. Christine spoke up and shyly said to the chef in French.

---

4 "My Dear Madam Penny Chatham I am so pleased you enjoy the Blackened Redfish. I learned how to prepare it from the master himself, Chef Prudhomme in New Orleans who would have been so pleased to hear of your enjoyment of such a special dish. He would also be impressed that you and your family went to the effort of going to where the redfish lives and harvesting them for your dinner tonight. I am in your debt Madame Penny. May God bless you and your family."

5 "The pleasure of your attendance is mine and may the enjoyment of your culinary creations bring pleasure to many others like it has to us, Chef Emile."

"Veuillez également accepter ma reconnaissance, le chef Emile. Le repas que vous nous avez préparé est magnifique et a créé une expérience merveilleuse pour nous tous. Ma famille serait fière d'un compatriote français avec un tel talent." [6]

The Chef, surprised by the return compliments in his second language gently bowed toward Christine and then to the other children and responded in like terms.

"La vie n'est pas complète sans l'appréciation de mes efforts par les autres et surtout par les jeunes esprits qui se sont réunis autour de cette table. Merci, Miss Christine." [7]

And he gently bowed again to Christine, then Sarah Jane and Sister Leah, and finally to Andrew Reardon, who laughed out loud and said, *"Merci,"* as he stood up and awkwardly returned the bow to his new friend the chef.

Finally, the Speckled trout dish was brought to the table. Emile continued, "Ladies and gentlemen, this is your final entre, speckled trout from the Jourdan River marshes as you well know!" The aroma of the broiled trout was great. Its white fillets were smothered in a sauce made from onions sautéed in butter and cooked with Sauternes wine from the Bordeaux area of France. When the sauce was nearly finished, slices of fresh squeezed lemon were added, and the garnish was placed on top of the trout. Once it was broiled, the sauce and fillet had a slightly grilled color, making the dish very attractive.

---

6 "Please accept my appreciation as well Chef Emile. The meal you prepared for us is beautiful and has created a wonderful experience for all of us. My family would be proud of a fellow Frenchman with such talent."

7 "Life is not complete without the appreciation of my efforts by others and especially from the young minds that have joined together around this table. Thank you, Miss Christine.

Since Andrew Reardon had helped with the preparation, he announced to the group, "You won't believe how good this dish is, and you need to know I helped in its preparation by stirring the sauce until it developed a certain consistency." As the others tasted the broiled speckled trout, they agreed it was outstanding, but so was the preparation of the other two fish dishes. Diners then had the choice of selecting a larger portion of the entrees or proceed to helping themselves to a bowl of wild rice, a platter of freshly grilled mixed vegetables which included carrot sticks flavored with olive oil, pepper and parmesan cheese, and young green beans cooked with vinegar, sugar, salt, and pepper.

Dessert was crème brulee, an old French favorite. It was chilled and served in small, white glazed ceramic bowls. The caramelized sugar on top was garnished with a small cluster of fresh mint leaves that Emile had brought with him. When the dessert was served, Andrew Reardon, again spoke up that he had played an important role preparing this dish as well, "The topping of the vanilla custard is burned sugar that I used a fancy blow torch that looked like my sister's hair dryer to create. I had to be careful to burn the topping just right so its flavor was complimentary to the custard."

Emile praised the budding dessert chef, "Your son and brother has many talents and in particular, a special gift for following directions to the 'T.'"

Sister Leah quickly responded, "Yes, Chef Emile, that is correct and he learned to be precise when carrying out chores because if he screwed them up, Poppa would make him do it again."

It was an outstanding meal and a time that brought the young Chatham family even closer together. Of course, Christine was included and felt the love and passion the family had for each other, and for her.

The next morning Jake Ingram came by at 8:00 am for coffee on the broad porch of the guest house. Through the early morning fog, views to St. Louis Bay and the big arching highway and pedestrian bridge looked like one of Claude Monet's impressionistic paintings. Hurricane Katrina and her thirty-five-foot-high storm surge collapsed the old bridge which left the village of Bay St. Louis remote and seemingly all by itself in the world. The new taller bridge which was storm surge proof reconnected the idyllic village to the other six sister cities of the Mississippi Gulf Coast. Each of the coast towns were no more than a few miles apart. The eastern most sister was Pascagoula, then there was Ocean Springs, Biloxi, Gulf Port, Long Beach, and Pass Christian before the great arching bridge took you to Bay St. Louis. The six seacoast towns were historic, and their commerce depended on the maritime and seafood industry. Tourism was beginning to become a big industry because of the seacoast character, plentiful seafood, and the abundance of renown graphic and ceramic artists who called the Mississippi coast their home.

Penny Chatham's efforts to get the water quality and salinity cycles in the Mississippi Sound back to their most productive historic levels was a big component of the renewed recognition of the Mississippi Sound which, in literary circles, was referred to as part of America's Third Coastline.

Serving her staff member a hot cup of black coffee that was steaming he replied, "Ahh, it smells like that Community Coffee that's made in Baton Rouge. I have had it before and loved the chicory flavor." After fixing his coffee with three sugars and a lot of cream, Jake began, "Well, Craig called me and told me he let the cat out of the bag. I admonished him for that. He did explain how beneficial a remote vacation spot is for you and your family especially at this time."

Speaker Chatham asked, "Did he give you an update on the president?"

Jake quickly answered, "No, he did not tell me much except that the president was in the hospital and Secret Service Director Camile Latady had dispatched six more Capitol Police to beef up your detail. They are on the coast and have already talked with Brent early this morning. There is no threat issue, but when the president is ill, it is just protocol to beef up your and the vice president's security. There is no telling where Vice President Hardy is and how security conditions have changed for him."

Penny looked at him but did not say a word. As good of an employee as he was, Jake did not know any more than what the public knows about the president and vice president at this particular time. He was aware that his direct supervisor, Chief of Staff Craig Gill, was privy to that level of information and had briefed the Speaker yesterday evening. At his entry level, his purpose was to inform Penny Chatham about the next leg of her adventure and he was enthusiastic about sharing that. "So, Madam Speaker, are you ready to go to a deserted island so far from the mainland that you can't see it?"

Penny was a little quiet and hesitant-looking as she asked, "Well Jake, how safe is it? I am not going to risk the lives of my kids. Pop and I don't mind taking chances, but I've got to know that the risks to our little brood will not be too extreme."

Jake smiled, "Your party will be the only group on the island. There will be four people we do not know that come with the large home you are renting. Two men are fishing guides, and each has their own twenty-four-foot-long skiff with twin sixty horsepower motors. They will be taking you and your family fishing anytime you want during the four days you are on the island. Another employee will cook all the meals for your family and, separately of course, for your security detail and me. He will also clean the large home when you are out exploring and fishing. The fourth person is an older gentleman who is known as the Mayor of Cat Island. He knows the history, both cultural and natural history of the island. Locals say he is a character!

"For the next three days you will reside in a spacious three-story home with broad porches overlooking the bayou that leads to the open waters of the Mississippi Sound. It has all of the modern conveniences including air conditioning and hot and cold running water. There are three bedrooms and a loft on the third story with fifteen beds in it. Your kids might prefer the two bedrooms, or they could bunk in the loft area. The main living area has a huge sectional sofa and other upholstered chairs, and there is a large dining table as well. The ground level beneath the elevated living quarters is a deck that is covered and contains a bar, different kinds of games like darts and hillbilly golf, and chairs and hammocks to enjoy the views and breezes in a shaded and comfortable environment.

"You will not believe how appealing this place is. I checked with previous guests including Gerald and Elizabeth Windham from Starkville who recently stayed there. He is a physician, and she is a schoolteacher and tennis coach. They brought their daughter and her family, and both families gave glowing reports. The employees and your security detail and I will reside in a two-story bunkhouse.

There is no cell phone service or television connection because of the island's remoteness and distance to the mainland. Your satellite phone, and mine and Brent's will be able to receive and to place telephone calls."

The Speaker and Pop, along with Andrew Reardon who had joined them on the porch took it all in and were impressed. They had never heard of the island getaway which was aptly named Pelican Roost, but knew part of Cat Island was privately owned and the rest of the island was part of the National Park Service's Gulf Islands Natural Seashore. However, there were no public access areas on the National Park lands that would attract adventurers, thereby keeping the isolated adventure inaccessible. "This place has got to be a dream experience", thought Penny Chatham. Pop was ready to go. He especially liked that there were two fishing guides in two boats which accommodated those who wanted to fish and those who wanted to explore the pristine natural beach along the island's south side.

Jake interjected one more advantage as though he was attempting to sell the Chatham's on the deserted island experience, "Three-mile beach on the south side is a totally natural beach with sand so white it is almost blinding, and it is within walking distance of the home. The beach is a product of large breakers from the open blue waters of the Gulf of Mexico." Penny Chatham, who had been continuously smiling while her trip planner described the island asked, "Ok, Jake, where do we sign up for this adventure?"

"Can you be ready to go by 11:00 this morning?" If you can, pack up and we will go by caravan over to the marina across the bay at Long Beach. Part of your security detail is already over there interviewing the fishing guides and inspecting their boats."

She asked, "What about food, do we need to pick up anything?"

Jake replied, "Everything is included. I provided a list of your family's favorite foods, drinks, and beer. There is a bar on the first level that is stocked. All you need is time, and an attitude ready for an adventure. I think there are trails on the island, and kayaks are provided to explore the inlets, marshes, and bayou. Of course, there is wildlife. We will need to be on the lookout for alligators, snakes, deer, and there is reported to be a pair of cougars which were once widespread in Mississippi. The Mayor of Cat Island who resides in the bunk house swears he sees and hears the big cats every so often. He says they move around in a stealth-like manner." After a short moment of silence, Penny looked at Pop and smiled. Jake anxiously said, "Are you still in, Madam Speaker? Will this be too much for you and your family?" She smiled again, this time at her husband who was an adventurer and skillful hunter and fisherman." Pop smiled back at his eager bride and said, "Heck, yes! she's in, and so are the rest of us, although I'm not sure Andrew Reardon will be ok with all of the diversity of wildlife that might be encountered when exploring the island by kayak and foot."

Andrew quietly spoke what was on his heart and mind, "I'm in, for sure, I'm in! This sounds like the coolest trip we've ever been on and I'm banking on getting a peek of a real mountain lion and alligators in the marshes! I know we always have Brent and others with us everywhere we go, but on the island could it just be us?"

Penny spoke up, "Let's see how it goes, Andrew. As long as we are quiet when we are out on the remote trails and move stealthily like the big cats, and when we take kayaks to get to some remote island point, as long as we are moving quietly, we have a pretty good chance of seeing wildlife. We need at least to have Brent with us in case there is a problem with wild pigs or something of that nature."

Smiling, Andrew said, "Thanks Mom, you are a real peach!"

Returning his smile, she said, "That's my boy. We will make it happen, Handsome." She did wonder though, where the "you are a real peach" thing came from. Flamboyant Chef Emile could have used that when complementing something Andrew Reardon did for him. Yes, that sounded like something he would have said.

Penny Chatham loved her children and worked creatively to meet their needs. She hoped they would always speak what was on their minds including their aspirations and even short-term dreams like striking out through the forest to catch a glimpse of a pair of Cat Island Cougars. As their mom, she would try to make their reasonable wishes happen just like in a normal family even though this family's mother happened to be third in line from the presidency. She was intolerant of being in a glass bowl and protected from everyone and everything. Her children needed to have the customary family experiences as she had as a child. Andrew Reardon's desire for family centered time exploring the five-mile-long deserted island was a reasonable request.

After the family packed up, they said goodbye to Christine, dropping her off at her parent's home on Second Street and Cedar Lane in the Bay St. Louis's Historic District. Driving over the big arching bridge allowed them to look down on the Jourdan River and marshes and reflect on their recent fishing trip.

On the twenty-minute drive to the Long Beach Marina to embark on a deserted island journey, they passed through the fishing village of Pass Christian which had an abundance of wooden oyster skiffs in its marina used for tonging the nearby oyster reefs. Tonging was the traditional way of harvesting oysters from their reef homes. After passing through "the Pass," as the locals called it, it was then on to the hamlet of Long Beach. As usual, there was a SUV with capitol police in front of their caravan and one about 300 feet behind the Chatham's rented van. Penny Chatham had talked to Brent while they were packing up to share Andrew Reardon's need for family privacy and a little less hovering by the security people. Brent had a young family himself and fully understood the need for a little slack, especially since they were going to a remote, deserted island twenty-five miles offshore.

Longleaf Pine Trees Native to the Coast

CHAPTER 11

A New Breed - Conservative and Liberal

Politically, the President and Vice President were strong advocates of conservative values. They received financial support from like-minded heads of industry and supporters who were dedicated to making economic changes to the country. Over the years, administrations elected to provide leadership had become labeled either very traditional or broad-minded. The two extremes had evolved to divide the country into two distinct beliefs which were branded either conservative or liberal.

Likewise, many of the nation's church congregations were labeled conservative or liberal. In the Southern Region of the country most were conservative because they professed traditional values and were cautious about change and innovation. Made up of self-confident individuals with strong beliefs, the churches were not opposed to change, but only after lengthy consideration and a thorough discussion of related issues. This group included Penny Chatham's family church.

Conversely, those who are liberal are defined as open to new opinions, respectful of individual rights and freedoms, and concerned with broadening an individual's knowledge and experiences. Being conservative implies resisting change. Many of the younger and newer politicians believed the conservative and liberal labels did not match their philosophy. While many politicians have adopted the label of one extreme or the other, political leaders like Penny Chatham from conservative states often embraced both conservative and liberal values, as did their constituents.

Speaker Chatham was the new breed of politician with both traditional and broadminded values. She was confronted with natural environments plagued with problems. Having knowledge of natural systems and how they had been affected by changes in climate and human interference, she was able to address the increasing degradation of natural environments and communicate with disenchanted citizens.

The current administration was committed to the preservation of existing conservative traditions and institutions and doing business as it has always been done. President Harrison, a known conservative had allocated large sums of money to support the fossil fuel industry. Additionally, he had opened national forest lands for the wood products and building materials industry.

Regarding energy, the President believed that the United States was self-sufficient with energy resources including hydroelectric, nuclear, coal, and natural gas. His party believes nuclear energy is remarkably safe and non-polluting, coal is abundant and clean, and hydroelectric is safe and non-polluting.

Taxing carbon dioxide emissions and adhering to requirements for reducing carbon dioxide would be damaging to the economy and result in higher energy costs and a greater burden to citizens. His party believed the idea that fossil fuels cause global warming and increase changes in climate was outlandish and the triumph of extremism over common sense.

Industry leaders who underwrote reelection of the President and Vice President supported their beliefs. In return, the administration was thankful for the unified support provided by heads of industry and returned that thanks through funding projects that directly benefit supporters.

—————————

In Washington, D.C, there was growing concern about the condition of President Harrison. His health was not improving; in fact, it was deteriorating. His blood pressure was climbing, and physicians were unable to get his high body temperature lowered. The President was still coherent but was totally bedridden and not regularly communicating with his staff. Not even members of his immediate family were allowed to visit him.

As a precaution, Vice President Hardy was sequestered deep in the foothills of the Blue Ridge Mountains. He was being kept current on conditions in the country and the state of the President's declining condition. Chief Justice of the Supreme Court James Roberts had been called to Camp David to explain to the vice president the details of officially becoming president considering Jim Harrison's declining health. Vice President Hardy was informed that if the President were to be incapable of carrying out his duties or were to die, Chief Justice Roberts would administer the Presidential Oath of Office to him and he would become president.

The Secret Service was also preparing for alternatives. Secret Service Director Latady ordered an armored limousine be prepared to ship to the Stennis Space Center Airport which was near the Long Beach Marina and the closest water connection to Cat Island. She had not yet given the word to send the vehicle but was fully prepared in case it was necessary. The Director also assembled a team of Secret Service agents to provide security for Speaker Chatham if that became necessary. Chatham would become second in line to succeed the President if Jim Harrison passed away. Thirty agents were being briefed about the geography of south Mississippi, the Mississippi Sound, and specifically about Cat Island, the destination for Speaker Chatham and her family.

Orientation of the agents was being led by two experts from the coastal region who had been flown to Washington on military aircraft. GIS expert Jonathan Cathcart from the Naval Observatory at the Space Center provided geographic orientation from an aerial perspective. Hannah Thomas, a naturalist from Pass Christian with detailed knowledge of the island provided all of its physical characteristics for walking, wading, and kayaking, and alternative water routes for departing the island. Besides instructing the agents on the description and hazards of the landscape, she explained the nature and potential suitability of nearby islands including Louisiana's Chandeleur Islands as a rendezvous place for terrorist organizations if an attack on Speaker Chatham was planned.

Director Latady's objective for the orientation was to ensure that there would be no geographic surprises for the agents. As Director of the Secret Service, she was always thinking ahead. If her agents were needed to provide secure conditions for the Speaker of the House of Representatives, they needed to be as familiar as possible with the barrier island's unique wilderness, as well as the Mississippi Sound from the island to the mainland. In the world of high-level security, the U.S. Secret Service set the bar for being prepared and making smart decisions. This situation was no exception.

Grove of Live Oak Trees

CHAPTER 12

King David's Bible Study

Given the grim situation of President Harrison's health and questionable continuation as president, an influential group of financial wizards belonging to a group known as King David's Bible Study convened to make a firm commitment to ensure that the flow of federal money to projects they supported would not be interrupted if there were a change in leadership.

More than half of the financial support for the election and reelection of the president and vice president had been provided by King David's Bible Study. Due to their generosity, this gathering of heads of industry played a major role in selecting federal projects that would receive funding and which environmental regulations needed to be loosened for the benefit of projects they championed.

The commitment of the Harrison Administration to support ongoing projects had to be carried through even if there was a change within the executive branch of government. Billions of dollars were at stake and that was too much to risk without assurances that changes in leadership would result in the continuation of federal funding commitments. Bets had been placed, and King David's Bible Study played to win!

The capitalists met in downtown Detroit, Michigan in a nondescript three-story, 1800's brick office building on Henry Ford Boulevard. This was a setting that would not attract attention as many of the most notable heads of industry rolled into town for a group pow-wow. Sitting around a long, two-and-a-half-inch thick rectangular table of old growth Chestnut cut from a Midwest Forest, a lovely young lady offered Bible Study members coffee or tea, either hot or iced. Charlotte was an attractive and smart looking brunette girl in her early thirties. Nearly six feet tall, the slim server had the figure of a university volleyball player. Tender confidence flowed from her mannerisms as she quietly interacted with King David Bible Study members. Her looks belied her polished and yet cunning ways as the personal assistant to Donald Anniston.

Visually, the movers and shakers were not unified in any way. Their ages varied, and the manner in which they dressed was very different from one another. Lawrence Mathis, a gentle looking man in his 60's was owner of a national line of nursing homes and retirement centers. He wore a fashionable brown checked suit with an open collar. For recreation, Lawrence enjoyed hunting white tail deer and wild boars. His elegant lake cabin in north Mississippi featured many of his most impressive mounts from around the country.

Carl Van Stovall, in his early 70's, was the largest stockholder in the Ford Motor Company and a committed proponent of the continued use of fossil fuel power. He had the build of one who was a daily runner and was dressed in straight cut Wrangler Jeans and a pearl-buttoned long-sleeved country western style shirt. For recreation, Carl tended his collection of spectacular, award-winning daylilies in a garden that had been featured in design magazines. His son Jakk was a landscape architect and regularly consulted with his granddad on design decisions for his notable Louisiana garden.

Loy Ray Vieters was the CEO of the Deep South Power and Drinking Water Company, one of the nation's oldest and largest utility companies. Loy Ray, as the group called him, was in his late 50's and was elected to the company's leadership position because of his skillful handling of controversial situations and his knowledge of the evolving attitudes about sources of clean energy. Whenever he had the chance, he prophesied that building energy efficient buildings was the most efficient way to save energy, declaring that most buildings could be built so they used 70-90% less energy than conventional buildings! His Detroit meeting outfit was Lucky Brand designer Jeans and a long-sleeved blue shirt from J.C. Penny. His socks were decorated with motifs featuring the sun and on his feet were 100% sustainable, black Allbirds Shoes made of merino wool from New Zealand.

Henry Oliver was an older, sophisticated philanthropist from the Dallas, Texas area. His manner of dress was a grey suit with a pale blue striped tie. He managed family oil money and was the CEO of multiple companies including chicken processing plants across the South and coal burning power plants in Virginia and Alabama.

He also had developed a vintage-style hotel chain situated in scenic locations including on federal lands and in national parks.

Donald Anniston, the Bible study group leader and the one who called the meeting, came in a pink polo style knit shirt with plaid Bermuda shorts and a hand sewn belt which featured images of Bibles. When anyone commented on the belt's uniqueness, he happily explained it was his Bible belt. Being from Alabama, which was in the middle of Bible Belt country, he was proud to wear it in public gatherings to show his allegiance to God and country. Aniston was a principal in a venture capital firm that owned companies and investments valued at thirty billion dollars.

Bringing the assembly of financial powerhouses to order, the Harvard business school graduate smiled big and genuinely, "Welcome to this early summer meeting of the King David Bible Study. I know you have been keeping current with the health of our president and have some thoughts on how we need to interpret existing conditions in our nation's capital.

"Just as we make investment decisions that benefit the country, we are here to sustain the nation's health and vigor by laying out a strategy for implementing those decisions. The agreements for implementation of the policies and projects already underway by our government must be carried through, despite what happens in the executive branch. In light of Jim Harrison's condition, if he dies and Vice President Steve Hardy becomes the President, it is imperative that we are all in agreement that the administration's current policies will be carried on."

There were reassuring smiles and nods of affirmation from around the table and several members spoke in support of Steve

Hardy's ability for keeping the country in good economic and social health. Don continued, "Those comments are comforting, but we need to make doubly sure that Hardy commits to support the projects the administration has ongoing and fund the future proposals we all agreed on as well. It would be unacceptable for him to make any radical changes if he assumes the president's position. That could be disastrous for us and harmful for the prosperity of the country."

Looking around the room as he slowly paced the perimeter of the long oval shape of the conference table, he queried, "Are there any objections?" Not hearing any opposition, he said, "Since we are in general agreement, I'm going to ask Loy Ray and Carl Van if they would meet with Vice President Hardy as soon as possible. After meeting with him, summarize your findings, and we will get Charlotte to share those meeting results with each member. If there are problems, some of us can sit down with the Vice President and do some arm bending. If it comes to that, I can arrange a meeting with Steve's chief of staff, Mike Anderson."

"Even if Jim Harrison pulls out of his spiraling condition and survives whatever it is he has contracted, his health will probably render him unable to meet the demands of the office. It's important for us to know his current condition on a daily basis. Charlotte and I will visit with his Chief of Staff Maggie Williams, and see what we can learn about the succession situation. Charlotte, who served you refreshments, will call each of you personally and keep you updated on his condition. If you are unavailable, she will leave a message for you to call her back. She will not leave you a recorded or text message on the president's condition."

The group all looked at Charlotte Hall who was striking in her snug fitting, two-piece suit that made her appear taller than she probably was. She smiled back at the highly successful group of businessmen with a look of admiration like being introduced to John Grisham. The Bible Study members returned friendly looks like older gentlemen with good upbringing would share with new female acquaintances. It was not at all like the scrutinizing look they regularly gave to their Bible Study leader Donald Anniston.

Charging ahead, Anniston continued, "What we do today sets the course for our country's economic and social stability as well as our bottom lines. Now, let us review the details of the administration's economic strategy. If there are changes that need to be considered, now is the time to bring them up."

Loy Ray Vieters, the CEO of the Deep South Power and Drinking Water Company jumped in, "Don, I just have to say, for our ears only, we are in a dilemma at Southern. If the country's dependence on our nation's established ways of producing energy were to change to reliance on renewal energy, that would be disastrous for our bottom line. Along with our hydroelectric plants, we have three older but highly productive anthracite coal power plants and one that is only six years old near Meridian, Mississippi. We also have the big nuclear facility at Savannah, Georgia. Of course, we cannot afford to disassemble and lose those major power producers."

Loy Ray talked openly. What he shared could have severely affected his businesses and the value of the company's stock. However, he knew he was with a team of like-minded business professionals, and like family brothers, they held each other's success in high regard and would keep his comments to themselves.

"Here is our dilemma, for your ears only, in our country and among other first world nations, there is developing a major shift from fossil fuels to clean, renewable power. Even steel and aluminum production now have a category for low-carbon metals, and in the U.K., low-carbon aluminum is available on a globally traded market. Some governments and large companies are buying it because their constituents are demanding it!

"It is the same with gasoline powered vehicles. I'm sure you are aware, and Carl, you can support me on this, all of the car and truck makers have electrical vehicles in production. We are beginning to be forced by a ground swell of public interest to provide clean energy, reduce our use of fossil fuels, and diminish the emission of CO_2 into the atmosphere. Power companies are responding. The fact is, there are large solar arrays that can provide this clean energy and send it to the power grid. However, it would be economically disastrous for our country to concede to the clean solar power voices at this time. It might be smart for the administration to help contain a dramatic switch to solar power as best as it can."

Smiling, with a smug look of confidence that there was staunch unity among Bible study members, Don Anniston said, "Thank you, Loy Ray, for the insight. It makes no sense to be in a country that is one of the few in the world that is energy independent and also has the general public asking for a switch to solar energy. We need to rely on our established technologies and use the natural resources with which we are blessed. As you said, we must contain the evolution or revolution to solar power, whichever way you look at it. Now, let's review President Harrison's policies for economic and social stability.

"Regarding the popular movement to establish a national commitment for reducing the use of fossil fuels, the current administration is not a supporter. Companies that produce and supply oil and gas to industry and homes would suffer as would our political party supporters who are investors in those industries. The cost of energy would rise and that goes against the Party Platform. If reducing fossil fuel use becomes policy, then we need to know that in advance of it being made public so we and our associates can divest themselves of energy assets. As we have expressed today, reducing our dependence on fossil fuels would not be a popular move for our Bible Study members who comprise the backbone of financial health of the party, if not the nation. We cannot allow that to evolve!

"The administration has clearly committed to support industry involved in moving goods worldwide. Continued funding of transportation related development is key to this effort. Money for upgrading ports and shipping facilities will make moving goods by water, rail, and air more effective and will support the bottom lines of our industries involved in worldwide trading. Continued support for this is clear." Looking around the room, Donald saw bright faces both nodding in agreement and showing no emotion at all. Both were good signs. If there was a concern or disagreement, this group would actively object by voicing their concerns, but there was no objection.

"Domestically, support for infrastructure is in the budget and federal money is beginning to be allocated for highway construction and the engineering for bridge planning and building projects. Party supporters are owners of large engineering and planning companies, and of paving and roadway construction companies. This is big and it is important. If you are not in it, now is a good time to consider becoming a part of the coming big money for infrastructure, both replacement of old projects and creation of new ventures. If you are unaware of these opportunities, contact your senators. There will be opportunities for you.

"Establishment of recreation opportunities for more tourism dollars will stimulate valuable land development projects and increase adjacent land values. We have six large reservoirs planned across the country that will be created by damming rivers which would provide these benefits. Party backers are investors in these large land enhancement projects and stand to benefit heavily from the national recreation projects. Henry, I'm sure you are in on these opportunities with your vintage hotels."

There was no verbal response but only a slight nod of the head. That was Henry's way of making sure the Bible Study meeting would not be any longer than it had to be. Most of his communication was through subtle movements.

"We need to be aware that opposition is building against damming rivers for these projects. Four of the reservoirs will be on rivers that tree huggers are calling wild rivers that have no dams on them. Opposition is stiff but that does not mean the reservoirs cannot be built. Our congressional representatives need to push these projects through to quell the opposition. Where we can help, timing will be important. Reach deep in those pockets and let's get those projects going. Our party platform states we need to use our natural resources wisely to create employment in rural areas of the country.

"As a matter of public knowledge, Mississippi and Louisiana's Gulf Coasts are benefitting from freshwater being diverted from the

Pearl River that borders both states. Senators Long and Knox convinced the President to provide 300 million dollars to provide more fresh water, reduce runoff pollution from the mainland, and for the creation of fresh and saltwater marshes to make the Mississippi Sound Estuary able to produce oysters again. Speaker Chatham stuck her nose in the project to make sure local mayors and supervisors did not benefit from any of that money with local projects like boat ramps and flood control levees. Instead, it was all spent directly on water quality enhancement projects with limited opportunity for investors. We don't need to get carried away with that tightfisted approach. Few of our investors benefitted from those changes. It is said the increase of seafood in the estuary two years after the project has made Penny Chatham a local folk hero. Her streamlined spending for water quality improvements could cut into our American way of doing business. We cannot let that kind of thinking dominate the way federal money is used.

"Investment in the building materials sector is supported by our Party Platform which has convinced congress to open national forests in the west, north, and deep south for harvesting old growth timber. There was opposition to clear cutting of these mature forests but our political power is strong and determined to make changes that would provide more money flowing to the truck driver, the wood cutter, and to the mills and construction industry across the country. This kind of effort provides jobs, jobs, and more jobs in rural areas where employment is slack. Opposition to the use of our renewable resources is growing. What is the big deal? The trees will grow back, that's why they call them renewable resources! We can't let that kind of thinking become commonplace because it will slow down our economy and limit investment opportunity.

"These are the high points for which we all need to be aware. This is the investment opportunity. Our money needs to be spent on vital projects that help stabilize and enhance national economic conditions. It is in this context that we will keep current regarding our dear President Jim Harrison's health, and Vice President Steve Hardy's commitment to existing federal pledges. It is imperative that current obligations are carried out and are not endangered in any way. We will protect the ideals of our party and how federal money is being spent, at any cost, and I do mean at any cost. Do I hear any amens from King David's Bible Study group?"

Amens were boldly shouted from all around the nineteenth century chestnut table that had witnessed many deals by those who pledged to stand up for the financial health and prosperity of the country. Satisfied with the unity expressed for safeguarding federal commitments of dollars, the mixed group made brief but pleasant conversation with one another, and then departed from Detroit.

As Donald Anniston left the meeting and was chauffeured to his private jet, he knew he had been right when he had encouraged his friends to organize their investment group after church bible studies. The camaraderie that builds in small study groups in churches and their firm dedication to ecclesiastical ways had transferred to this group of businessmen who were all dedicated to their capital ventures.

He remembered suggesting that King David from ancient Israel be chosen as the Bible Study name because David had come from humble beginnings. Several in the group could relate to his progressing from an unpretentious Bethlehem shepherd who became the armor bearer for King Saul who slew the Philistine giant, and then became one of Israel's greatest kings. Anniston's satisfaction was reflected in his face as he walked across the tarmac toward his plane.

Sea Oats

CHAPTER 13

Charlotte Hall and Camille Latady

Charlotte, of course, knew details about the discussions in King David's Bible Study. She knew of what the seemingly benevolent group was capable and that they were not as compassionate about supporting the American Dream as they were their own personal assets. Through her working for Donald Anniston and her acumen when establishing personal contacts in Washington, she was privy to first-hand accounts on the condition of President Harrison. The unanswered probability of his impending death or his inability to carry out his duties as President of the United States was the gold for which she was seeking.

Charlotte Hall understood that tumbling blocks of power in the White House could affect leadership in the federal government. More importantly was the viability of projects already funded and would they continue. Of course, she was fully aware of the edict of King David's Bible Study for maintaining the government's commitment to existing projects regardless of who the president was as long as those that contributed heavily to get the president elected, lavishly benefitted. It bothered her to consider what that obligation could mean to the wellbeing of Penny Chatham if conditions changed and she inherited a major leadership role in the executive branch of government.

The Speaker of the House impressed Charlotte. She had worked tirelessly on projects which she believed would be good for the country and was seemingly honest in all of her dealings. Her support of ventures to restore the Mississippi Sound estuary and the Lake Pontchartrain Basin was impressive. Those rural wilderness areas were populated by some of the most contentious people in the United States and Speaker Chatham had managed to convince them to work together for the benefit of marine life and wildlife in Louisiana and Mississippi.

The proof of her energy, drive, and positive outlook to implement changes on the ground were beginning to be clearly evident two years after modifications to the Pearl River Basin. Additional freshwater flowing into the Mississippi Sound had returned saltwater to its original brackish condition and provided for a vigorous return of wild oysters.

The oyster reefs had created more marine life biodiversity. Their form diminished the forces of wave action and reduced shoreline erosion. Daylight extended to greater depths in the clearer water increasing phytoplankton for oysters and marine life in the lower level of the food chain. Wild oysters from the Mississippi Sound were coming back and were once again available at Felix's and Acme Oyster Bars in the Vieux Carre.

Along with the increased fishing opportunities for oystermen, seafood processing plants were once again canning and shipping products harvested from the Mississippi Sound. Major increases in blue crabs were a boom for processing plants around Lake Pontchartrain in Louisiana. Returning the salinity of water in the estuaries to their historical range created many beneficial changes for marine life, the coastal edge, and for fishermen.

While Speaker Chatham had great zeal for restoring damaged natural environments, she was also a proponent of reducing the nation's heating and cooling energy needs through slowly changing buildings to be responsive to natural processes like the daily and seasonal movement of the sun and the change of seasons which would save the amount of energy they used. Citizens saved money, and using less energy reduced the amount of carbon dioxide being emitted into the atmosphere.

In her talks, Chatham preached the benefits of a rectangular building shape with the long side facing south to absorb wintertime sunlight and reduce heating costs. The length of its roof overhang on the south side would allow the low angle of winter sunlight to warm the south side of the building and stream through the windows to heat the indoors.

That same overhang would block the high angle of summertime sunlight from striking the building's south side. Along with tree planting on its east and west sides, summer sunlight would not strike the building, thereby significantly reducing energy costs for indoor cooling.

As a graduate of Stanford University in California, Charlotte understood and supported the possibilities for creating low energy use buildings. She had become aware of living sustainably in a physics course which focused on energy efficient building design where the class used Regenerative Design Techniques, a book by professors at Mississippi State University.

Charlotte was impressed with Penny Chatham's determination to create a grass roots movement to educate home and business owners about the growing impact of relying entirely on fossil fuels for energy. It was an exciting new frontier that spoke to the brainy Charlotte Hall. With the remote possibility that the torch of government leadership would be passed on to the Speaker of the House, Donald Anniston's Personal Assistant was not going to be the one to cause her to stumble.

Penny Chatham was third in line to the highest office in the land but could easily become second. The possibility existed that she could even succeed to the most influential leadership role on the planet. Charlotte could not ever allow King David's Bible Study to prevent Penny Chatham's succession to a higher office. That would violate her environmental ethics and her decency as a human being.

These thoughts distressed the Stanford Graduate in Environmental Studies. She wondered if Don Anniston even knew what degree she had earned. He only introduced her as his personal assistant and a graduate of Stanford University. Her trophy looks and a degree from Stanford was how she was recognized. For a while, that plus the $175,000 a year salary was fine with her, but as Penny Chatham's movement for building sustainably gained in popularity, she felt compelled to help her, or, at the very least not to stop her vital crusade dead in its tracts.

Through her contact with a criminology professor at school she sought to determine who might be a key government official to share information with about the King David Bible Study group. She thought someone should know about their plan to stop any individual or group that would affect the Harrison administration's support and funding for existing and planned projects should there be a change in leadership in the executive branch. This resistance to change would be carried out at any cost.

Her former professor had explained that the current administration's circle of wagons in Washington was very tight and that a government agency that was apolitical would be her best bet. A close friend who was a senator in Tennessee, said the only division in the judicial branch of government that was unbiased was the Federal Bureau of Investigation. Even more independent of political inquiry and persuasion was the Secret Service.

While in Washington, D.C., after having met with President Harrison's publicity director where she got a very disturbing account on the president's condition, she decided to walk to the nearby headquarters of the Secret Service. Determined to go to the top and visit with its director, she convinced herself that now was the time to see if anyone in the federal government would be interested in her insight and compelling information.

Arriving at their control center she met a brick wall. The uniformed agents outside of the building would not even let her walk into their headquarters. She tried her best to get an audience with Director Camille Latady through telling the agent in charge how important it was to have just a few minutes with the director. What she had to share was of national importance. The agent whose favorite word was "no," was enjoying the spirited conversation with the tall, slim, and good-looking brunette. He asked, "Tell me, Charlotte, what would I be able to tell our director that would convince her to take a few minutes out of her busy day and visit with you?"

Sensing the agent who was also in his early thirties was enjoying their conversation and delighting in challenging her motive to see the director, Charlotte put on her most serious face, paused, and then said "King David's Bible Study."

The agent just stood there smiling. After a pause, his smile turned to one of concern. He responded in a questioning manner, "King David's Bible Study?"

She responded, "Yes, tell her King David's Bible Study." The agent who was in his mid-thirties calmly stared at this uninvited guest and continued to wonder about the mental condition of the athletic stylish beauty.

"Yes," said Charlotte. Pausing, she continued, "I believe she will take the time to talk with me a few minutes if you just tell her King David's Bible Study."

The calm, uniformed Secret Service Agent looked carefully into the eyes of this confident, and yet determined beauty to see if there were signs of derangement. Confidently, the visitor gently smiled as the guard stepped back and looked her over good. Receiving a text, two nearby agents walked up to take Charlotte to an area behind a nearby screen and do a thorough physical security check. Apparently, someone in authority inside the building watching a video of the conversation with Miss Charlotte Hall decided she was being persistent enough to warrant additional evaluation.

"Miss Hall," the desk agent said with authority, "may we search you for weapons?" She calmly nodded ok.

"Leave your purse here on the desk. It and you will be examined by our security people." The two plainclothes agents gently guided her behind a high masonry wall that served as a security check screen where she was swept with a metal detector and patted down for plastic explosives. An agent with plastic gloves wiped her hands and forearms with a moist cloth taken from a sealed bag. They placed the cloth back in the bag, sprayed it with a reagent, and sealed the bag. When they were convinced there was no chemical contamination on her hands, the female agent said, "Thank you, Miss Hall, let's go back to the security desk."

Agent Parker who had first encountered Charlotte Hall said, "Thank you for your patience. I told Director Camille Latady there was a distinguished young lady that wished to talk with her. I asked you what could be said that would convince the director to visit with her and I shared those four words with her. Normally the Director does not have visitors and hardly ever meets with the public."

Charlotte anxiously interrupted, "And what was her response?"

The agent responded, "After I told her the four words, she asked to meet with you in the first-floor secure briefing room. You've got your five minutes with Director Latady. Go with these two agents. We will keep your handbag here at the front and you may pick it up when you leave." Smiling at the young secret service agent she said, "Thank you. You have done a good deed for your country."

Returning her very sincere smile, Agent Parker, with his lips pursed, gave her a subtle grin and uttered so she, but only she, could hear it, "Go for it, lady." Her tenacity and honesty got her a meeting with the one leader in the federal government without political bias that had the ability to act on information of potentially national importance. Charlotte Hall was relieved to be able to divulge the extent to which King David's Bible Study would go to stop Penny Chatham from ascending to a higher position of influence in the federal government.

Smiling to herself and rejoicing within, the unexpected visitor was escorted by the two plain clothes agents to a small conference room within the interior of the building. When the agent knocked on the solid wood door of the briefing room, a pleasant female voice said, "Please come in." Having her first look at the emissary of the most powerful group of investors in the country, Director Latady said, "Please sit-down, Miss Hall. Agents, close the door behind you if you will."

The ladies sat at either end of the eight-foot-long wood conference table. The room was quiet, very quiet, like it had thick insulation in the walls and a ceiling that prevented transfer of any sounds. Charlotte noticed there were no ambient noises including nearby street noises. Director Latady was in her forties and dressed in a gray two-piece suit. Her complexion was an olive color and Charlotte thought she appeared to be of French Creole descent.

The two alluring powerful women smiled as they looked at one another. Finally, Director Latady said, "Thank you for taking time to go through the hoops to visit with us. We have to be very careful nowadays regarding unannounced meetings."

Charlotte smilingly responded, "I understand completely. Director Latady."

The Director of the Secret Service replied, "Please, Charlotte, call me Camille."

Charlotte smiled and responded, "Of course, Director Camille." Continuing with her introductory thoughts she asked, "Can this conversation be off the record?"

"It can, Charlotte, and at your request, it will be," replied the Director of personal security for the President and Vice President and speaking clearly with complete thoughts as though every word of the ensuing conversation would be information important to national security and documented for future reference. Camille Latady waited calmly but also with anticipation to hear what the personal assistant to the leader of the influential group of businessmen had to share.

"First, I chose your organization with which to share this information because I needed to confide in someone within our government that does not have a political bias. I did my research, and it was either going to be the FBI or the Secret Service. I know of instances where an FBI Director had expressed political openness toward one of our political parties and that makes him biased when you hear what I have to say."

Camille Latady smiled and slightly shook her head up and down in affirmation to Charlotte's conclusion. Charlotte continued, "So, I feel most secure sharing confidential information with the U.S. Secret Service. Are you and your organization apolitical?"

"Yes, we are, Charlotte. We could not be in charge of our clients' security if there were political biases that might taint how we act in split-second life and death situations."

Charlotte glanced down at her folded hands, and then looked up with a red flush on her face staring at the government figure to whom she was about to confide extremely foreboding information. Finally, she quietly spoke as though what she had to say could be heard only by the lady across the table, "The King David Bible Study group has made a decision to combat Speaker Penny Chatham's way of thinking and prevent her from becoming president should that become a possibility. I know it's a long shot for her to become president due to succession, but I thought someone in our government needed to know that if that transition did evolve, it would be vigorously contested."

Camille sat silently, looked down at the brightly polished table-top and breathed deeply. She looked up and said to Charlotte, "This is between you and me. President Harrison's physicians say he is critical and may not live for more than two or three days." Charlotte put her hand to her mouth in distress. Shaking her head up and down the Director continued, "We are in the process of transporting the Chief Justice of the Supreme Court back to Camp David to administer the oath of office and transfer the office of President of the United States to Vice President, Steve Hardy. This puts a little more pressure on your Speaker Chatham. "

Camille was all business now that she felt like she had confidence in what her unannounced visitor had to say. "Tell me the names of those in the Bible study group and which members are the most hostile toward Speaker Chatham." The personal assistant to Donald Anniston did as she was asked. Camille then got all of Charlotte Hall's contact information including taking a cell phone facial photograph and one focused on the fingers and palm of her open hand.

"Thank you, Charlotte Hall. You are a brave United States Citizen, and we value your being concerned about the peaceful transfer of power. I will be in touch with you. What is the contact of a dependable college girlfriend with whom I can set up a phone call with you if needed?" Charlotte complied with her request.

She was then escorted out of the building by two agents, past the security desk to pick up her Burberry Handbag, and then to a waiting unmarked car which would take her wherever she needed to go. As she walked past the building's guard desk, she winked at the handsome uniformed guard whom she first met. He smiled and gave her a subtle one-fingered salute that suggested respect and admiration for whatever she had come to share with the Director of the world renown U.S. Secret Service.

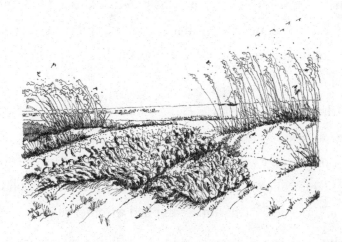

Sand Dunes, Sea Oats and the Mississippi Sound

CHAPTER 14

Cat Island Bound

As the Chatham family was pulling into the Long Beach Marina, a cell phone message to Pop informed him to follow the lead security SUV and pull the family van right next to it. The family was not to get out until the second SUV of their security detail pulled up on the other side of the van and an agent would open the door for them. They were to stay in place until that occurred.

Pop thought the tightness of the distance between the vehicles was a little uncomfortable and he was concerned about the apparent increase in cautiousness. However, he told the family to wait, not exit the car. Once Brent opened the sliding door, he said, "Ok, Madam

Speaker, your boat is ready. I will walk you to the boat. Your family will be escorted by other agents."

Penny Chatham asked, "So, Brent, what's up with the extra attention?"

He responded, "I think it is just Washington exercising a little more awareness of Penny Chatham. Probably just an exercise to keep us all sharp." As they walked down the marina boardwalk, she looked back to make sure her family was being taken care of. Sarah Jane was walking close beside a security guard named J.T., and Andrew Reardon and Sister Leah were holding hands and walking next to Linda Jack who was not a regular with the Chatham family detail. She had been assigned to this Gulf Coast trip after she recovered from the West Nile Virus which she contracted on duty in South Carolina when Speaker Chatham was speaking at a national conference. Once you've contracted West Nile, your body is immune to the virus and Linda Jack had completely recovered.

Penny hollered back, "You kids do as you are told, or we will drop you off somewhere between here and Cat Island!" Looking back at Linda Jack she shouted, "Glad you are back, Linda. Are you feeling good? I didn't know you were down here."

Linda smiled back and said, "Excited to be here, Madam Speaker. I'm back in the saddle now from the virus. It was tough, but hopefully I'm like you, tougher than the opposition!" Penny Chatham smiled and gave her a thumbs up.

Michael Bergeron met them at the skiff that would take Penny to Cat Island. He was a fishing guide and the one who was in charge of the island's home and all of the experiences offered at the guest lodge. He was a big, powerful looking man with broad shoulders and dark hair. Pleasantly he said, "Madam Speaker, we are pleased you have chosen to experience the Mississippi Sound with us. You and your family will have a great time, and hopefully, mother nature will provide plenty of successful fishing activity for you." Penny smiled and simply said, "Thank you." Her mind, sensitive to the extra precautions was elsewhere, primarily on the safety of her family.

As she was helped into the skiff by Brent, he told her, "You will be going in this boat with me and J.T. He will be joining us as soon as your family has boarded their skiffs." J.T. was near retirement age and the oldest of the capitol police agents. Always a pleasant agent with a happy attitude, he seemed to know people everywhere they went. The family knew J.T. from their many travel experiences. Brent explained to Secretary Chatham, "We are dividing up your family in three skiffs because of all of your belongings and gear, and to accommodate the increased security for which Washington has asked." The Speaker was quiet and looked back at her family. But because she had occasionally been the recipient of increased security for seemingly no obvious reasons, she took the conditions in stride and relaxed.

Pop and Sister Leah got into the next skiff along the pier with a slim, wiry, and talkative fishing guide named Bob Collins. He was all smiles and explained how much time it would take to get to the island and the speed at which the boat would travel to get there. A security agent named John Russell would travel with them. He was a quiet guy and like J.T., was a regular on the Speaker's security detail when she was traveling.

Andrew Reardon and Sarah Jane were joined by agent Dorothy Belle in the third boat. She was in her 50's and was caring and motherly which slightly irritated Andrew who was feeling like he was nearly grown up and didn't need any extra care. This skiff was a DMR marine patrol boat and was driven by a DMR police officer.

As the group pulled out of the Long Beach Marina harbor the Chatham family felt as though they had left the world behind them. The stiff sea breeze blowing in from the Gulf swept all the restrictions on their lives behind them. The southeast wind was strong enough to extend a flag horizontally, causing white caps to form on the waves which became higher the further they traveled away from the mainland.

The whole departure thing was beautiful, except her family's personal security had been on her mind since they pulled up tightly between the two capitol police SUVs at the marina. That was odd. She also noted each capitol police officer boarded their skiffs carrying a black padded rifle case. On her previous travel experiences, there had never been such a show of heavy arms. Maybe that level of security was necessary because they were going to a deserted island twenty-five miles from the mainland. Or, maybe that was not the reason?

Penny Chatham sat bouncing along in the fast skiff with a Capitol Police officer on either side of her instead of Sister Leah, Sarah Jane, and Andrew Reardon. Her eager son would have probably been rambling around the boat checking out other places to sit. Most likely he would have settled in on the seat in front of the driver's console all by himself, taking in the expanding view of the increasingly bigger and wider expanse of water. In that location, the sights were the best and a light spray from waves hitting the bow on the charging boat would cool is face, arms, and legs. He, no doubt, would be thinking of the pirates of Barataria and brothers Jean and

Pierre Lafitte that the professor had briefly mentioned to him before the Spanish dagger debacle unfolded.

It had been a few years since he had chosen to sit beside his mother. There is a time in many boys' lives when they leap from the nest to grovel around on the ground and create a temporary mess of their lives, or find a way to create good things and become outstanding contributors to their communities. Penny Chatham hoped for the best for her little pirate Andrew Reardon. She hugged and loved on him as much as he would let her, which was infrequently.

As the three twenty-five-foot-long saltwater skiffs sped southward toward an island that you could not yet see but knew it was out there, four more DMR marine patrol boats joined them, two on each side of the family skiffs. The family vacation had seemingly become a flotilla of security personnel. The Speaker was now fully aware of the dramatic increase in security and would talk to Jake Ingram about it once they got settled in on the island.

Through an early summertime fog that happens when a cool spell moves in over the warm brackish water of the Mississippi Sound, a long stretch of tall, longleaf pine forest began to emerge. Expansive salt marshes and white sandy beaches bordered the southern side of the island. The marshes were part of nature's planting design creating a broad, lime green base on which the stunning pine trees sat. The Speaker's boat led the entourage of skiffs now slowing their approach to the edge of the island. The form of a small inlet appeared from within the broad base of salt marshes providing a welcoming feeling. Penny was excited finally to see an opening that would allow them to get into the interior of the deserted island and arrive at the three-story home.

Mike Bergeron, the skiff driver and experienced fishing guide announced, "We are entering Jean Lafitte Bayou. It will wind around a while and take us to the lone home on the island. I think you will be impressed. Our guests have always been pleased with our deserted island accommodations. Penny Chatham hoped Agent Bob Collins had told Andrew the name of the bayou, as she quipped back to Mike, "So am I hearing it right that we are going to rough it a little bit?"

The fishing guide and Cat Island host laughed, "Well, I will let you tell me if where you will be staying is challenging and rough in any way." He was smiling big as though his new guest and her family were going to be shocked out of their drawers.

As the skiff glided through the bayou creating only the slightest wake, the view to their accommodations was slowly revealed around a bend of salt marsh grasses punctuated with marsh elder shrubs and swamp red maple trees. Ahead, now finally in full view, the gorgeous three-story home with a deep balcony across its front sat on an elevated grassed clearing forty-feet from the edge of the bayou. To say it was impressive was an understatement. The Speaker softly reacted, "Not in my wildest dreams would I have guessed there would be this kind of accommodation on a deserted Mississippi island twenty-five miles off the coast!"

Mike Bergeron looked back at her and smiled saying, "I think you will like it. With all you've done to improve our coast, you deserve it, Mrs. Chatham."

Indeed, the Speaker of the House of Representatives was astounded by the beauty of the fashionable three-story home. There was nothing rough and weathered looking about it. The skiff pulled up to a pier constructed of large wooden timbers that stretched along the bank. As her chief of security Brent helped the agile Secretary step onto the wooden pier she turned and said to her fishing guide, "I am truly amazed Mike Bergeron, this is beautiful!"

Mike just smiled and replied, "It is called Pelican Roost." Fishing guides are generally laid-back men of few words. They make up for their words with their action helping people catch fish and keeping them safe from fish hooks, snapping jaws with rows of teeth, and dorsal fins which at times, can be flying around from fish flopping on the boat deck like thugs in a knife fight!

As the other boats pulled up, agents J.T. and Dorothy went into Pelican Roost to evaluate conditions. Providing security for the Speaker meant thoroughly checking the lodge to ensure a safe environment. The big home had three bedrooms and a loft on the third story with fifteen single beds to accommodate families who might have an abundance of kids. There was a large, open covered deck beneath the home with hammocks, chairs, a refreshment bar, and plenty of games such as darts and Hillbilly Golf. It was a shady retreat for Mississippi's July and August heat. On top of all of the sanctuary's amenities, it was on a deserted island, in the Mississippi Sound, and too far from the mainland to receive cell phone calls or have television reception. Even on a clear day, land could just barely be seen!

When the Speaker's security came down from inspecting the house interior, they gave the ok signal for the rest of the family to begin their own exploration of the island tree house as Andrew Reardon loudly called it as he got off the boat. Pop had been reading to him and Sister Leah about Robinson Caruso before bedtime. As they walked up the board walk, they passed a dozen or so large, domesticated brown rabbits eating grass and hiding beneath the boardwalk. The rabbits were unbothered by the new guests and friendly enough to let the kids who were overwhelmed by their presence, feed them grass and clover, but not pick them up. Mike Bergeron had brought a few over from the mainland anticipating that they would be a novel addition to an already fantastic homestead! They were a hit with all of the Chathams.

Penny and Pop walked up into the second story of the home to the living quarters. It contained a large kitchen and dining space, and a huge lounging area with sectional sofas located in a two-story living room with floor to ceiling windows overlooking the bayou. They put their baggage in one of the three bedrooms on that level. The kids, not surprisingly, chose the loft on the top floor of the home where they had a choice of selecting their bed among the fifteen that were in the big open space. Their views from the loft balcony overlooked the large living room and beyond through the two-story windows to the Cat Island marshes, Jean Lafitte Bayou, and a mature slash pine forest. Putting their travel bags on their favorite bed, they rushed downstairs to go out onto the porch off the living room that stretched across the front of the house. It was lined with rockers and chaise lounge chairs that provided panoramic views to forests, the bayou, salt marshes, and distant views across the Mississippi Sound toward the mainland.

Fishing guides Mike and Bob met with Penny and Pop and shared with them the island schedule. They could have their meals prepared and served at the long kitchen table whenever they wanted. When the group was ready to bathe, they needed to tell their hosts so they could turn on the hot water heater. Interior air temperature would be held at 76 degrees Fahrenheit unless guests preferred that to be changed.

The menu for lunch that day was boiled shrimp and fried chicken tenders with a garden salad, green bean casserole, macaroni and cheese, and a congealed strawberry dessert. The hosts needed thirty minutes notice so that the table could be set, and the chicken fried.

The plan for dinner that evening depended on what they caught while fishing the marshes that afternoon. If they got skunked, there would be rib eye steaks and hamburgers with baked potatoes and boiled corn. Dessert would be banana pudding.

Penny and Pop were overwhelmed. They were ready for lunch and asked if after lunch would be a good time to go fishing. Mike assured them, "We nearly always have good luck with speckled trout any time of the day and sometimes redfish too. We are ready to go whenever you are and fish as much as you want. In the mornings, we can be ready to go as early as 5:30 am."

Penny thanked them for being so accommodating. She asked, "We would also like to explore the island and see all of the different kinds of landscapes. Is there anyone who can escort us along the trails?"

Mike chuckled and said, "For sure, we will take you where you are willing to go. However, there are no trails on the island except the ones the animals created. We can go where they go, and we can make our own. To see the seven-mile-long island, we will have to begin our exploration with kayaks of which we have plenty." This was beginning to sound like just what the Speaker wanted, a real adventure. She needed to clean out the cobwebs in the attic of her mind and make room for new thoughts and challenges. Mike asked, "We have eight kayaks. Will that be enough including your security detail?"

It was common for the capitol police assigned to guard the Speaker of the House to become less visual once the Speaker arrived at a destination and a secure environment had been established. "My detail will probably not join us on our explorations. It will be just my family of five and you."

Mike suggested, "I will be more comfortable if Bob Collins joins us too. You never know what might pop up to slow us down a bit." The Speaker liked the unsure nature of being on the deserted island. It was exciting and very different from her routine in Washington. But she was fine with adding Collins. She said she would keep Jake Ingram appraised of their island exploration schedule. He was on the island, and like the security detail, would be near but not noticeably around. For this part of the trip, Brent with the capitol police provided him with a satellite phone for better security so that communication would be expedient if necessary.

Penny Chatham called Jake Ingram and asked about the increase in security and the additional Department of Marine Resources Marine Patrol boats. He was unaware of any changes in Washington but promised to call and check on it.

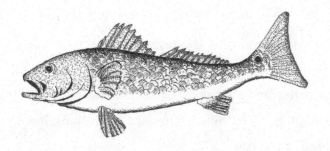

Redfish Prowl Mississippi Sound Marshes and Nearshore Grass Beds

CHAPTER 15

Fishing the Marshes

After lunch, the family prepared to go on their guided fishing trip to the north side of Cat Island which was lined with salt marshes. Small bait fish and crabs were attracted to the marsh environs and fishing beyond the perennial grasses would put the fisherman's minnows right in the middle of the feeding action. While it was a 30-minute boat ride around the west end of the island to get there, for the Chatham's, it was like taking the scenic route. In order to accommodate casting and bringing in fish to the boat, they split into two groups with the fishing guides. Pop and Sister Leah went with Bob Collins and Penny Chatham, Sarah Jane, and Andrew went in Mike Bergeron's boat. On the way they passed a cluster of steel I-beams protruding six or seven feet above water. Sister Leah, intrigued by the flooded ruins of something asked, "Mr. Bob, what did that used to be?"

He shot back over the sound of the twin 75 horsepower motors, "It was an elevated house with a very bright light on the peak of the roof called a beacon. As a lighthouse it warned boaters of shallow water at the western end of Cat Island.

"So, did someone live in the lighthouse?"

"Yes, they did. The Boudreaux family had two boys and a cat. When the weather was good the boys took a boat into Long Beach to go to school. Early paintings of the Cat Island Lighthouse depicted the white wooden house nestled into a small, sandy island with native sea oats and marsh grasses, Rosemary shrubs, and clumps of Spanish Bayonets. The family also had a skiff and a pier for when friends came to visit. While the boys didn't have much of a yard, they pretended Cat Island was their backyard." Leah was fascinated with what those kids' life must have been like living way out in the water on a small island.

About five miles beyond the western side of Cat Island lie Louisiana's Chandeleur Islands Penny could see pale, greenish blue lines on the western horizon. They are located on the west side of a deep pass used by large boats to enter into the Gulf of Mexico from ports near New Orleans

From a distance, shrimp boats could be seen gently pulling their large nets strapped to horizontal booms that extended from each side of their vessels. Elegantly shaped Chandeleur boats were probably anchored just off the small spits of sand and grasses. The bed and boat accommodations they provided attracted adventurers to fish the islands for days at a time. In addition to comfortable sleeping, lounging, and dining areas, it was standard for the Chandeleur Boats to carry from six to eight skiffs that could be launched by a winch for fishermen to explore the multitude of little islands and try their luck fishing. As part of the experience, on-board chefs would create outstanding seafood dinners centered around what their guests would catch.

Once the Chatham fishing party rounded Cat Island and were heading due east, they were treated to close up views of miles of shallow water populated by clumps of lime green smooth cord grasses, the predominant emergent salt marsh grass on Southern and Eastern coastlines. Cruising into a southeast wind with the boat motors wide open, nearby schools of lady fish could be seen hitting the surface creating large areas of disturbed water. Mike, the fishing guide, said "You can throw your line with a minnow on it into the school of ladyfish and catch one-pounders from now until the sun went down. They are fun to catch but not so great to eat."

Sarah Jane was overwhelmed with the beauty of the place, "Mike, this is gorgeous! The light green salt marshes gently undulated back and forth from the southeast winds and our boat waves are magical to look at. It's unlike anything I've ever seen!"

Speeding toward their destination, the gentle up and down rhythm of the view of the landscape and the skiff hitting waves molded by the southeast winds was so relaxing that Andrew Reardon, commented with a glazed look, "It's just like the hanging moss in the live oak trees. If you watch it blowing in the trees or stare at the marsh grasses swaying back and forth, after a while, you will want to lie down and take a nap! Add that to the feel of the rhythmic beat of waves hitting the bottom of our boat and you might be down for at least an hour!" He was a talker and liked to postulate things that always had an effect on someone's psyche.

His mother said, "You know, Andrew Reardon, I don't remember you being sleepy on our trips, and for that matter, hardly ever in your sweet young life." He shot back the cutest, kindest smile meant only for his mother. Their exchange of looks where full of unsaid words of love and respect meant only for each other.

Sarah Jane quipped, "All right you two lovebirds." Andrew's face flushed red from embarrassment, but he had no retort. In his mind, he was number one in his mother's eyes.

Mike Bergeron slowed the edgy skiff down to a crawl, faced it squarely into the sea breeze, and cut off the big motors. He then moved to the bow of the boat and lowered the trolling motor. As he quietly maneuvered the eager fishing party to a hundred feet out from the edge of the island's salt marshes, Andrew snapped out of his drift toward sleep and said under his breath as though he was talking to himself, "It's time to put on our predator hats." Collectively they were all dreaming about having tug of wars with some big speckled trout or redfish, and maybe even something bigger such as a blacktip shark which inhabited brackish, subtropical waters!

Mike selected Penn spinning rods with open face reels for each of them. They were equipped with a #2 steel hook and a ½ ounce weight to enhance casting the bait to about fifty feet beyond the shoreline. As he baited their hooks with live bull minnows, he quietly gave them directions where to cast their bait. Penny Chatham made the first cast. He instructed her to reel up the line so it was taut and so she could feel a fish taking the bait. "When he pulls on the line, don't jerk it. Let him have it. Count to five before you set the hook, and then really jerk it hard. Once you have set the hook, the rest will be up to your instincts. When you reel it in and it gets near the boat, I will be there to net the fish. Be sure to play the fish. Don't horse it in. You don't want to lose it. Remember, no fish means you will have lunch leftovers for dinner."

Andrew Reardon probably knew more about what the fishing guide instructed than his mother did. He was quite sure about the instructions not to horse the fish in. He made a mental note to show his mother what that meant when he caught his fish. Confidence was never a short suit for Andrew Reardon.

Once rods were baited, Sarah Jane and Andrew each cast toward the marsh. Mike helped Sarah Jane after her first cast went over her mother's line and half the distance it was supposed to go. Andrew said, "Good try, Sarah Jane, maybe in about fifty more casts you'll get the hang of it." She politely ignored his dig.

Penny Chatham, in her most reserved and kind reaction curtly said, "One more comment like that, Young Man, and I'll kick your cute bottom." Andrew and Sarah Jane both smiled sweetly at their mother who often threw out comments like that, but only to her children, and then mostly to Andrew Reardon who needed the most instruction. The children then targeted each other with devil-inspired sneers.

Watching the beauty of the salt marsh swaying back and forth along the shoreline while waiting for a jerk on their line, they were impressed by the mature long leaf pine forest up beach from the marsh and the irregular line of shrubs between the forest and the marsh. The shrubs were mostly marsh elders which could tolerate both salt and fresh water and were the transition to the pine trees on higher ground. Above the marsh elders were wax myrtle shrubs which were once depended on by colonists for making candles from their fragrant, waxy berries. The fishermen noticed the abundance of birds flitting around in the shrubs which, no doubt, were providing opportunities for nesting as well as the enjoyment of the flavorful berries. Penny made a mental note to come back and hike along this picturesque south shore and experience its seldom seen impressive old slash pine forest.

As the mesmerizing views along the south shore was creating a level of comfort brought on only by nature, Andrew Reardon's fishing line began to slowly move toward the east, parallel to the shoreline. As his rod tip gently curved from something on the other end of the line, Sarah Jane heard him counting. Quietly he said, "One, two, three, four, five!" At five, he pulled hard on the line. Sarah was impressed. It responded by pulling back with a serious tow like he was pulling on the leash of a mature rottweiler or one of those new, large Labradoodle dogs.

The fight was on. As the rod bent nearly double, Andrew lifted it up to give more of the rod's shaft room to bend in this fight with an unhappy and unknown sea creature. After a long struggle pulling to the right, it reversed its strategy and turned to pull the other direction. Andrew reeled in slack line as he skillfully played his fish, trying to keep pressure on the monofilament line to prevent the marine creature from getting off. As it fought, Andrew Reardon's strategy was to get him near enough to the boat for Mike to net. Once it got within netting distance, it splashed the water's surface and made a mad dash straight out away from the boat. Line rolled out from the drag on the reel which made a whirling noise. This was no small fish. Andrew continued to hold his ground and reeled back the line he lost. As the aquatic challenger began to tire, his young opponent began to reel in and pull the unknown sea creature toward the front side of the boat. Mike carefully positioned himself along the side of the boat and to the left of the novice saltwater fisherman.

As the fish came close to the side of the boat and could be seen a few inches below the water's surface, Mike stated, "Wow, you've got a trophy Redfish!" Those words thrilled the fishing crew. Andrew said nothing. His pursed lips were intense on landing this very large beauty caught feeding along the salt marshes. Mike gently slipped a 30-inch diameter net beneath the behemoth redfish and with his two big hands lifted it over the gunwale and onto the boat deck.

"Andrew Reardon, look what you caught! That is the biggest redfish I have ever seen!" said Penny Chatham.

Sarah Jane had her iPhone out taking sequential pictures of fighting and landing the fish. "Nice job, brother," she said.

Andrew looked at his mom and sister and with a very satisfied grin said, "Thanks." He was overwhelmed. Earlier fishing trips taken with his daddy had prepared him for this proud accomplishment. For sure though, this was an especially big thrill because he was fishing with his mom and big sister. His momma understood her young man's quiet and reserved joy. Yes, it was because he caught a big fish, but it was more so because he had conquered a significant creature of nature's aquatic world. Andrew Reardon also realized that was a world especially important to his mother who was gifted in convincing others to work together to create conditions where creatures like the large redfish could flourish. Besides knowing how to work together with the right people, it took an understanding of how all of the components of the marsh and marine water ecosystem work together to create ideal habitats.

After pictures, including one of Andrew struggling to hold up the big fish along with his mother and sister, he asked the patient fishing guide, "Mr. Mike, can we let him go?" Penny Chatham smiled as tears welled up in her eyes. She thought how wonderful his experience was in landing this beauty, and how thoughtful her ten-year-old son was about releasing this masterpiece to live and maybe even fight again. This would be a picture that would go into Penny Chatham's Family Pictures Inspiration Album on her desk in Washington.

"Of course," said Mike, and they all watched as he gently released the giant back into the brackish waters of the Mississippi Sound. Putting his arm around Andrew Reardon's shoulders, and with a tight hug he said, "You are a true sportsman. I am very proud to know you."

Andrew smiled at Mike and said, "Thanks." It would take a while for the boy to get through the excitement of landing the big fish. Once he did, he was full of advice for his mother and especially his sister Sarah Jane. One day he wanted them to have a similar experience. Their catching a redfish or speckled trout even half that size would be just fine with him.

The trip back around the island and past the ruins of the old Cat Island Lighthouse was comforting. About twenty minutes from the welcoming setting of Pelican Roost, the family became anxious and couldn't wait to get there. It was their home, if only for a little while. The late afternoon sun was at their backs and they were taking in the warm colors against the unusually bright green needles of the slash pines. This was a time of day for which photographers sit and wait. Dark shadows behind the tall trees accentuated their change of color from green to an orange glow, creating a stunning picture.

Sarah Jane was wearing out her cell phone taking pictures of the quickly changing shapes and colors of the late afternoon landscape.

Once back at the lodge, they all gathered around their successful afternoon's catch for a picture, much like the baseball and softball pictures taken of their kid's teams. It was a glorious photo with 28 keeper fish laid out in a semicircle in front of the Chatham's. Everyone in both skiffs had caught fish that afternoon and all were giving the details of their fish stories. The big prize, however, went to Andrew Reardon. He only had cell phone pictures taken by his fishing guide and his sister, but his redfish was twice the size of any of the other fish landed that day.

After pictures were taken of the day's catch, the family was introduced to Chef Tony, a tall and skinny guy in his late twenties. He smiled and said very little as he did not like to be the center of attention. Mike bragged on Tony as the best chef on Cat Island which drew a pretty good laugh from the Chathams in as much as they were the only guests on the entire island.

Tony explained he would accommodate the family's schedule for all of the meals and could even prepare any special dishes they enjoyed. He shared that he learned to cook from his mother and she had sent a big glass jar of buckeyes which are chocolate covered peanut butter balls for the family to enjoy.

Chef Tony asked Pop and Penny Chatham, "Well, what would you like your island chef to prepare for dinner this evening?"

Penny looked at Pop and said to the kids, "What about speckled trout?" They were all excited to enjoy the fruits of their afternoon labors.

Penny asked Chef Tony, "Can we have our trout some baked with lemon and butter and some fried? I think the kids might enjoy that."

He clicked his cowboy boot heels together and with a smile he snapped, "Baked and fried it is, Madam Penny! We can have your feast ready in about forty-five minutes which will allow time to freshen up. The mayor of Cat Island turned on the hot water tanks when we saw you coming up the bayou from fishing so there will be plenty for showers. The mayor is a clever man in his eighties who is the caretaker for Pelican Roost when no one is here. You will see him sitting around visiting with us so feel free to come introduce yourself and visit with him. He is here year-round, has been through hurricanes, and is intimately familiar with the critters that make Cat Island their home."

Chef Tony told the group the rest of the fish would be cleaned and iced down to be taken back home. Penny said they would not be able to carry them back because of living so far away but to be sure and serve them to her security detail and staff member Jake Ingram. "As you request, Madam Penny, we will cook them up for everyone!"

Magnolia Hotel – 1847 in Biloxi

CHAPTER 16

A Few Moon Pies

The specially prepared meal of fresh caught broiled speckled trout for the adults, and boneless strips with extra crispy cornmeal batter fried to a golden brown was a hit with everyone! The kids even went back for seconds on the fried trout. Prepared with the hearty meal was a green bean casserole with crispy fried onions on top, and baked asparagus with a cream sauce. When they traveled, dessert was always part of the meal along with decaffeinated coffee after dinner for Pop and Penny. Because of the freshness and excellent quality of the meal, anticipation of what Chef Tony would come up with for dessert was high. As he cleared the table, Sister Leah and Andrew almost pestered the talented cook about what was going to be for dessert, and even whether or not there was going to be a dessert, and if so, what the heck was it going to be! Tony was tight lipped. His only comment back to the barrage of dessert related questions was, "Hmm, let me see, I think there were a few Moon Pies left over from the group that came last week. Let me check and see if they are still here."

Sister Leah, a lover of any flavor of Moon Pie responded, "That's fine with me! They are the best way I know of to finish a meal. Are there enough to have two?" Andrew Reardon looked squinty eyed and pursed his lips at the prospect of a Moon Pie as a consolation dessert instead of something fancy. He was hoping for something in the same ballpark as the outstanding island meal Tony had just served. However, he did not object because Moon Pies were at least a dessert!

Dragging out the anticipation of a sweet way to end this superb family meal, Chef Tony returned from the kitchen and replied, "There were no Moon Pies left from last week's crowd. Y'all give me just a minute while I look around and see how we might finish this Cat Island fish dinner. I should have been smarter and whipped up something that would match the quality of that meal." Reading between the lines, Sister Leah and Andrew Reardon had a feeling the option of a Moon Pie might not have even been what Tony had in mind to end a meal where his diners had gone out into the wilderness and harvested the main courses.

After a really long minute in the kitchen, which heightened the anticipation of what was to come, Chef Tony walked out to the dining table with a fresh baked strawberry cake that was still warm, and a big bowl mounded high with round scoops of vanilla ice cream. The family helped themselves to slices of moist cake and as many scoops of vanilla ice cream as they desired. All through this final course of the meal, it was quiet around the long Pelican Roost dining table. The dinner with its surprise dessert was an outstanding way to end a memorable day of fishing, not to mention a justified reward earned by those who worked hard to contribute to the table fare. Before they were finished with their strawberry cake and ice cream, Penny Chatham asked that a group picture be taken with Chef Tony to go in her inspiration picture album.

After the feast, the family retired to the gallery that stretched along the entire front of the home. The deep and fully shaded balcony was lined with plush rockers, club chairs, a large glider, and four over-sized chaise lounges with thick cushions. The early evening summer sun had become a golden ball sinking fast on the broad horizon. Soon the tops of the mature longleaf pine trees would be washed with that same gold color that was reflected on the ripples in the bayou. Prevailing southeastern winds had shifted to due south, spreading a gentle breeze across the Chatham family who were scattered across the porch in their favorite lounging spots like blackbirds on a powerline in the waning days of fall. Like the birds, they sat relatively still, only occasionally chatting with one another.

The peace and family unity comforted Penny Chatham. Life was good. This was a very special time for her and her family. Through reflection and soft conversation, they quietly relived the excitement of the boat trip over to the island, and on fishing the marshes along the island's north shore. The wildness of nature surrounding them on all sides was spellbinding and encouraged appreciation of one another. Sister Leah fell asleep with her head resting on her mother's shoulder. Bedtime was sneaking up on all of them. The island had sapped their energy and dulled their alertness. Andrew Reardon whispered almost inaudibly, "We need to huddle up and rest together like this more often." Pop looked at him and winked. That usually meant a good idea was suggested and he would work hard to make it happen again. Experiencing the setting of a June sunset with a gentle southerly breeze lightly brushing over their balcony was hypnotic. They were all together, and they were safe and healthy.

Breakfast was at 7:30 the next morning. By that time, bright summer sun was already peeking through the boughs of the slash and longleaf pine trees that surrounded Pelican Roost. Getting up early would have been at 6:00 am when the gold in the rising sun could be seen through the trees. On Cat Island, it was a dark, moody looking gold color like the eyes of a wild cougar or bobcat. Pop always encouraged getting up early enough to get more done during the day, and especially to enjoy the magic of the rising sun. Sister Leah often asked about that magic. "I've been up and have seen the sunrise, but I never noticed any magic."

Pop smiled and told her for sure, there was magic. "Baby, it is expressed in the color the early morning sun paints the Great Maker's landscape. It is nature's way of always changing and providing variety for its inhabitants, instead of staying constant. Mother Nature starts out at daybreak with a deep, intense golden color and all of the detail we see in the landscape is a silhouette. That color slowly gets lighter and brighter, until nature's artist finally packs up her colors and allows the transition of the traditional daytime color of the landscape to occur. You can only see ten to fifteen minutes of her "plein aire" artistic expression in the morning, and again right before the sun sets in the evening."

"So, daddy, I think I can see your point", postulated the first grader. "That would be magic in anybody's book. I'm guessing Mom Nature was extra busy yesterday evening splashing color in the western sky as the sun was setting. I did think it would have been a beautiful painting, at least the brief glance I saw of it. I'm wondering if part of her magic might also be putting some sand or grit in our eyes that makes us sleepy and causes us to close our eyes?"

Pop looked at his sweet little girl child to see if she was being serious or was trying to catch him in a lie, but she was dead serious. Pop replied, "That could be part of it, Sweet Baby. I'm thinking she carries her grit in a special leather pouch for use after her evening painting spree because I have never felt like closing my eyes during her magical morning painting demonstrations." That seemed to satisfy inquisitive Leah Chatham.

Over morning coffee on the balcony, Penny asked Pop, "What plans do you have for the day? Is more fishing on your wish list?"

"That would be fine," he said, "But I also want to explore the island and do something different like setting out some crab traps or even tonging for oysters. Tonging is something I've read about but have never done. Do they even do that around here?"

Jake Ingram walked up the boardwalk from the staff guest quarters and hollered up to the balcony, "Good morning Chathams. Are you ready to inject some real diversity into your island activities?"

Penny Chatham momentarily thought, "Oh no, there is a situation in Washington and we will have to cancel the rest of the trip and return home!"

Pop, not even considering there might be a calamity on the horizon said, "Sure eco adventure planner. Come on up and have a cup of coffee with us. But, don't bring any bad news with you." Jake smiled as he bounded up the staircase to the second floor dressed in pressed khaki hiking shorts and a long sleeve, peach-colored Columbia fishing shirt. A leather and cloth belt with repeating redfish on it made his outfit sparkle.

Coming through the glass doors to the balcony from the plush living area, Penny said, "Stop by the kitchen and pour yourself a cup of coffee. Milk is in the icebox. It's Community Coffee with chicory from Baton Rouge. I think you will like it."

Jake said, "Ok, thanks. I'm beginning to like your regional coffee. It's in the same category as cheese toast for breakfast and Uncle Ben's corn grits smothered in butter. I'm adjusting, in fact, I'm enjoying the changes."

"Help yourself to the grits too and cheese toast if there is any left," invited Penny Chatham.

The breakfast guest was one staff member who had proven himself consistently proficient at tasks to which he was assigned. That was expected by the Speaker's chief of staff but the careful attention the Coast Guard fellow gave to clients interacting with the Representative's office was outstanding. As a conduit to Representative Chatham between citizens seeking to solve a problem, Jake Ingram was a good listener and able clearly to convey their concerns. Clients felt comfortable with him and confident he would be capable of communicating issues which they wanted Representative Chatham to consider and work toward solving. A good example of his prowess had been the Pearl River Basin project that directed additional river water to the Mississippi Sound to restore brackish water conditions that brought back the wild oyster population. The outcome of those changes had restored the economic and ecological health of an entire region!

"Come over and pull up a chair. What diversion from our routine of fishing, eating, and porch sitting do you have for us today?" asked Penny.

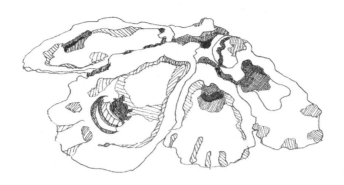

Oysters - Fresh Shucked

CHAPTER 17

Tonging

After sitting down in an inviting wrap around club chair, Jake Ingram took a sip of coffee and a couple of spoonsful of buttered grits. As he scanned the spectacular view westward across the bayou and salt marsh, he said, "There is a naturalist along the coast named Hannah Thomas. She is the authority on Cat Island and the Mississippi Sound Estuary. We asked her if she would consider arranging a trip for your family to nearby oyster reefs to tong for oysters and she has agreed. In the three years since the nutrient rich water from the Pearl River has been diverted into the Mississippi Sound Estuary, Mississippi oysters have become plentiful once again, and we thought you should have a hands-on experience to see that achievement yourself. If you want to try tonging for oysters, we can arrange for that and a photographer to be with you?"

Penny Chatham said, "Definitely, yes, Pop was just talking about oyster tonging. For sure we would like to do the tonging, but no to the photographer. We want to keep this at a family vacation level and besides, we can take our own cell phone pictures. We would love to meet this naturalist and my kids would enjoy socializing with her. When do we go?"

"I have tentatively scheduled her to be here at 12:00 noon if that works for you," said the trip planner who had been challenged to make sure there were plenty of surprises along the way. Nodding in a very relaxed manner and further stretching out on the cushions of a chaise lounge, the Speaker's body language indicated all was good.

Pop said, "It's a go for us Jake. Thanks for coming up with all of your wild ideas. We never know what challenging things we are about to be dragged into!"

"Ok", said Jake, "Tony will make a picnic lunch and pack some drinks to take on the expedition. We asked Miss Thomas to arrange for two wooden oyster luggers with open decks for tonging and each will have a crew of two oystermen. In case there are mechanical problems, we are going with two boats so we still have transportation. Hannah Thomas and the oystermen are excited to be doing this for you since they knew that you have been the lead legislator for restoring the Sound's brackish water."

"Thanks, Jake," smiled Speaker Chatham, "Don't forget Senator Long in Louisiana and Senator Knox in Mississippi were also big players in bringing folks to the table on that one," she replied from her now nearly prostrate position on the thick cushions of the chaise lounge.

Jake said, "Yes ma'am, they were key players. See you at the pier a little before 12 noon."

The family was enthusiastic to be going oyster fishing as Andrew Reardon called it. The outfit for tonging oysters was to dress in long pants and long-sleeved shirts as it was a dirty job. Picking through oyster shells and encountering an occasional irritated blue crab brought up from the bottom demanded protective clothing for the job.

Two oyster luggers and their captains, along with Hannah Thomas arrived at quarter to twelve. They were all smiles and looking forward to meeting Representative Chatham and her family. The Speaker did not need an introduction as her image and accomplishments were known throughout South Mississippi and Louisiana. She was an icon for the restoration of the Mississippi Sound Estuary. The oystermen were rugged looking men in their fifties with sun baked faces and hands. They thanked her for restoring the oyster habitat which was totally gone from the estuary three years ago. Penny smiled and thanked them for speaking up during the trying times when working with Louisiana to get the flow of Pearl River freshwater back into the Mississippi Sound, and restore conditions back to what they were during the heyday of seafood production.

Jake then introduced Speaker Chatham to the unpretentious naturalist Hannah Thomas, whose technical knowledge of disturbed conditions in the estuary had been crucial to implementing changes in the Mississippi Sound. "Hannah Thomas, this is Speaker Chatham, her husband Jim, and children Sarah Jane, Andrew Reardon, and Sister Leah." The modern-day coast explorer and naturalist was tall and sporty looking, and exuded an air of confidence when meeting the Speaker and her family.

"As the Pearl River keeper, her organization is the voice of the Pearl River and Honey Island Swamp ecosystems." Hannah smiled, stepped forward slightly, and reached out a hand to Speaker Chatham. Brent with her security detail put out his large hand, blocking the friendly handshake gesture.

Penny smiled at the moderately surprised new acquaintance and said, "Sorry, Hannah, security gets like this sometimes. I know who you are and respect the knowledge and drive you provided when we were creating the plans for restoration of the Sound. You were invaluable to the success of the changes that were made and instrumental in regulating the additional freshwater necessary to keep our brackish water within the most productive range for oyster production. We admire the contributions you are making on behalf of the Mississippi Sound Estuary."

Hannah smiled at the Speaker who was an exceptional leader of environmental causes along the coast, and said, "We are ready to head out for an afternoon of tonging the oyster reefs if you are?"

"Well, let's go," Speaker Chatham excitedly replied, "We are really looking forward to this." Turning to her eager ten-year-old expert fisherman she asked, "Who do you know that has ever been oyster tonging?"

With a surprised look he raised both shoulders and held out his hands with their palms up and said, "Hmmm, maybe Pop?"

His daddy looked at him and shook his head smiling and said, "No, handsome, this will be a new adventure for me too."

Sister Leah interjected, "I have probably been at some point in my life, but I can't remember it. The technique for catching the shellfish will come back to me once we are near the oyster reef. Don't worry Andrew Reardon, I will give you some pointers when we get there."

He shot back, "Whew, I thought I would be going into this blind but Leah, you have lifted a load off of my shoulders knowing I will be getting some fishing tips from you. Thank you, sweet sister."

"Don't mention it, handsome brother," shot back Sister Leah.

Penny Chatham, who was moderately embarrassed at this sarcastic banter between siblings, turned and said to the River Keeper and the oyster guides, "We are all thrilled to be going and learning about tonging. Let's get going before World War three breaks out."

After two security officers with long satchels loaded with security gear boarded one of the oyster luggers, and the family and a security officer boarded the other boat, the oyster fishermen pushed off. Hannah Thomas who was on board with the Speaker's family instructed, "We are going to an old oyster tonging area called St. Stanislaus Reef which is exclusively limited to harvesting oysters by hand with tongs, unless you can dive down to the reef and chip them off with a claw hammer. You don't see that done much anymore except by some of the recent immigrants to the coast who are used to harvesting in that manner. Oysters have come back like gang busters throughout the Mississippi Sound Estuary. After three years, they have matured to their largest size which is perfect for harvesting and eating."

Andrew Reardon asked, "So the oysters need really salty water in which to grow?"

The River Keeper who was in charge of that salty water explained, "Oysters need only a little bit of salt in the water in which they grow. Three years ago, water in the Mississippi Sound Estuary was either too salty or didn't have enough salinity, and over a period of years all of the oysters died.

"So, Miss Hannah, tell us exactly what is an estuary?" asked Sarah Jane.

"Estuaries are bodies of water along coastlines that rivers flow into creating the slightly salty conditions we call brackish water. Long and narrow barrier Islands separate our big estuary from the really salty seawater in the Gulf of Mexico which is usually thirty-three parts salt per 1000 parts of freshwater. You can just about float in open sea water without paddling your arms. The brackish water in the estuary between the barrier islands and our mainland histori-cally ranged from eight to seventeen parts salt per 1000 parts of freshwater which was ideal for the culture of oysters. Our Mississippi Sound oysters were also plentiful because the river water that once intermittently flowed into the estuary to dilute the sea water was full of organic matter and nutrients which fed microscopic algae which was the main meal upon which oysters feast."

"The delectable bivalves can live in water that is thirty-two parts salt per 1000 parts of freshwater, but they have to be protected from predators like the oyster drill snail which will move into an oys-ter reef when salinity rises above fourteen parts salt per 1000 parts of freshwater. They feed on oysters through drilling through their shells. However, the predator snail cannot survive in water salinities below fourteen parts salt per 1000 parts freshwater."

"When salinities drop below eight parts salt per 1000 parts of freshwater, a pathogen called Dermo, or technically Perkinsus marinus, will move into the oyster reef and kill the oysters. I know all of this sounds confusing but the bottom line is that oysters have a salinity cycle range they depend on for health. Now let's see if I have really confused you. Tell me, what is the range of salinity that is ideal for the health of oysters?"

The children of one of the most respected political environmentalists in Congress looked blankly at the renowned naturalist. They were not expecting to be quizzed on marine aquatic science. Finally, Andrew Reardon offered, "If it were my oysters, and I wanted them to live a healthy and happy life, I would make sure the saltiness of the water would never go below eight parts salt or over fourteen parts salt per 1000 parts of freshwater."

"Great answer. You are right, Andrew." The Pearl River Keeper reached over to give him a reward hug but paused as a large arm from the onboard security agent moved between her and Andrew Reardon. She asked, "Isn't it ok to give him a hug for his correct answer?"

The agent, now with his open hand on Andrew's chest gently nudging him backward, smiled and said, "No ma'am, not at this time."

Sister Leah chimed in, "Its Andrew Reardon, not just Andrew." She said it in an irritated manner that let the renowned naturalist know she was probably asking questions too complicated for kids her age.

Penny Chatham kindly said to her youngest daughter, "Stick to the questions your teacher is asking."

Sister responded, "Ok, Mom, I was just watching out for Andrew's feelings."

Her mother retorted, "Its Andrew Reardon, baby." This evoked a hint of a smile back from her precocious daughter.

All eyes, which were momentarily diverted on the minor family playful spat, went back to Hannah Thomas. "Andrew Reardon's answer that a salinity range between eight and fourteen parts salt per 1000 parts of freshwater is ideal for oysters was correct. However, they can tolerate short periods of lower and higher salinity levels safely. Since salinity depends on how much water flows through the Pearl River Basin, when there is a heavy rainfall like three to five inches over a twelve-hour period the river will discharge large amounts of water into the Mississippi Sound that could dilute the salinity level down to eight parts salt per 1000 parts of freshwater and lower. By contrast, when there are extreme periods of drought and the flow of river water diminishes, salinity can rise above the fourteen parts salt per 1000 parts of freshwater for short periods of time. In either extreme, oysters will survive when brackish water salinity moves outside of the ideal range as long as those conditions don't last too long."

Continuing her condensed marine science ecology lesson, she shared, "Every day there is a low and high tide in the Mississippi Sound. During high tide, really salty water in the Gulf of Mexico flows around the barrier islands and moves into the Mississippi Sound Estuary. This is the source of salt our oysters depend on. Hours later, at low tide, water in the estuary flows southward around the barrier islands. This regular cycle of the tides is another factor that maintains the salinity levels needed by our wild oysters."

"Can you describe the oyster drill again, Miss Hannah", asked the Chatham's oldest daughter.

"Sarah Jane," responded the Pearl River Keeper. "it is a snail that feeds on oysters through drilling through its shell so it can eat the oyster. If the normally brackish water in the estuary stays too salty for too long, like for a month or more, oyster drills will multiply and eat all the oysters in a reef."

"How big are the oyster drills?" asked Sarah Jane.

"They will fit into the palm of your hand." Replied Hannah. Again, quizzing the students she asked, "A healthy oyster reef depends on a certain range of slightly salty water, and that level of saltiness is what?"

Not to be outdone by her siblings, and to wipe out any lingering suspicion of having a bad attitude, Sister Leah quickly quipped, "That would be eight to fourteen parts salt per 1000 parts of freshwater. It is not enough to float in but oysters love it!"

"Excellent, Leah, you are right!"

As the oyster luggers worked their way toward St. Stanislaus Reef which was about ten miles toward the mainland from Cat Island, Andrew Reardon said, "I think it is time for our lunch break. I'm hungry!" Everyone was eager for their sack lunch made by Chef Tony, the Pelican Roost chef. As Pop was passing out the sack lunches to the other boat, Andrew asked, "What's on the menu for dinner Pop?

He eagerly responded, "Po boys! You have a choice of either a fried shrimp or fried oyster po boy on Reising's French Bread. They are dressed all the way and are still warm," Pop proudly announced.

"They are also cut in half so you can trade sandwiches and try both kinds, and there are mini containers of cocktail sauce." After Pop gave po boys to the boat captain, Agent Brent, and Hannah Thomas, his eager brood got their lunches. They were used to waiting until guests and older visitors were first served. As the po boys were unwrapped, the trading began. Jake had made sure there were plenty of Barq's Root Beers and bottled Niagara waters to go around. Quiet settled over the boat and all that was audible was the diesel engine rhythmically chugging its way to St. Stanislaus Reef. Anticipation of 'catching' some oysters, however that was done, was on the minds of the fishermen.

As Hubert St. Pe, moved the lead oyster boat over water that the captain hoped was above the large Telegraph Reef oyster bed, he shouted for crew member Hannah Thomas to throw in the water what he called their highly sophisticated listening device so he could 'hear the oysters talking to one another'. He explained to the young passengers, "When that sonar device picks up transmission between oysters, we will hear a 'ding' and that will be the location of the reef." Freckly Hannah, as the captain called her, threw in a heavy round steel ring attached to a 30-foot-long blue polypropylene rope. In its former life before becoming a sonar device, the steel disk was used in the braking system of a truck.

Penny Chatham asked Pop, "Didn't we see something similar in St. Thomas used in a steel band?"

"Yes, we sure did. They had one sitting on a wooden stand and were beating on it to keep the rhythm tight." Pop traveled a good bit and had a wide variety of experiences and interests. He had gone to school at Louisiana State University and Harvard University where he had studied geography and environmental design. In one of their courses on sustainability, they used the book Regenerative Design Techniques. It explained how to create buildings that required very little energy and home landscapes that produced large amounts of vegetables and fruit. His wife Penny had taken a similar course at Mississippi State University called Design of Sustainable Communities where that same book was used in the class. Living sustainably played a big part in how the couple first got to know one another.

The low-tech reef locator was slowly pulled across the mud and sand bottom until it hit a mound of oysters cemented to one another and created a melodic ringing, kind of like an older door bell. Some reefs were three and four feet high and hundreds of feet long. As the steel brake disk started bouncing over the reef and the rope jerked back and forth, Captain Hubert hollered, "We there, Freckly Hannah?"

She Responded, "Shut-er down Captain. I believe we've hit pay dirt!" A yellow polystyrene buoy half as big as a basketball with a weight on the end of a rope was thrown overboard to mark the spot where they would begin to tong for oysters.

Focusing on the three children on board, Hannah Thomas eagerly asked "Are y'all ready to catch some oysters?" The fit looking naturalist knew a great deal about the ecology of the Mississippi Sound and the Honey Island Swamp through which the Pearl River flowed. Having red hair and a fair complexion, she wore tan Carhart pants and long-sleeved denim shirt with the insignia of the Pearl River Keeper Organization on it. She wore a wide brimmed straw hat to keep the sun off her face and reduce her assortment of freckles to a minimum. She looked like she knew how to catch oysters, and she did.

Sarah Jane commented, "Miss Hannah, you look like a professional oyster tonger if there ever was one."

Speaker Chatham answered, "Yep, you sure do. We are ready when you are to start catching oysters. I have no idea how to get them from the reef to the boat but am excited about learning."

Sister Leah added, "I hope these will be as good as the oysters in the po boys we had for lunch!"

Hannah smiled and started to put her arm around the shoulders of the little orator without a shy bone in her body, but pulled back, recalling Agent Brent's admonition for no touching any of the Chatham family. Instead, she began the quest by saying, "Ok, you bunch of novice oyster tongers, let me begin by saying three years ago there were no oysters remaining in the Mississippi Sound Estuary. You heard it right, there were no oysters left in the Mississippi Sound. After years of wild swings in the salinity level of the water, predators moved in along with disease and wiped out the entire population. Your momma and Senator Long in Louisiana dedicated themselves to understanding why that was happening and how the problem could be fixed. And now, we have oysters again. Thanks to the two of them."

Pausing, the personable naturalist looked grateful at Penny Chatham and said, "Thank you Representative Chatham, and to Senator Long, for bringing back our estuary. We are excited to be here with you and be part of your getting a good look of the results of your handiwork."

The Speaker smiled and said, "Thanks to you too, Hannah Thomas, for providing all the grass roots support to make changes happen and for advising the rest of us about what needed to be done to restore our seafood population." Her children looked at their momma and then at the naturalist. While they didn't understand the depth of knowledge and perseverance it took to make restoration of the huge estuary happen, they saw a look of deep appreciation for one another in the faces of these icons of environmental leadership along the Mississippi and Louisiana Gulf Coasts.

Hannah Thomas confidently said, "Ok, let the chase begin. Captain St. Pe, can you give us some pointers?"

The experienced oysterman took over with the confidence of an experienced high school history teacher. "We are going to catch these oysters with a tool like the Indians used hundreds of years ago. My people, who are of French background, landed in Biloxi's Back Bay in 1699. Indians showed us and the Spanish settlers that came later how to harvest the delicious beauties within the hard shells we are going to break away from their reef home and bring up to the boat to take home with us." He had the attention of all of his trainees.

"As you saw, we pulled our brake cylinder along the bottom until it hit the hard mounds of oysters we call a reef. Now that we found it, we will use tongs to pry a few oysters away from the top of their reef. The reef is like a large apartment complex that houses a lot of people, except this time the people are oysters." Andrew Reardon looked puzzled at the wise fisherman, wondering why he had to explain how a reef for oysters was like an apartment high rise for people. But he kept his queries to himself.

Eager to know more, Sister Leah asked a question of compassion, "Will it hurt them to break their shell away from the oyster reef?"

"No, it won't, Shorty," replied the oysterman. Continuing to impart the 'how-to' for catching the stationary oysters, he began, "The tool the Indians used was a tong. It is made with two sticks crossed in the middle with a rake on the end of each stick or handle. You can buy them either twelve, fourteen, sixteen, or eighteen feet long, depending on the depth of the reef. An eighteen-foot tong is good for fourteen feet of water. Where we are here on Telegraph Reef the water is only eight feet deep so we can use a twelve-foot tong. It will be easier for you to handle too."

"Begin by standing along the boat's edge. Holding onto the tong handles, ease the rake down the side of the boat to touch the bottom. Then spread the handles back and forth to open and close the rakes. That will break off oysters that are cemented to the reef and catch them in the rakes. After spreading the handles back and forth five to eight times on the surface of the oyster reef, and if the rakes feel heavy like you have jarred lose some shells, lift the handles and rakes straight up and pour the shells out on this stainless-steel table top. Our culling table is where we will go through our catch, keeping the oysters that are at least three inches wide, and pushing the rest of the shells and smaller oysters back onto the reef where they can grow for us to catch next year."

"I've got three sets of tongs. Miss Penny you and your baby can tong on the north side of the boat, Mr. Chatham, you and Andrew Rearview stand on this side." Andrew heard the mispronunciation of his name but decided to let it pass as he wanted to get on with it and catch come oysters. "I will work with Sarah Jean on the back of the boat."

"Ok, crew, get with it. They are paying $49.99 for a thirty-two-pound sack of large three-inch, fresh caught, raw oysters. Let's get 'em and get some jingle in our pockets!"

Andrew Reardon, never one to pass up an opportunity to react added, "Sounds good to me. I could use $50.00."

Sarah Jane commented from the back of the boat, "Bet I catch some before you do, Rearview!"

As he was a little ticked the mispronunciation of his name came back up, he said, "Good luck Jean, you're going to need it!" That demanded a terse reply but Captain Hubert St. Pe with whom she was oyster fishing ignored the backtalk and said, "Ok, Sister, let's get over that and concentrate on breaking some oysters off this reef."

The confident seventh grader replied, "Aye-Aye Captain."

Hubert St. Pe whispered, "Let's go, Sarah Jean, let's show little rearview and the rest of them how it's done." She giggled but concentrated on spreading the tonging handles back and forth, trying to knock some two and three-year-old oysters off the reef.

After spreading the sticks back and forth about ten times, the tongs began to get heavy with oysters filling up the rake. "Captain S.P., I think we've got some. This rake is getting pretty heavy."

The venerable oysterman responded, "Ok, Sister, bring it up slowly, making sure to keep the sticks together so the rake doesn't empty before we get our catch in the boat." Sarah Jane did as the Frenchman said. The rake was heavy, especially pulling it up eight feet from the reef surface, but she was able. "Now before you bring it out of the water, shake the rake up and down to get the mud off the shells." After she did that, Hubert helped her lift the rake full of shell and oysters onto the culling table. The tongs made a big smacking sound as it hit the shiny stainless-steel surface of the table. She looked at her instructor thinking she might have done something wrong. He said, "Good Job, Sarah Jean, don't worry, that was the sound of big money hitting the table!"

As the metal rakes were spread and its contents poured onto the table, two blue crabs righted themselves from beneath the rubble of shell with their pinchers wide open facing Sarah 'Jean' and ready for battle. Andrew and the others who came to the table to see what they caught were fascinated with the large crabs. Captain Hubert St. Pe was not surprised at all and began, "Ok, Sarah, put these heavy rubber gloves on so you don't cut yourself. Next take this culling iron, pick up the live oyster shells, and knock off the empty shells they are attached to. The two metal flanges at the top of the culling iron are three inches apart. Any oyster smaller than that we will throw back so it can grow larger."

Sarah Jane did what he said, picking up oysters and knocking off the empty shells connected to the live oysters. When the live oysters were smaller than the space between the flanges, she pushed them off the culling table and back onto the reef. When she was about finished with culling through the oysters and shells, she had five keepers that were three inches or more in size. Finally, she said, "What about those crabs, are they going to try to pinch me?"

The captain shook his head and said, "No, my Cherie, they are enjoying looking at you working hard and out fishing your younger sister, your mom, and ole Rearview over there. Nudge them over the edge so they can get back home to the reef."

After that comment, Andrew Reardon decided to put it into high gear as he went back to his and Pop's tong and more intensely than before, moved the tong handles back and forth and brought up the second rake of oysters. It was a good catch as well. Penny Chatham and Sister were the third to bring up their tongs full of shell. Brent, cautiously watching the Speaker, smiled at their success. He never spoke or interjected into the conversation or activity. That was not his job. He was there to watch and make sure the Speaker was safe and in a protected situation.

Tonging successfully for several hours, they had a basket nearly full of large oysters. "You got a little more than half a bushel of big, fresh, Mississippi Sound oysters," said Captain S.P. as Sarah Jane called him. "I believe when you have your oyster dinner tonight, you will taste the beauty and health of our estuary. You done good, and may God bless you peoples."

As the old oysterman bowed his head in reverence and respect, he held his arm up like a country preacher praying for his flock and said in his family's native language, *"Dieu a souri à nous tous avec ta présence."* [8]

Sarah Jane just smiled at the compliment or kind thoughts he expressed. She could tell from his demeanor and the inflection in his voice it was a caring thought.

Dinner that evening featured fresh oysters harvested from the Mississippi Sound Estuary as the main course. Like the day before,

---

8 "God has smiled on all of us with your presence."

the afternoon on the open waters of the Mississippi Sound Estuary depleted everyone's energy level but not so much so that the lively family did have enough energy to bathe before dinner and seat themselves around the long lodge-like wooden table. The authentic gulf coast oyster dinner set before the family featured fresh vegetables and oysters prepared in five different ways. Of course, macaroni-and-cheese was included as that was always a favorite of the younger diners. Dessert that evening was a choice of chocolate or lemon meringue pies, and a banana cream pie. Penny Chatham said to Pop, "Wow, Jim! Does it ever end? Wonderful food fresh from the Sound, close-up marine life encounters, a crazy good family, and a job that has outstanding perks!"

The family ate like there was no tomorrow. There is something about catching your own food that endears fishermen and hunters, and also gardeners to take special interest in preparing and enjoying what they worked hard to catch and grow. In this case, Chef Tony did all the preparation and even dressed for the special dinner. In honor of Speaker Chatham and her influence in nearly single handedly bringing oysters back to the Mississippi Sound, he dressed in a real chef's outfit, complete with the white toque. That dramatic act was in admiration of the effort expended by Representative Chatham for the benefit of the good people along the Gulf Coast and for the abundance of aquatic creatures in the great Mississippi Sound Estuary.

Salt Marsh and Tidal Inlet

CHAPTER 18

Assigning Kayaks for the Flotilla

At the Walter Reed National Military Center Hospital in Bethesda, Maryland, concern for the life of President Harrison was growing. He had been hospitalized for five days and recently had slipped into a coma. His medical team was not optimistic about his recovery. If he did regain consciousness, it was probable that he would be mentally incapable to govern the country, at least for a while. Since Jim Harrison was unable to carry out the powers of the office of president, those duties had been shifted to the Vice President who was cloistered at Camp David in the Appalachian Mountain region of western Maryland.

While Speaker Chatham and Pop were having coffee on the balcony of the Cat Island Lodge talking about yesterday's outstanding tonging and oyster dinner experience, Jake Ingram came to the boardwalk in front of the home. He quietly spoke so as not to wake the rest of the family still sleeping from yesterday's oyster tonging adventure, "Madam Speaker, you have a phone call from Washington."

"Do you have your satellite phone with you, Jake? I am charging my phone's battery."

"Yes, ma'am, I do," replied Jake. "I'll bring it right up." Walking briskly up the steps to their ample balcony, he said, "The plans for the day are to explore Cat Island by kayak and walk through the longleaf pine forest to Three-mile Beach on the eastern side of the island. Many have said it is the most beautiful, natural beach on the Gulf Coast and probably the least accessible too."

Speaker Chatham replied, "We are ready to go. The kids will be especially excited about getting a little dirty and maybe seeing some wildlife! I can probably get everyone ready to leave as early at 8:00, right after breakfast. Does that work?"

Jake replied, "Yes, that timing will work great with the plans I made. The naturalist Hannah Thomas that was with us yesterday will be here at 8:00 am. She asked that the fishing guides prepare the kayaks for launching as exploration of the island will begin on water and work toward the old longleaf pine groves on the western end of the island. Hannah Thomas will lay out other hiking options depending on the stamina of your family members. She knows the island like nobody else and is the best one to go with you."

Penny Chatham gave Jake a thumbs up as he handed her the phone. Not a fussy, detail person, one of her greatest assets was to surround herself with really capable people that could take an idea or plan a trip and give options from which the Speaker of the House could choose.

Changing the subject back to her responsibilities in Washington, Jake said, "Your Chief of Staff is waiting for your phone call. If you need me to go with y'all on the island journey, I can help with your kids and carry the satellite phone?"

"Thanks, Jake," replied Penny Chatham, "I think that's a good idea. Would you mind kayaking with Sarah Jane?"

Jake smiled and said, "I would love the opportunity and Sarah Jane would probably enjoy me as a kayaking partner, being a Coast Guard Academy graduate and all. I have been in canoes and all kinds of boats, but never in a kayak. However, I do know it is a narrow watercraft which is propelled by the use of double-bladed paddles. The boat is native to the Alaskan Eskimo people and has cockpits in which to snugly sit. In the far north, a splash cover over its bow prevents icy Greenlandic water from washing into the boat." Penny Chatham smiled at his brainy explanation of the kayak and was pleased at his willingness to be a buddy with her blossoming teenager.

After returning to their bedroom, she placed the call to her Chief of Staff in Washington. "Craig Gill, tell me how things are going in the Swamp?"

"Good to talk to you, Speaker Chatham, how are things in your swamp?" replied her chief of staff.

"Outstanding, we are actually on an island, but the Honey Island Swamp is about twenty-five miles north of here," she replied. She knew that would throw Craig off a bit. The northeasterner, like Jake Ingram, was straight as an arrow and to him anything in the South was either near a swamp, right beside a swamp or in a swamp.

"We are not doing so well in Washington", he shared. "The president is gravely ill. He is now in a coma as we speak. The Vice

President who is at Camp David has been given the authority to take over his duties until he is healthy again. President Harrison's condition is touch and go. He might not make it. That's my opinion. You know, they are not revealing much, actually nothing at all on his health nor what is causing his illness."

"I see", replied the Speaker. "I will call Connie and talk with her. Poor thing, the job is so taxing and now to have her husband in such bad health. Craig, have you heard anything at all about how he contracted whatever it is he has?"

"There is no update on his health," replied Craig. "I called Maggie Williams, his publicity spokeswoman, and she says the medical team is closed-mouth. They are not telling anyone anything, not even her. As far as she knows, even his family has not been able to see him and does not know about his condition."

"They are not even able to go to his room and see him?" replied a very surprised and concerned Penny Chatham.

"No Ma'am, not at all," replied Craig

"Ok, anything else," the Speaker curtly said with an air of impatience. She almost always became annoyed when being told something that she did not want to hear.

"No ma'am," replied Craig. "I will call when there is more news."

The Speaker hung up. She opened a locked leather case beside her bed and got out a small notebook with names and contacts and called Connie Harrison. A sad and exhausted voice answered hello. "Connie, I am in Mississippi, but I've been keeping up with you and Jim."

"Oh, Penny, he is not doing well, not well at all! I don't know what's wrong with him and they won't even let me on his floor at the hospital to see him! The doctors say they think he has been poisoned but they cannot confirm that." replied Connie Harrison, now sobbing.

"Connie, I am so sorry. Are your kids there with you?" replied the Speaker.

"Yes, they are here, but they can't see Jim either!" she replied.

Penny Chatham replied in a very sincere manner, "You call me If I can help in any way, Connie. We are saying prayers for you and Jim."

She had the utmost concern for her friend who was a member of her sorority in their old college days. Penny Chatham sat on the edge of the bed reflecting about the president's condition. She was sad for what the family was experiencing, but there was also a tinge of fear for herself and her own family. If the president's health did not improve, Steve Hardy would be sworn in as the next president. If something happened to Steve, that overwhelming responsibility would fall on her shoulders as Speaker of the House of Representatives. Her office was third in line to succeed to the office of president. She did not want that. She had been elected to manage and improve conditions for her constituents in the State of Mississippi. This included her people that lived in the country and in the cities, and even along the edge of the swamps.

Then the full House of 435 Representatives had voted and selected her as their voice for working with the President and members of the Senate. Being Speaker of the House of Representatives was a really big honor. However, a huge number of expectations go with honorable positions. She was doing her job admirably as well as keeping up with needs of her congressional district in Mississippi. Maintaining peace among house members and effectively communicating with the senate and president was complicated and challenging. Nevertheless, she loved it and was very good at meeting those challenges.

The thought of all these responsibilities ran through her mind in the desperate moments after calling poor Connie Harrison and hearing about Jim's dreadful situation. As she evaluated the possible changes to her job and family that could happen, Sister Leah came into the bedroom and demanded, "Momma, do you have your hiking boots on? Should I wear mine? I think I need some help dressing for our island exploration journey daddy told us about." As the voice of Penny Chatham's sweet baby girl got louder and higher in pitch, young Leah exclaimed, "This could be the most exciting escapade I have ever been on and I want to dress right for it! Momma, can you please get upstairs to our room right now!" Penny Chatham thought of the book they had been reading together at bedtime, Cornelia and the Audacious Escapades of the Somerset Sisters. She smiled at her young scholar's developed vocabulary and wondered what her cherished baby would become one day. With her mother's love and attention, she could be whatever she wanted.

It was overwhelming to think about the job of being President and managing a young family all at the same time. It wouldn't be fair to her kids. That just could not happen. Penny Chatham had a wonderful life. Her thoughts came back to reality as she walked up to the loft with fifteen beds and an incredible view that stretched from meandering Jean Lafitte Bayou to the west side of Cat Island's salt marshes and longleaf and slash pine forests. Sister Leah had selected the bed in the loft that was right in the very center of the front row of single beds facing west through the two-story windows. "Ok, Big Shot, I hear you are going to be Pearl River Keeper Hannah Thomas's right-hand helper. For that awesome responsibility little lady, you will need some long pants, your long-sleeved Columbia fishing shirt for the briars and mosquitoes, light weight socks and those rubber high-top boots for jumping in and out of kayaks and following trails through the old pine forests. If we have to pass through any stands of waist high saw palmettos, the boots and pants will be perfect. Did you bring that wide brimmed canvas hat that keeps monkeys from climbing in your hair?"

Penny tickled her youngest and as she squirmed, Leah responded, "Heck yeah, that hat will protect me from all kinds of tree climbing mammals, and keep me from getting my nose and cheeks sunburned." Looking inquisitively at her mom she asked, "What are you wearing on your head to protect yourself from the boundless variety of woodland creatures creeping and crawling out there, and probably some falling from the trees?"

Her mom quipped back, "I'm hoping you will walk right in front of me and they will jump on you first!" Again, her mom went for her most ticklish spots.

After prolonged giggling and twisting that made a shamble of her freshly made bed, her youngest child looked into her momma's eyes and in a sincere and loving manner, she said, "I will be right behind Miss River Keeper herself; so, Momma, you will be third in line and doubly protected, I promise. I will not let anything get you." Tears welled up in Penny Chatham's eyes as her always surprising daughter gave her a sweet and gentle hug. Times like these were among the many high points of having children and taking them through many different kinds of experiences so that they learn and appreciate the love that a family has for one another.

At a little before 8:00 am, the group was gathering in the sandy front yard dotted with sporadic tufts of grass here and there. The domesticated large brown rabbits were there too to make sure the grass didn't get out of hand and to see the Chatham's off on another adventure. As the fishing guides pulled out the single and double kayaks from beneath the ground floor decking, Hannah gathered the group together to discuss where they would go and the manner of transportation they would take to get them there. "Miss Penny, would you like to be in a kayak by yourself or with a partner?" Hannah asked.

Penny said, "I thought Sister Leah and I would go together."

Leah shot straight up from petting the long ears of a domesticated rabbit named Harold and said, "I don't think so Momma. Remember, I told you I need to be with the River Keeper. She and I have connected, and I will be there to offer guidance so the trip will be exciting and challenging, but not dangerous. Brent doesn't have to go with us, does he?"

Speaker Chatham's thoughts turned to the as yet undisclosed events unfolding in Washington. She looked at her assertive young future leader and said, "Ok, as long as that works for the River Keeper, and yes, Brent has to go with us Baby, and maybe even one or two of Brent's other friends." Looking at her chief of security she said, "Are y'all good with going in individual kayaks?"

"Of course, ma'am," replied Brent.

Picking up the pace as the group was preparing to depart, the renowned Gulf Coast ecologist began assigning kayaks by pointing out the three boats for the Capitol Police Security Detail. She and Sister Leah would take the lead boat and the other two-person kayaks would carry Pop and Andrew Reardon, and Jake Ingram who the Speaker had invited would go with Sarah Jane. Penny Chatham would have the freedom of being in a kayak by herself. That was the group of ten who were now anxious to set out and explore Cat Island. As they were pushed off from the pier in front of the guest house by the fishing guides who stayed behind, the Speaker's security detail evenly spaced themselves throughout the four family kayaks. Earlier, while the group was loading their gear into the slender boats, Penny and Pop noticed the security men placed rifles and automatic weapons in their kayaks before departing. Andrew Reardon, of course, also noticed the irregularity of the extra fire power and was anxious to know why. As they pushed off, he asked "Brent, will we be on the lookout for those mountain lions that are on the island? Is that why you brought so many guns?"

"Yes sir, Little Man" he responded. If we have an encounter with a cougar, I don't want to be the one blamed for not having the firepower that would stop it dead in its tracks instead of allowing it to attack and drag one of us off into the underbrush." That was all Andrew Reardon needed to hear. His not responding to Brent was a clear affirmation of Agent Brent and his heavily armed buddy being on the trip.

Moving northward up the bayou from Pelican Roost, the formation of the flotilla of explorers was erratic-looking as most of the travelers were not experienced kayakers. However, they quickly learned to paddle their boats in a steadily forward direction. When they came to the cut off on the bayou that led northward to the Mississippi Sound, Hannah the River Keeper and Sister Leah paddled westward through a narrow opening into a brackish pond lined with marsh grasses that extended toward the base of the 150-year-old longleaf pine trees that ringed the south side of the marsh.

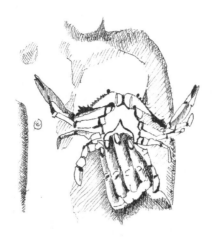

Boy Holding a Blue Crab

CHAPTER 19

Unusually Exotic and Primeval Looking

Back in the nation's capital, the personal assistant from King David's Bible Study had been busy seeking to learn more about President Jim Harrison's condition. Her endearing personality and persistence usually took her a long way when finding out information. This time, however, there was no up-to-date news on the president. No one from the White House or Executive Branch would share anything. Charlotte did find out from a close friend at the Judicial Branch, that someone, probably the Supreme Court Chief Justice had been summoned to Camp David. She interpreted that to mean the president was weak and incapacitated and chances were strong that he was unable to carry out his executive duties. If that were true, it would not be long before the vice president would make the declaration that President Harrison was unable to fulfill his obligations as President and he, Steve Hardy, had been administered the oath of office and taken the reins of the government.

A call to Don Anniston was made to inform him of the situation and probable events that would play out through the coming days. "Thank you, Charlotte. I agree, I'm thinking you are spot on. Keep me informed about anything the vice president says about government issues and about the president's health. I need you to make a phone call to each of the Bible Study members and share with them your thoughts about how all of this is probably going to play out. They will want to make some business decisions based on your information."

"I'll get right on it, Mr. Anniston", replied Charlotte, "and I'll keep plugging away with my contacts for more solid information. However, I feel sure this is the direction it is going. I'll call you when I know more."

Don Anniston was not worried about the possible transition of Steve Hardy to president. Both he and Jim Harrison had the same ideals as the Bible Study group, and both had been very appreciative of the financial support provided by the close-knit group of corporate leaders and venture capitalists. During the first election, all monetary needs requested by both men were met by the group. With that kind of unlimited backing, the administration made sure advantages of exceptional value were returned as pay back to the Bible Study members. The extraordinary significance of the study members in the upcoming election was a given, even if Jim Harrison was unable to be part of the ticket.

Meanwhile, the kayak flotilla departed from Pelican Roost northward down Jean Lafitte Bayou at about 8:15 in the morning. The weather was perfect for an adventure through the deserted island's marsh inlets and pine forests. By midday, the temperature had climbed to a warm 88 degrees that would have normally caused explorers to break into a sweat. However, the group was air cooled by a brisk sea breeze out of the southeast. The wind blowing through the evergreen needles of the old pine trees made a rhythmic whispering sound that instilled a sense of peacefulness. Contributing to a dreamy, carefree feeling, the long strands of Spanish Moss swayed back and forth in the 200- year-old live oaks stretching northward over the edge of the salt marsh.

After the first hour on the water, the scenery became unusually exotic and so primeval looking that the Chatham's clamored to beach their crafts to get a closer look and take some pictures. It was coastal scenery that had not been touched by mankind. Pop had been commenting that this exotic looking landscape was probably how the coast looked when Sieur d'Iberville and his party of French explorers beached their sailing vessels in the shallow water of Back Bay Biloxi and walked to dry land to establish a French settlement in 1699.

Finally, Andrew Reardon issued an ultimatum for the flotilla to pick a spot on the idyllic sandy shores for what he was calling an absolutely essential pause for an up-close inspection of the ecology! He kindly but persistently had been hounding River Keeper Hannah Thomas about taking a shore break because they needed to get some driftwood and make a brief nature call, but not necessarily in that order. She was fine with taking photos and the 'ecology pause' but reminded Andrew he was in a kayak and she was curious where he was going to put any keepsake driftwood he found. He said that if Brent and his men could put big game rifles in their kayaks, he could probably stash some driftwood somewhere in the one he and Pop were using.

As the flotilla of seven kayaks quietly and cautiously glided toward an opening in the salt marsh grasses that would take them to their rest stop, Hannah Thomas abruptly whispered in a forbidding and hushed guttural tone, "Pull your paddles above water, now, and stop moving. Freeze where you are."

Her threatening warning caused the gliding flotilla to stop all movement, wondering why and what was wrong? Up ahead, the travelers saw a dark shape clearly making a move from the sea oats covered sand spit to open waters, sliding between loosely spaced clumps of stiff salt marsh grasses. The dark object was the width of a thirty-year-old tree trunk and had the coarse texture of the bark of a longleaf pine tree. Once it reached knee deep water, the thirteen-feet-long gliding tree trunk-like object was a few yards beyond the front of Hannah Thomas and the Speaker's kayak. Hannah shouted out loud, "Sister, drop your paddle and pull your arms inside the kayak. Speaker Chatham, drop your paddle, do not move and hold tightly to the edges of your cockpit!" Before reaching the shallow draft kayaks, it dropped beneath the water's surface and picked up speed, barely clearly the bottoms of the vulnerable kayaks floating above its prehistoric body.

At the same time, she reached inside her Kayak and pulled out an eighteen-inch-long knife with a pointed blade out of its leather case that she had tapped with duct tape to the underside of the hull in front of her cockpit. The three security guards pulled out their 45 caliber hand guns with extended magazines and held them pointed upward in case they would need them should the large alligator capsize one of the kayaks and attack one of the occupants.

Because of the restrained motion of the flotilla, and because of the number of the kayaks, the prehistoric lizard-like reptile vanished without incident in the depths of the tannin-colored water in the marsh pool. The swirl created by such a large creature in the shallow water caused the lightweight and shallow draft kayaks to move and bump into one another. Hannah Thomas directed the flotilla stay close to one another and beach their craft together on the sandy shoreline. The armed capitol police agents got out first to make sure the area was safe. Once securely on shore for their "ecology break," the group carefully explored the sandy spit and dunes in small groups for safety.

The western end of the island's long brackish pool with its meandering bayou was surrounded by salt marsh meadows on the south side and eight-foot-high undulating mounds of washed-up sand covered with sea oats all along the north side. Throughout the sandy barrier that faced the mainland, spectacular pieces of sun-bleached driftwood had washed up and were scattered on the beach and in between the sand dunes. After the party beached their watercraft and crawled out to stretch their legs, Hannah Thomas told the group, "This pretty sand barrier along the north side of Cat Island, as you speculated Pop, is probably what the natural edge of the Mississippi mainland would have looked like when Biloxi was discovered by French explorers in the late 1600's."

"The beach and sand dunes were created by a southeasterly sea breeze and waves that carried and deposited the same kind of white sand you see along Mississippi's coastline. A mound of sand washes up daily along the shoreline during the rising tide. When the tide falls, the mound dries out and stiff breezes blow loose sand upbeach replenishing beach sand that had been used for building higher and wider sand dunes. As part of the natural beach establishment process, sea oat grasses establish on the dunes and hold the sandy mounds in place. When there is a tropical storm or hurricane, sand dunes protect what is behind them from damaging storm tides and surging waves. During extreme weather events dunes can be damaged and even flattened by storm waves. Have no fear though, because the roots of the sea oats extend down into the original level of the beach and the restoration of beaches and dunes begins again."

Sarah, surprised that beaches were always beaches because of the daily renourishment by Mother Nature asked, "So, the washed-up sand continually maintains the sand on the beach?"

The River Keeper responded, "It sure does, Sarah. However, that washed up sand has to be held in place by native grasses and herbaceous plants otherwise the beach will continually lose sand and eventually become an eroded shoreline. That's what happened over time along Mississippi's beachfront. If there were salt marsh grasses along the coastal edge like once existed along our mainland's man-made beaches, they would grow the beach wider as the grasses trap washed-up sand. As the trapped sand grows in elevation, the area evolves into a dry sandy beach. Coastal ecologists profess that almost any salt marsh eventually becomes a beach."

"In our situation here, the dunes are protecting a large marsh pool which is a highly productive nursery for crabs, fingerling redfish, and speckled trout among many other marine creatures." Sarah Jane, a seventh grader with an avid interest in biological sciences, was particularly impressed that the marsh pool they had been boating on for the past hour was a highly productive nursery providing a diversity of aquatic life for the Mississippi Sound Estuary."

She asked, "So what if there was no more brackish water and salt marshes along our coast?"

The Pearl River Keeper replied, "Scary answer, Sarah. In short, there would be no more biodiversity along the coastal edge and the amount of shrimp, oysters, redfish, and speckled trout, among many other important marine creatures would diminish, drastically. The outstanding speckled trout and red fishing along our coast would disappear. The local oyster bars would close, and seafood po boys would become hard to find."

Describing how mankind often ignores the benefits of natural cycles, the experienced River Keeper explained, "Under the direction of the local government, mounds of sand on the mainland built by the gentle and persistent winds from Mother Nature are regularly flattened by motor graders and tractors pulling rakes to make the beach temporarily wider and give it the appearance of the wide and barren beaches found along the Alabama coastline. Waves eat away at the temporary sand beaches along our coastal edge, eroding one and one-half feet of loose sand every month.

"The natural beach along our mainland could look just like where we are standing, complete with long stretches of bright white sand, sand dunes filled with sea oats, native beach grasses, and driftwood galore all without maintenance by mechanical equipment." Looking directly at Andrew Reardon she said, "Along the mainland's highly maintained twenty-six miles of beach, you would be seriously out of luck collecting driftwood, seashells, and even the occasional doubloon from the days when there were pirates!"

Andrew had just returned from walking around a five-foot-tall mound of sand with hands full of driftwood sticks bleached white and a two by four with rounded edges that he speculated must have washed up from Costa Rica. Excitedly, the four-foot-six-inch tall fifth grader responded, "I am with you Miss Hannah, all the way. Of course, I like natural beaches and stuff to beachcomb, but right now my biggest problem is to find a way to take these driftwood treasures back. They are too cool looking to leave out here where no one will see them."

Smiling at the boy Hannah Thomas had a grin that said, "There is no doubt in my mind that this little guy will wind up being an ecologist, or artist with his keen interest in objects found in nature." The River Keeper wound up her beach biology illustration to the group with a simple, hypothetical question. "Tell me what you think. Which beaches are the most appealing, these on Cat Island that have many varieties of beach plants and mounds of sand courtesy of Mother Nature's handiwork, or the flattened, barren beaches along our coastal edge created by heavy machines propelled by fossil fuels?"

"Who would have ever thought the beaches in Bay St. Louis could be as pretty as these," commented Sarah Jane. "We spent some time on their beach a few days ago and I did notice it was flat and there were no sand dunes. I guess if you never saw what a natural beach could be, most people would be ok with the wide-open flat beach. They probably think that it is the natural beach!"

Penny Chatham spoke up, "I agree with you and Sarah Jane. If people have never seen Nature's idea of a natural beach, then they would think the flat beach without natural grasses is the way it should be. They might not realize that every eight years or so the Harrison County Industrial Board has to pay $11,000,000 for contractors to pump sand back in from offshore, and the state pays $3,000,000 a year to for the Sand Beach Department to continuously rake and grade twenty-six miles of beach to be flat. Hannah, where does all of that sand that naturally washes up on the beach go?"

The Pear River Keeper responded, "When beaches are raked each week to remove native emerging grasses and shrubs trying to grow in the sand, part of the natural strength of the settled sand is removed. Raking creates a six-inch-deep layer of fluffed-up sand that is easily moved by the wind and washed away by rainfall. When beaches are graded flat, sand along the water's edge washes away from wave action because there are no plant roots to hold the porous material in place. Once it is separated from our beaches, it is carried away by the littoral drift, which is the natural movement of water from east to west along the coast."

Continuing, Hannah Thomas disappointedly stated, "Studies have shown the beach loses three feet of width each month from wave erosion. Wind erosion blows some of the loose sand from constant raking onto the adjacent highway. Simply, sand provided naturally by Mother Nature is lost by wind and wave erosion. Pumping in sand to renourish the beach and cleaning the highway of windblown sand is not only unattractive but very expensive. Relying on nature's natural cycles is a better way of managing coast beaches. The long-term effect of pumping sand from offshore to replenish eroded sand is coming to an end. In many places along the twenty-six miles of our manmade beach, there are no longer sand reserves out in the water to use for pumping back onto our eroded beaches!"

There was a round of clapping and verbal support of what the Pearl River Keeper had learned about standard beach management procedures, and the future beach management changes that were inevitable. The group was fully surprised that nearshore waters along Mississippi's coastal edge had been depleted of offshore sand from the periodic loss of one-hundred feet of beach width every eight years that which was lost by uninformed management. Sister Leah leaned over and quietly said to Hannah, "I want to be like you one day. Do you think there would be a place for someone like me?"

Hannah Thomas looked down and smiled sweetly as she thought about putting her arm around her kayaking partner, but didn't. "Of course, Sister Leah, there will be a strong need for smart and concerned people like you. The environmental health of our country cannot survive unless we have a whole bunch of Sister Leah's to take care of our natural environments and demonstrate to others how that should be done." The little first grader smiled and looked straight ahead. She was proud and touched by the River Keeper's words of support.

Travel planner Ingram had arranged for small, waterproof canvas coolers for each traveler packed with snacks and drinks to be placed in the kayaks. There were bottled waters, cut up apples and grapes, and small cellophane bags with Cheeze-Its. Along with their snacks, lunch was prepared by Chef Tony and placed in the bottom of the coolers. Reusable black ice on the very bottom kept the trip food cold and dry. The intrepid explorers walked around and looked at Mother Nature's artwork as they devoured their snacks.

Looking at the sand mounds and sea oats, seeing driftwood of all kinds, and examining the ephemeral pools of water here and there between the dunes was fascinating and enjoyable. All commented how they had never seen a real natural beach and loved the unusual and surprising look of landscapes created by nature. Hannah commented how popular the coastal edge would be with this kind of biological diversity. "Beachgoers could walk for miles through an easily accessible beach environment totally created and managed by nature. An interesting part of letting Mother Nature be in charge is after each tropical storm or hurricane, there would be changes. Never again would the beach be static. Instead, it would be ever-changing just like all environments in the natural world. "

Winding up their exploration of the north side beaches and marshes of Cat Island, the trip leader announced, "Ok y'all, it's time to pack up your survival totes and squeeze into your kayak. That includes you too, Andrew Reardon. You remind me of a university archaeologist, who collects natural and cultural treasures from remote and untraveled locations in the world to take back to civilization for interpretation and display."

Andrew heard his name mentioned and looked up in time to catch her comment on interpretation and display. "No need to worry, Miss Hannah, most of my treasures will go on my window ledge back home in Georgetown. Only my friends will see my stuff, and they will think it's neat. I would like to get a group of my buddies together and talk to you about taking us back here, without my parents and Brent and his guys. Maybe we could even spend the night on the beach?"

That produced a big smile from the River Keeper who responded, "Ok, Cabeza de Vaca, give me a call when y'all are ready."

Andrew made a note to ask Sister Leah to help him find out who the heck was Cabeza de Vaca! "He" or "It" sounded important, someone or something of which a bright fifth grader should be aware.

The group pushed off from the beach along the northern edge of the long salt marsh pool. Because the prevailing southeast winds were being calmed by the mature pine tree forest, the water in the marsh pool was calm, and in places smooth as glass. The flotilla looked experienced and confident. In anticipation of what lay ahead, they were quiet and focused on reducing their interruption of natural sounds in the marsh pool environs. Other than swirls of fish and reptiles along the edges of the salt marsh and the occasional hawk's irate call announcing the presence of intruders, all was quiet and peaceful. Penny Chatham and her fleet of adventurers were the trespassers in this remote and fully natural landscape. The only man-made sound was the slick swish of paddles cutting into the brackish water and propelling the kayakers forward. They were all keenly observant of the island's jungle-like character while keeping a sharp eye out for any more encounters with alligators.

Diesel Powered Shrimp Boat

CHAPTER 20

Onward Through the Dark Forest

The coast ecologist broke the tranquility of the journey and said, "We are headed to the western-most point of the island where we will beach our kayaks, disembark, and proceed into the dark forest by foot. Remember, even though most of this island is owned by the National Park Service, there is no public access or trail system. There will probably not be any signs of previous island guests, except maybe a pair of cougars which are also called mountain lions. They have been seen on the island but never together. The travelers listened to the naturalist and paddled on, paying greater attention to their primeval surroundings and soaking up the character and sounds of the ancient landscape through which they were traveling.

The hiss of their paddles carefully scooping water along with the whisper of the smooth sliding kayaks through the brackish pool was a wonderful sound. Great blue herons, regularly spaced out along the shoreline about the distance from home plate to mid center field, eyed the flotilla but did not leap into the air in fear. Instead, they just observed the intruders moving through their home place. Some had probably never seen floating people slithering quietly through their marsh pool. The occasional juvenile alligator was seen in the shadow of the salt marsh grasses near the shoreline. Their eyes and snout peaking above water concealed what was floating below the surface of the water.

Red winged blackbirds squawked, possibly to alert the animal kingdom to the presence of royalty in the flotilla. A tribal leader in the pack of humans on the marsh pool had returned the flow of river water back into the Mississippi Sound Estuary which generated a revival of aquatic life including the reappearance of wild oysters. A commander in the exploration party had the ear of aquatic and avian life in the Honey Island Swamp. These benevolent humans and their pack returned the balance of nature which had been altered by mankind for selfish reasons and disregard for wildlife. All in the pack gliding through the brackish marsh pool, through a divine revelation, felt the respect of the wildlife bystanders.

Penny Chatham quietly told the group that she had often observed animals showing appreciation of efforts when people were making changes for their benefit. "In fact," she said, "their show of gratitude often occurred when we were planting salt marsh and sand dune grasses, and native trees on areas of barren beaches where they used to exist naturally. As we planted sea oats and salt marsh grasses, the ubiquitous sea gulls were curious and happy about the plantings, flying close by and twisting their heads watching what we were doing. Acrobatic black skimmers were not bothered by our presence as they went about teaching their young how to scoop up shallow water for tiny brine shrimp and floating oyster larvae only a matter of feet from where we were digging. They all knew we were toiling for their benefit, restoring their natural beaches and salt marshes!

"Even when we were inspecting the Pearl River in the Honey Island Swamp, extra attention toward our party was consistently given by Kingfishers and Osprey. After the restoration of the flow of Pearl River water eastward to the freshwater-starved Mississippi Sound, the big blue herons and brown pelicans by their undaunted presence exhibited affection to my coworkers and me."

Drawing near to the westernmost spit of land on the island, they found the idyllic scene became more attractive and inviting as they came closer to the landing. It was like preparing to insert the party's seven dark-green and orange-colored kayaks into the scene of a fine painting in a museum where the artist had captured the drama and feelings radiated by the landscape. And now here it was in real life; a sculpture that was crafted by nature's wind, waves, sun, rain, and tropical storms waiting for the group to experience.

As they beached their watercraft, the explorers were quiet, probably not unlike D'Iberville's party in the late 1600's, as they anchored their sailing vessels and gently sloshed through knee deep water to the splendorous beauty of the subtropical shoreline across the bay from the Biloxi peninsula. Each of the current-day travelers was overwhelmed by the beauty and drama of the Deep South weather-beaten landscape that was inviting them to come see its beauty and get to know its inhabitants.

The nearly naked sand spit was sparsely clothed in pieces of bleached and weathered driftwood and clumps of constantly swaying sea oats which had sent up their bloom spikes for the benefit of the bees and perpetuation of their species. The lone Spanish Bayonet plant, escaped from someone's ancient island garden, stood proudly erect ready to inflict man or beast with a puncture or gash. A well-used path, no doubt frequented by possums, deer, swamp rabbits, or even the island's pair of cougars, led southward in the direction of a mature longleaf and slash pine forest.

After tying up their kayaks, the group walked toward the forest. It was midday and the heat of the June sun beat down on their bare and thinly clothed skin. Their bodies, composed of 85% water, were like cups of liquid heating up in the sunlight. Shade in this case was imperative for them and vital for all mammals at 30° North Latitude. Tree limbs and dark green pine needles would intercept the life-giving sun thereby giving the party comfort and enabling them to continue their discovery of the deserted island.

In order to get to the shade, they walked up through fragrant marsh elder and bayberry shrubs densely growing on a small bluff. As the travelers got a toehold on the steep bluff as they climbed upward, they would reach back and pull those behind them up the steep incline. Hannah and Sister Leah went first. Then Brent, went up and nodded to the other two officers that it was safe for the Speaker to climb upward. Pop was told he could help his wife and son up the bluff. Sarah Jane went up on her own. When she got to the top of the bluff she held on to the trunk of a shrub and held her open hand out for Jake. He proudly took it and scrambled up the bluff. He could have made it on his own but was fine with Sarah giving him a hand. She was a very agile and strong seventh grader. Once the shrubby hillside was behind them, they came to a dense saw palmetto glade. In nature, each plant species is located according to the areas' available moisture. The palmetto palms did not need as much moisture as the shrubs and dominated the area up to the long leaf pines which were able to tolerate variable moisture conditions.

While following the beaten path of the animal run, they continued beneath the thickly growing saw palmettos. The agile and versatile Hannah Thomas pulled out a machete from its holster on her side and began to cut back palm branches so that her group of human travelers could walk through in a single file. The thickly growing saw-tooth palms thinned as the deep shade of the pine trees began to cover the ground. Finally, they were able to spread out a little as they walked along a slight ridge that curved eastward.

"Once we get into the forest," the River Keeper shared, "keep your eyes open for big cat animal tracks, their droppings which is called scat, and trees which have scratches on their trunks. Their scratched marks define their territory visually and leaves their scent from glands on their paws. Their tracks are four inches wide and three inches long. They have four toes in the front and a heel pad in the back. Their scat is like that of a house cat except it is five inches long and usually contains hair and bone fragments. They scratch a place on the forest floor just like a cat does before depositing their scat. We might also see partially buried prey that would be evidence of their presence. Cougars are solitary animals that move through the woods in a very stealthy manner."

The group was quiet and listened intently, including Andrew Reardon who usually had a comment to share. "It's important to stay with the group and not go off on your own," directed Hannah. "If another nature break is needed, let the group know and we will keep a look out for trouble. Andrew Reardon and Pop in the back, are you with us?"

Andrew felt like he had been singled out for the 'nature break' comment and retorted, "Of course, we are, Cougar Tracker. Why wouldn't we be?", he replied. Immediately Pop put the squeeze on the young boy's shoulder quickly prompting, "Sorry, Miss Hannah, I apologize for being a smart ass."

With that comment Pop picked up his kayak partner and threw his torso over his shoulder and with his right arm around his legs said to the group, "I think we have our most vocal adventurer under control. It is highly unlikely he will be straying away from the group." Andrew Reardon said nothing. He knew his daddy loved him and he was in the safest hands he could be in. He thought about his comment to the River Keeper and made up his mind to keep thoughts like that to himself and try not to think about offering creative remarks on the rest of the trip.

The Pearl River Keeper resumed describing other natural phenomena, "There is also the possibility a bird species called the Ivory Billed Woodpecker could be nesting on this remote end of the island. It is almost two feet long and has been seen in Arkansas and on the island of Cuba, as well as in the Honey Island Swamp through which the Pearl River flows. The woodpecker feeds on larvae that looks like grub worms and are located beneath the bark of trees. As the largest woodpecker in the world, the ivory billed bird is on the critically endangered species list. The Honey Island Swamp reserve is less than twenty-four miles from here as the crow flies so it is not beyond reason they might be nesting on this island because of its inaccessibility."

Andrew Reardon laughed out loud from his position of bobbing up and down while being carried. He thought using crows and woodpeckers in the same sentence was odd and downright funny. Pop reached up and put his hand on the boy's rear, again gently squeezing to warn him to calm down and keep his comments to a minimum. Andrew got the message and again softly apologized to the River Keeper, "Sorry, Miss Hannah."

Continuing, Hannah said, "The slash pine and longleaf pine are native to the Mississippi coast and its barrier islands. They once provided plentiful amounts of wood and turpentine but the barrier islands are now almost totally owned by the National Park Service and commercial harvest of wood has stopped."

"Slash and longleaf pine wood is dense and strong and is a very popular building material. Most pine wood harvested in the South is labeled Southern Yellow Pine and includes the slash, longleaf, and loblolly pine trees. The strong tree grows fast and can withstand hurricane force winds, and even storm surges that can flood an area for eight or more hours. It is remarkable that their roots can be submerged in salt water that long. During Hurricane Katrina, which had a thirty-five-foot storm surge that lasted for six hours, many old pine trees on Deer Island near Biloxi died because the storm was followed by six weeks without rain. That was unusual and a drought that lasts that long after a storm surge is very rare. Trees flooded by the storm surge need the rainfall to dilute the high salinity water accumulated in the soil around their root systems."

There was no comment, even from Andrew Reardon. Hannah continued talking about the slash pines. "Let me share one more thing about these beauties." She stopped and was slapping a thirty-inch diameter trunk and pointing out marks a few feet above the ground on the old tree called cat whiskers. "These diagonal lines were once deeper cuts into the trunk that directed the flow of tree sap in the winter to flow out of the tree and down into buckets. The thick, yellow sap contained a resin that would become turpentine after being taken to a mill for processing. Turpentine was a valuable chemical and used as a solvent in paint, varnishes, shoe polish, and even in medicine."

Andrew Reardon, in a weakened voice from needing a lunch break, injected, "I know about turpentine Miss Hannah. My grandmother gives us a spoonful of it with some sugar in it when we have a really bad cold."

Hannah looked at Penny Chatham for verification, who pursed her lips, cocked her head and shook it up and down in confirmation of Andrew Reardon's remark. She followed, "She sure does. So far it hasn't hurt him that I know of, but he doesn't get many colds, thank the Lord."

At a bluff on the south side of the island, there were peaceful views overlooking a salt marsh and intermittent clumps of underwater grasses beyond the marsh which was similar to where they fished a couple of days ago. Hannah offered, "This looks like a pretty good place to stop. Anyone ready for a lunch break?"

They were famished and as they found a place to sit on the forest floor covered with pine straw, Sister Leah said in exhaustion, "Thank you, Fearless Leader. We are all about to die. I'm ready for a root beer. I'll bet Jake Ingram was thoughtful enough to make sure those Barq's drinks were packed in our lunches!" Jake did not react to her comments because he did not know what kind of drinks Chef Tony packed. However, for Sister Leah's sake, he hoped there was a bottle or two of Barq's Root Beer.

The salt marsh at the south edge of the pine forest stretched for two miles. Beyond the marsh grasses you could see large areas where the water was agitated with fish hitting the surface. Hannah pointed out that they were lady fish and were feeding on fingerling mullet. "Large bull reds and black tipped sharks are there as well smacking the surface feeding on the ladyfish. If you like to catch a very active fish that will give you a big fight, throw a lure or line baited with a bull minnow into the midst of the school and you will catch ladyfish until your arm and hands get tired." That suited The Chatham children just fine. They asked their Pop if they could come back tomorrow in the fishing boats and just catch ladyfish. They liked the idea of non-stop action and besides Sister Leah didn't like the idea of keeping anything she caught anyway.

"You bet we can. I will talk to Mike and Bob about arranging an outing tomorrow morning at 6:00 am", replied Pop. Sister Leah looked at her older sister and rolled her eyes but said nothing. The canvas cooler had a cold Barq's Root Beer in it and she was concentrating on enjoying that. She glanced at Pop and gave him a look of 'Don't bother me with the details. Just keep me happy.'

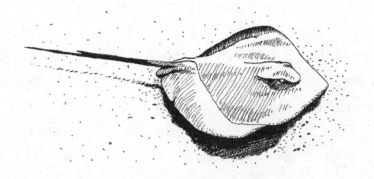

Sting Ray Feeding along Marsh and Beach Edges

CHAPTER 21

Hannah Thomas Ecologist

After a lunch of tomato sandwiches, with plenty of mayonnaise liberally seasoned with salt and coarse pepper, the group was ready to go. Packing up their canvas coolers and being sure to leave no trace of having had a picnic lunch, Penny Chatham was eager to keep enjoying the different landscapes on the island. She asked, "Tell us where we are going next, Hannah."

The ecologist and trip leader responded, "The island is five miles long and three miles wide. So far today we have traveled about two and one-half miles on the water and two miles through the pine forest. We will continue to walk through the forest and be on the lookout for signs of the cougars and evidence of the Ivory Billed woodpecker. The cougars are probably in the forest somewhere waiting until dusk when the other wildlife is getting up and starting to move about."

"The Ivory Billed Woodpeckers which are bigger than a crow might be actively feeding in the woods prying larvae from beneath the bark on dead trees. They also eat fruit, nuts, and seeds. As we walk, and if we are quiet, we might hear one. They make a noise when feeding that sounds like someone blowing on a clarinet mouthpiece, or a tin trumpet. An ornithologist friend in Florida named Dr. Jerry Jackson went to Cuba and found evidence of the rare birds feeding on larvae in trees. He observed large swaths of bark stripped high up on the trunks of dead pine trees."

"Did he see one," asked Sarah Jane?

"No, he didn't," replied Hannah, "and he was in the remote pine forests of western Cuba for two weeks. However, he heard its repeated tin trumpet call several times while exploring the forests. I think they might also be on Cat Island. This is great habitat for them and there would be very little disturbance from people." The group was pumped to see or at least hear the Ivory Billed woodpecker. Seeing one of the cougars, however, was not high on Sister Leah or Sarah Jane's list. A picture on a website would be enough for them.

Hannah continued, "Once we get to the southeast tip of the island, we will leave the pine forest and go down into an extensive area of rippling mounds of sand dunes covered with sea oats. It is a scenic, dynamic transition to a lower elevation where we can carefully walk along the edge of a small salt marsh pool to get to the sand dunes. The pool and dunes will be on a three-mile-long sand beach that faces southeast toward the waters of the Gulf of Mexico. I think you will enjoy the dramatic beauty and great landscape diversity in this final leg of the trip."

Pop said, "Sounds great. I think we are all ready to go."

Sister Leah, staring up into the fearless face of their intrepid leader asked, "Final leg? What about our kayaks, Miss Hannah? I left some cool rocks and shells I picked up on the beach in our kayak and I have to go back and get them. It's imperative I get those keepsakes because I was going to make momma a necklace with one of them for her birthday!"

Hannah, who was in her early thirty's, unmarried, and did not have kids, was touched by the passionate plea from her boat mate. She kneeled down, looked her in the face and gently reassured the group's youngest traveler, "Don't you worry, Little Island Cougar, our boats will be towed back to Pelican Roost and will be there before we get there. Your treasures and birthday gift will be waiting for you."

That was fine, well, almost fine with Leah. She replied, "Good thinking, my fellow sister of the forest, but I would rather be called Ivory Woodpecker than little cougar. Because my brother Andrew Reardon likes to sneak around and stay up late, he has more of the characteristics of a cougar and might better deserve that nickname." Andrew Reardon was ok with the title. He was pretty tired and unable to contest that title or any other.

As the group prepared to depart the bluff, Andrew Reardon, nearly exhausted, stood facing his hiking partner with his arms up in the air ready for a lift up to his daddy' shoulders. Looking down, his daddy grinned and said, "Ready to roll, "Amigo?" Returning that invitation with a big grin, Pop interlocked his fingers and put a temporary stirrup down to help his favorite son hop up to his perch like someone getting on a horse.

With an elevated view higher than any of the hikers, Andrew cautioned, "Be careful of low hanging limbs that could bump and possibly knock me off my roost."

The edge of the forest was near as they could see bright light ahead. As they were approaching the end of the animal run which had the makings of a hiking path, the naturalist River Keeper reminded them their trail was established and shared by island mammals of all kinds. It belonged to the animals; human beings were the uninvited guests. That thought instilled respect and thankfulness to those that created and used the trail.

The hikers were about to experience the abrupt change from dense pine forest to brilliant white sand and many mounds of dunes. Here again, changes, and especially abrupt changes in the landscape occurred because of elevation differences and the availability of moisture in the soil.

As they approached the end of the old pine forest, their curiosity was heightened by the dramatic change in the landscape. Emerging from the dark, cooler environs of the dense pine forest and out onto a bright, treeless area brought smiles to the faces of the travelers. There were marshes, a very long beach, and sand dunes covered with sea oats. Immediately, the unobstructed stiff sea breeze cooled the perspiration from their arms and faces. Squinting was mandatory in order to see because of the brightness of light reflecting on the white sand. The radiation from the sun was refreshing and provided a cooling effect as it and the impatient sea breeze evaporated the perspiration from the bodies of the travelers. While the transition from the deep, dark forest to the bright open dunes was theatrical, its sensory perception was welcoming.

Abandoning the thickly growing slash pine forest and moving toward the spectacular beach, they walked down a short path of densely growing saw palmettos. Following the animal run, Hannah, again cut palm fronds away from the middle of the path so her travelers could proceed without getting cuts and gashes from the saw teeth on their stems.

Once they had passed through the palmetto glade, the next challenge was to get down to the beach level by navigating down a seventy-five-foot-high mound of sand. The party held hands to avoid slipping and tumbling down the tall wind-blown sand piled up against the edge of the forest. Agent Ryan who played high school and college football was first to go down the steep animal trail to check its stability. He strong sense of balance allowed him to stay erect the entire distance down the steep path. When Brent was satisfied the sandy descent to Three Mile Beach was relatively safe, Hannah Thomas and he went down the steep slope with Penny Chatham between them holding their hands. They made it with a moderate amount of difficulty. The Speaker lost her balance and landed on her rear about half way down and took Hannah Thomas with her. Their laughing sounded like a combination of cackling with some punctuated screams as they rolled over and over until stopped by Agents Brent and Ryan. Continuing to laugh and point the finger at who it was that lost their footing and caused the human avalanche, they got back to their feet and continued down the slope.

Sister Leah, now apprehensive about going down the sandy slope held tightly on to her daddy's hand as they were next. They both slowly eased down the steep trail and when Pop's feet slipped out from under him, they both rode the rest of the way down to the bottom on their bottoms. That drew a vigorous reaction from the group who clapped and cheered them on, complimenting them on their loss of balance and inability to negotiate a steep slope. While Pop laughed, Sister Leah demanded she be reunited with her Kayak partner for any forthcoming terrain challenges.

Next, Jake and Andrew Reardon went down with Sarah Jane in the middle. She tried to shake off Andrew's hand attempting to get her brother to lose his balance and tumble down the mound. It would not have been a dangerous fall but would have been one where sand would end up in his ears, shoes, and probably down his shirt and hiking pants. He was not ready for that and would not let go. Instead, he landed at the bottom of the slope vertical and on his feet!

Finally, Agent Dorothy, who Sister Leah called Momma Dorothy, came down the steep animal trail. Half way down she decided to go the rest of the way like she was going down a very tall sliding board. As she landed at the bottom, she jumped up on her feet with a big smile and bowed to the audience. The party clapped for the outstanding style and athletic skill exhibited by the Capitol Police agent.

The explorers then passed through dense thickets of wax myrtle and marsh elder shrubs, interrupting the daily routines of the many birds that called the evergreen shrubs home. Being located above the high tide line, these shrubs could withstand windblown salty water and occasional submersion from storm tides. Once they passed through the shrub zone, there lay before them a stunning, eyelevel view of undulating sand dunes and a long flat beach facing toward the southeast.

Several noticed it was similar in appearance to one you might see on Alabama and Florida's coastline that fronted on the Gulf of Mexico. The dazzling, panoramic view of the three-mile-long natural beach from their elevated vantage as they emerged from the pine forest hushed them to silence. Now being face to face with the dunes, beach, and the large breakers from the Gulf, the explorers were momentarily silenced by awe at the sight of Three Mile Beach. Nature's scenery muted all casual conversation. The island troopers just stared at the wild and awesome spectacle fronting the Gulf of Mexico.

Overwhelmed by the drama of the scenic wonder, Penny Chatham eventually broke the silence and said, "Nature's magnificence is always surprising and diminishes the challenges and disruptions in my mind. I am thankful for this tranquil experience, Hannah Thomas. It is doing wonders for enhancing my capacity for hopefulness and intensifying my appreciation for how our natural landscapes positively affect all of us. We are a country with an abundance of scenic wonders and maybe we need to recognize and make more of them available for our inspiration." A few amens were quietly spoken in recognition of the Speaker's thoughts.

All valued Penny Chatham's comments as they were affected by the beauty of the beach landscape as well. She drew her thoughts to a close by saying, "The beauty of wild, natural landscapes is always a pleasant surprise and takes us, if only a short while, away from our hike through daily commitments. That experience increases our positive outlook and makes us emotionally stronger."

The Cat Island party recognized Speaker Chatham's powerful abilities for uniting people with nature and even greater abilities to work wonders such as returning brackish water to the Mississippi Sound Estuary. They were proud to be with this simple, family person who was plugged into a formidable position helping to govern, at least in a small way, the 300 million people in the United States and the wonder-filled country in which they lived.

Once down at the beach, no one could resist walking along the waves crashing along the shoreline. Shoes and socks came off and pants were rolled up to enjoy this dynamic change in the normally calm and quiet Cat Island landscapes through which they had boated and walked since they embarked on their journey this morning. Andrew Reardon and his sisters were amazed at the sheer quantity of shells scattered within the surf line and were stuffing their pockets with keepers to bring back home. Sarah Jane was using a canvas hiking bag she got when subscribing to the National Audubon Society Birding Magazine. She gently admonished her mother, "See, Mom, this is why I brought this canvas bag, not just because it was stylish!"

Penny Chatham smiled and put her arm around her first daughter who was about to emerge fully into her teenage phase, "I should have known better, my Daring Explorer. You always have multiple reasons for every decision you make. You've got all of your bases covered, all the time, Sweet Girl!" Sarah Jane smiled at her mom and gave her a quick peck on her sunburned cheek that glistening with sweat.

Hannah Thomas led the group northwestward away from the beach walking through fields of Spartina patens, a salt marsh grass that grows above the high tide line. Also called Salt Hay, the lime green grass had thick, two-foot-long shoots of leaves and stems with narrow seed pods. It provided strength to the sandy soil in the upper portion of the beach which was above the high tide line. It also trapped windblown sand moving across the barren lower beach.

Behind the fields of salt hay, sea oat grasses had established on six to eight feet tall sand dunes that were twenty-four feet wide. There were multiple lines of dunes with shrubs and some had small trees growing in the depressions between the dunes.

After walking a mile and a half, and enjoying the bright, open nature of the wild, Cat Island beach, Hannah asked, "Anyone interested in heading back to Pelican Roost? I have a feeling Chef Tony is going to have Virgin Pina coladas for the young folks and grown-up versions for those of us a little older. Andrew Reardon asked what they had in them. "Do you like fresh pineapple and crushed up ice?"

"I think I might. Right now, anything with crushed up ice would be good", responded the obviously exhausted ten-year-old explorer. Of course, a comment like that opened him up to ribbing from his siblings.

"How about some washed-up seaweed with a few crushed sand crabs sprinkled on top?" offered Sister Leah.

Andrew Reardon quickly reacted, "Ahh, you always bring up your favorite drinks, Sister. Why don't you broaden your pallet of afternoon refreshments and come up with something new instead of the same old refreshments you always drink." Sister Leah knew not reacting to her brother's unkind comments would be the best response. "Let him simmer in his fatigue juices," she thought to herself.

Penny Chatham looked back at Leah and winked. She quietly commented, "Good job, Sister. I believe you won that disagreement." Her youngest and most gifted child smiled and offered a quick salute back. She recalled the Bay St. Louis police saluting her mom and thought that was so funny. Saluting the most precious person in her life was always followed with a giggle which her mom loved and, if she was close enough, would pinch her six-year-old cute daughter in the side, eliciting even more giggling.

Leading the barrier island exploration team back in the direction of Pelican Roost, Hannah Thomas walked a broad arc through the beach landscapes and finally westward toward the towering slash pine forest and the shade it afforded the beginning-to-be-weary explorers. The comforting qualities of the retreat offered full protection from the elements of hot June weather and high humidity. There would also be air conditioning, showers, fresh clothes, and hopefully the refreshments the River Keeper had anticipated might be served to the dedicated band of Cat Island Explorers.

On the one-and-one-half mile walk back, the conversation began to build along with the excitement of returning to their three-story shelter that afforded panoramic views of marshes, inlets and open water which eventually met Mississippi's coastal edge. Even though you could not see the mainland, it was reassuring to know all of the protection afforded by human settlements and their colorful variety would still be there when they returned, ready to serve and provide that basic need of human interaction. Hiking and kayaking all day through primeval landscapes made you think of what life would be like without being part of that variety and unable to see and visit with lots of people every day! Losing that experience would not be enjoyable, and in fact, might be devastating to a sound and creative mind.

Thinking of home and reconnecting with friends and her challenges as Speaker of the House of Representatives was now creeping back into the thoughts of Penny Chatham. She and her family had experienced one of the most remarkable and enjoyable natural landscapes in the country. Through the exceptional guidance of Hannah Thomas, they came to know the beauty of the island and its natural processes that kept it healthy and intact. They learned about its diversity and about the different landscapes that were profoundly dependent on each other.

Remembering a famous line by Dr. Martin Luther King, Jr., Penny Chatham said to herself, "I too have been to the mountaintop." And she had. "I have seen and experienced firsthand the results of working hand in hand with the people of Louisiana and Mississippi three years ago. I thank God for the conciliatory attitudes of the players and the progress we have made together!" She shivered while walking the trail back to Pigeon Roost just thinking about what had been accomplished in three years.

Seeing a physical change in her mother, Sarah Jane asked, "Momma, are you alright? Is the heat getting to you?"

Penny Chatham responded, "Yes, Baby, I am fine. Actually, I'm better than fine. This trip with y'all has been the highlight of my past three years!"

Her maturing daughter responded, "You will be all right, Momma. When we get home, we can get one of those grown-up iced drinks and you and I can sit on the balcony and talk about things."

Her momma of thirteen years looked back at her oldest daughter and said with watery eyes, "I'd like that, Sweet Girl. I'd like that very much!"

Clutching her daughter's hand tightly, they walked together along the edge of a canal that had been dug in the 1930's to provide access to the valuable slash pine timber. As they got closer to Pelican Roost, the landscape began to be more open and settled looking. That was fine with the hikers. They loved the wilderness character they had experienced that day, but all were ready to land at Pelican Roost and enjoy all of the amenities it offered.

Never one to give up or forget a discouraging comment, Sister Leah shouted back to Andrew Reardon, "Hey, Antron, you still going to have one of those seaweed and crushed crab smoothies?" Antron was one of his favorite video game characters and she thought that might get a rise out of him. But there was no response. There was no retort like she was expecting. He was one who could come up with a backhanded response faster than anyone she knew of. Looking back at the end of the hikers, she saw her usually energetic brother slumped over Pop's shoulder again, his head bobbing up and down. He was dead to the world with exhaustion.

Arriving at the three-story lodge, they made plans to clean up and rest, rest, rest for the remainder of the evening. Chef Tony greeted them as they walked up. "Pina Coladas are on the drink menu this evening. Any takers?"

"Yes!" Exclaimed the travelers, almost in unison. Pop asked, "Could we shed these dirty clothes and get a little more presentable?"

Chef Tony said, "Of course. I'll bring up some pitchers and tumblers to the balcony in about thirty minutes?"

Sister Leah answered for her daddy, "Sure, that will work, Chef Tony. We could all use some of your magic water for our souls, as well as a rest for our weary feet." The six-year-old loved to take charge of a group. After the all-day adventure, she was bright and alert, unlike her brother who was still in a collapsed state on his dad's shoulder.

Tony replied, "Ok, Short Stuff, you got it. I'm going to make a very special Pina Colada especially for you." That was fine with Leah. She like to ruffle feathers and throw out a few shocks every now, and then to bring attention to 'the shortest girl in the crowd' as she often called herself.

Oyster Beds Exposed During Low Tide

CHAPTER 22

After the Wilderness Expedition, A Call from Craig Gill

On the mainland, the press was being briefed about the passing of President Harrison. The nation was shocked. One news correspondent asked what was it that took the president's life. Maggie Williams, his press secretary, replied, "His physicians are still determining the cause of death."

A reporter from the Wall Street Journal bluntly questioned the whereabouts of the vice president and his health. The articulate and quick-witted Maggie smiled at the reporter and said, "You know the answer to that Mr. Rusty David, my boss was President Harrison and that was enough to keep me plenty busy. I don't keep up with the vice president. You will have to check with his press secretary, although

I'm sure he is in fine health." But he wasn't. The reporter would not get that from his press secretary, at least not yet.

Checking the satellite phone when Penny Chatham got back to her room, she saw that she had been getting calls from her chief of staff since early that morning. Five calls since 8:30 am meant something was up. She feared the worst, of course. After such an incredible day and week of highs, of course it would be offset with a substantial issue needing her attention. Surprisingly though, she was not irritated like she would normally be by a call from Washington while on her part vacation and part work trip. With this tolerance and amicable attitude, a call back was placed to Washington.

She had unwound from many months of long hours of networking with her congressional peers and providing motherly care to her precious but demanding children. Her family burdens were no different than those on most moms. Pop was a capable take-part dad, but there were things only a mom could do, and matters Penny Chatham wanted to do. She was capable of balancing her work demands with the responsibilities of being a traditional mom.

Being a representative of her people and helping to solve their problems, as well as working toward improving their relationship with their environment was her day job. As a political figure, she had evolved into a powerhouse of change for harmony between man and land. That was all good, but this was also her time to be a mom and she was not going to give up that wonderful, rich experience. Penny Chatham had a big heart and had the attributes of being a regular, down to earth person with a family that was often included in occasional aspects of her job such as their trip to Tanzania and this remarkable foray into the swamps, estuaries, and maritime forests of

Louisiana and Mississippi. Her trip to the coast, primarily, had been to evaluate changes made to restore the production of seafood in the coastal estuaries with federal assistance. But, she was also expecting to have an adventure with her family to spice up her life, and she had found it.

Her reputation as an attentive mother and a dynamic politician was appealing to the public and terrific for her polling numbers. Nevertheless, her recognition of the grass roots support that was building on her behalf was unimportant to the busy congresswoman. What she cared about the most was including the everyday person in understanding seemingly complicated environmental decisions and making choices that benefitted both man and nature. People liked to be included and asked their opinion, and Congresswoman Chatham was flat good at that. She was never one to drone on about possibilities and complicated issues. Instead, she wanted to learn from her constituents. That practice worked and produced two important outcomes: alternative solutions to the problem evolved, and the positive reputation of Penny Chatham! All of these thoughts were running through her mind as she waited for Craig Gill to answer her call. "Speaker Chatham, I am sorry to tell you this, but President Harrison has passed. He died in his sleep early this morning." There was dead silence on the other end of the call from the remote confines of an uninhabited barrier island off the coast of Mississippi. Penny Chatham sat on the edge of her youngest daughter's rumpled bed in the sleeping loft looking out over Jean Lafitte Bayou and the placid marsh pool through which they traveled by kayak this early morning. From her view thirty feet above ground level, she was thinking about how peaceful it was to be surrounded by trees and the calmness and serenity of a wild landscape created and managed by Mother Nature.

Her chief of staff knew his boss well and anxiously put his emotions on silence through the long pause which he knew would come. The passing of Jim Harrison would be a major loss to the Speaker because he was a friend in addition to being the country's most important leader and a world renown figure.

Slowly and softly Speaker Chatham replied, "Tell me, Craig, how is his wife Connie taking the loss?" She had been hoping the phone call was about a problem with some aspect of the application of her Sustainability Bill, or maybe that a key member of her staff had taken another job. She was not expecting to hear that her dear friend's husband had died! Presidents never die in office. How could that have happened?

"I have not heard", he replied. "I do know that the floor with the president's hospital room is sealed off and those who tended the president are being quarantined. The family was not able to see President Harrison before he died and are still unable to see his body. Of course, all of this is confidential."

Penny was upset. This was awful news that she could not fix. Her can-do attitude that got her to the level of Speaker of the House of Representatives was that she could fix anything with knowledge and public support. She told Craig, "I will call Connie. Could you send some flowers to the White House? Select something simple and fragrant, like a small bowl of white roses that can be set on a table; nothing big and showy."

"Yes ma'am, I will. And Madam Speaker, Donna just handed me a note for you to call Camille Latady. She is the Director of the Secret Service and says it is urgent for you two to talk."

"Of course, it is, Craig. I understand and will call her when we finish talking. On another note, I'm sure Jake will tell you about today, we have just emerged from an all-day exploration of the island's marsh pools, jungles and natural beaches. We started in kayaks and ended on foot. As physically taxing as it was, we all hung in there because of the incredible beauty of this wild place. I say all, Andrew Reardon flat wore out and fell dead asleep toward the end of the hike. Pop had to carry him the last three miles on his shoulders. Today's exploration has been an astounding experience."

Continuing to be positive in spite of the bad news, she said, "You need to meet the naturalist we hired three years ago as the Pearl River Keeper for the freshwater diversion project in the Honey Island Swamp. Her name is Hannah Thomas and she is fully in charge of making the best decisions for the flow of water from the Pearl River basin into the Mississippi Sound. Write her name down and remind me when we get back that she needs to be recognized for having such an effective handle on managing water quality for both the Honey Island Swamp Wildlife Sanctuary and the Mississippi Sound Estuary. The Lake Pontchartrain Basin Foundation needs to be recognized as well. Charles Delgado and Tasha de La Houssay are doing great work and are including the Mississippi Sound Estuary in their monthly evaluation of water quality and marine life. Take a look at the Hydrocoast Maps they are putting out. I'll have Jake send you the URL for it. The color graphics and brief narrative provide an overall look at the variables that contribute to the ecological health of Lake

Pontchartrain, Lake Borgne, and the Mississippi Sound Estuary. Call Jake and y'all come up with some alternatives for how the Lake Pontchartrain Basin folks can be credited for their continuous efforts that have helped restored the productivity of those estuaries."

"I will, Speaker Chatham, and you be sure to return the Secret Service Director's call. She has called me three times today and once while we have been talking. It must be urgent."

"I will do just that Craig," replied the Speaker. "My mind is clear. I'm ready to get back on a fast horse and ride." Penny Chatham then called Connie Harrison and expressed her concern. The family was distraught and saddened to the greatest extent possible. Penny Chatham's call helped. In times of greatest need, it was important to have close friends call with their comforting concerns.

Pelican Chick Carved Tile by Christine Codling

CHAPTER 23

Camille Latady

After taking a few deep breaths and getting a glass of ice water to sip on for a few minutes, Speaker Chatham called Camille Latady. The call went straight to the director who answered, "Speaker Penny Chatham?"

"Yes, it is, Director Latady."

The director cut to the point at hand, "Since President Harrison's death, Vice President Steve Hardy has been sworn in by the Chief Justice of the Supreme Court. You are now next in line for the office of President. If anything happens to render President Steve Hardy incapable of fulfilling his presidential duties, by law, you will be sworn in as the next President." After a prolonged pause where there was no reaction, the Director retold the fact of the matter, "The Speaker of the House of Representatives is third in line to the office of President. You are now second in line."

Penny Chatham had been expecting to be notified about the line of succession. She knew all about what the Director of the Secret Service was telling her. It was irritating to be reminded what the constitution says about succession. Part of her job was to be fully competent on the laws governing the executive and legislative branches of government and of that she was very knowledgeable. As a member of the legislative branch, she was the one house member selected by her peers to lobby the president and senate on behalf of the 435 member House of Representatives. It was essential that she was knowledgeable of the legal bounds on how the president and congress react to one another.

Her irritation with Director Latady was growing because she was telling her what she should know and already knew, and it was also because she really did not want to hear the facts of the situation with the passing of President Harrison. She liked things like they were. Going back to Washington and building momentum for implementation of her sustainability bill was a big enough challenge and that was where she wanted to put all of her efforts.

She did not like the remote possibility which the additional burden of presidential succession placed on her. Traveling to the Deep South to review progress on the provision of additional freshwater to restore brackish water in the Mississippi Sound Estuary cleared her mind and firmly convinced her the monumental efforts of orchestrating Mississippi and Louisiana to work together to restore once highly productive ecosystems were worth it. Going back to Washington to continue working on her existing projects was a rewarding experience she was looking forward to having. She did not want a lecture on other responsibilities that were being thrust upon her.

Finally responding, "I hear you, Director Latady," "What else do we need to visit about?" Trying to soften her irritation she continued, "We are winding down our visit with constituents here in Louisiana and Mississippi and preparing to go back to Washington."

The director of the secret service, hearing and ignoring her irritation said, "Because of current conditions, as we speak, I am sending thirty additional Secret Service Agents to Long Beach, Mississippi, to join six agents sent last week to become educated on the ground about the island on which you are staying and the Mississippi Sound. Those initial six agents were briefed by a local expert named Hannah Thomas over a two-day period on the terrain, water, and culture. They were sent by me to ensure your safety in an area with which we were totally unfamiliar. As a precaution, I also sent an armored limousine yesterday for your safety. It is at the Stennis Space Center."

Now really annoyed, the Speaker replied, "My safety? Do you think my safety is compromised in any way?" she pointedly asked, now with growing concern. The Speaker was initially irritated with the Secret Service Director because she thought Washington might be overdoing it a bit. But the safety issue was a bigger deal. Her kids and husband were traveling with her and to expose them to any issue where their wellbeing was a concern was not in the cards for Penny Chatham. She was a small-town girl from Mississippi with a beautiful and loving family, and their health was not supposed to be compromised in any way by her government job.

"No, Madam Speaker, not that we know of, but it is protocol. At this time, you are second in line to the Presidency. Therefore, you will be protected by the Secret Service, at all times. The additional agents will be landing at the Stennis Space Center airport in an hour and thirty minutes. The airport has been closed to all other air traffic except that related to your safety. The six agents on the coast that were briefed by Hannah Thomas will be at Pelican Roost in Department of Marine Resources Patrol boats by 8:00 pm."

"I see", replied the Speaker. "Any more good news?"

The Secret Service Director was direct and dry. She would not debate whether or not provision of armed security and intrusion into the Speaker's personal life should be up for discussion. Continuing, she said, "Our task force director on the ground in Mississippi is named Charles Parks. He will be contacting you this evening for a brief introduction after they arrive on Cat Island. "With a gentler tone Director Latady said, "We are here to ensure the safety of you and your family Speaker Chatham. Either you or your staff trip planner Jake Ingram can call me at any time, direct. Enjoy the rest of your trip."

Penny Chatham was exhausted by the phone call. After the all-day excursion on Cat Island, she had been ready to stretch out on a chaise lounge on her second story balcony and soak in the natural beauty of the island. For her last evening in this unique and rugged natural setting, she dressed up more than usual by putting on a beige billowy blouse with natural shell buttons. The pants she selected were off white and loose fitting with a drawstring around the waist. She told Pop she was shooting for the "I am unhindered and unconstrained" look. Her sunburned face reflected that feeling as she declared, "I am totally fascinated by this deserted island in the Mississippi Sound and I am spellbound by the island's constant sea breeze. If anyone disturbs this wonderful feeling I am having, Agent Brent Rupard with my security detail will lock them away in a dark and dank utility shed."

Her calm and tolerant husband responded, "Well, all right, Laura Croft." Then he turned and positioned himself in a chaise lounge toward the other end of the balcony.

As she sat down at the opposite end, still miffed about Camille Latady's phone call, Chef Tony walked over and offered her a tall tumbler of an exquisite looking Pina Colada garnished with a thick, round slice of fresh pineapple cut to fit on the glass rim. "Would you prefer a traditional Pina Colada or a virgin one?"

She answered, "I'll take the scandalous version Tony. After my exceptional and awe-inspiring island jaunt today, only the extreme version will do!"

As Penny Chatham was finishing explaining to her family who had gathered on the balcony how the island experience affected her mind and senses, Hannah Thomas bounded up the stairs. Everyone was glad to see her again. Penny and Pop had extended an invitation for her to stay for dinner and spend the night as they were all departing in the morning. She was excited by the invitation and as a natural beauty, didn't have to do much to look refreshed. She had changed into light green brushed cotton cargo pants and a pale pink long-sleeved Colombia fishing shirt that was most likely bought for style and not for fishing.

Sister Leah, overjoyed to see her kayaking partner shouted, "Miss Hannah, Miss Hannah, I hope you can stay with us for our last evening here on the island, please" she pleaded. "Come sit over here by me!"

Rescuing the River Keeper from the exuberance of her youngest daughter, Penny Chatham said, "Come sit over here," she said patting the floral cushion on the unoccupied chaise lounge beside her. "I hear you have been educating some rough characters from Washington about the island's character and the ins and outs of the Mississippi Sound." Hannah looked at the Speaker and smiled but didn't say a thing. After a short pause, the Speaker said, "Its ok, I live with having to have security. The director of the Secret Service told me you were acquainting her people over at the Stennis Space Center with the island and Sound from a geographical standpoint. Thanks for doing that. No one knows the area like you," she said smiling as the two of them now shared knowledge of her covert meetings with secret service agents from Washington.

"We are very proud to have you as our River Keeper," continued Penny Chatham. "Ben Posadas with the Mississippi State University Extension keeps me up to date on the increases in commercial seafood and of the extra money being spent on recreational fishing like we are doing on this trip. Is the seafood productivity of the Mississippi Sound coming back like it was in its heyday of the 1960's and earlier?"

"Yes, it is Madam Speaker," replied Hannah Thomas. "We are now having exceptional oyster and shrimp landings like those that were recorded in 1965!"

"That's great, and please call me Penny. After our eight-hour island exploration jaunt and your being like a second mother to Sister Leah, I feel like we are family. My kids think so too. Sister and Sarah Jane adore you and want to be like you." Hannah was enjoying the encouraging comments and stretched her long self out in a very casual and comfortable position on the chaise lounge next to the Speaker of the House of Representatives. They sat and visited about how many different kinds of ecosystems there were on the island and the impressions those landscapes made on the day trip explorers.

Penny Chatham was especially interested in the impressions her family and Jake had gotten from the different kinds of untouched natural landscapes and whether they would affect their feelings toward one another and even people they did not know. She wanted to know if experiencing wild and stunning landscapes created a general feeling of optimism? Also appealing to the River Keeper, she asked, "Is there anything more important to the experience than just seeing the wildness in today's island landscapes? Wandering through them is having a powerful effect on us as friends and family, and I'll bet it influences our general outlook toward people we don't know but with whom we will be interacting. Maybe it brings us together as a bigger family of mankind?"

Knowing something powerful came out of today's backing trip, the Speaker continued, "I'm baffled Hannah, I'm really confused! Just what is this wild island thing doing to us, or for us? Are we more afraid in any way, or is it binding us closer together and showing how interdependent we are on one another? Today's events moved me. I also have more respect regarding how nature keeps a clean and attractive house and I'm now more knowledgeable about the physical cycles and interrelationship of creatures in her arsenal of equipment and cleansers to keep those island landscapes so attractive and appealing.

"Sitting here drinking these pina coladas I can honestly say, that after today, I feel like I can better relate to nature's wild creatures. We are the true representatives for the pelican and otter and even the cougar and ivory billed woodpecker. However, until we walk where they walked, how can we ever have effective dominion over the animals on the land and creatures in the seas? Today we paid our dues. We flew with the pelican and waded the shallow marshes with the blue heron. Something happened today, Hannah, to all of us regarding our feelings toward nature and for one another. I think it enabled us to have a higher regard for each other and for the wild landscapes and their inhabitants."

Hannah Thomas was enjoying listening to the rambling thoughts of her new politician friend as she enjoyed the tequila, lime juice, and triple sec in her icy end-of-the-day Margarita which Tony had made for her. Finally, she responded to the litany of queries espoused by her colleague sitting beside her in a plush chaise lounge. "You cannot go into the wilderness and not be impressed. If you are quiet and observant, you will see and feel more than the one who casually walks or boats through a wild landscape only looking but not paying attention. To get the good stuff, you have to listen and move like a wild creature cautiously moves through that landscape. You have to put yourself into their skin to be one of them."

Seeing that Penny Chatham was hungry for her knowledge and absorbing her every thought learned from face-to-face contact with creatures of the wild and the plants, soil, and water which surrounds them, she continued. "Most people have not had the opportunity to experience a wild landscape. When they do, and to get the most out of it, they need to move slowly and cautiously, and be aware of the natural environment and wonder about the powerful cycles that shaped it."

"Oftentimes, I suggest they begin their journey as a bird, mammal, or fish and convince themselves they are going to revel in that experience from the vantage of the animal they choose. I know that sounds crazy, but it enhances the awareness and enjoyment of what's around you more so than just seeing its beauty. As a wild creature, they will see and experience nature's beauty with both a sense of dependence and caution. If I am with a small group, I tell them to pretend they are part of a pack or family of an allied species moving through the landscape together, relying on one another for food and safety. As part of that pack, they are to communicate their feelings and desires to their family members as they travel, just like Andrew Reardon did today while taking a nature break to collect driftwood. "

That is just what the Speaker of the House needed to hear. It had been a long time since she had experienced a wild landscape where nature did all of the creation and maintenance. Her sense of enjoyment, camaraderie toward the others in her group, and dissipation of fear due to the safety of the closeness of that group were reactions that gave her strength and optimism. As one who had the authority to seek greater restoration and availability of wild places for the benefit of many more people, she needed verification of the benefits from today's trek through Cat Island's many ecologically distinct landscapes.

For Penny Chatham, the day-long exploration of the island was monumental. Those kinds of experiences shared with others would create a greater awareness of returning back to nature some of the responsibilities for keeping her landscapes healthy, productive, and stunningly beautiful. She was now convinced and firmly determined to make wilderness experiences more available to others.

Mississippi Sound Oysters Canned in Biloxi

CHAPTER 24

Turmoil in Washington

In Washington, D.C., the Stanford University personal assistant to Donald Anniston was busy making early morning phone calls to Bible Study members to inform them of President Harrison's passing. She had heard about his death from the White House Press Secretary at 5:30 am. It would be seven hours later before a special news bulletin made the news public.

Keeping her information brief, Charlotte Hall said, "Hello, Bible Study member, this is Charlotte Hall calling to inform you that the President died this morning at 5:30 and Vice President Steve Hardy was sworn in by Chief Justice Burger shortly after the President's passing. Hardy is now in full control of the country and is currently cloistered at Camp David in Maryland. Donald Anniston does not expect there to be any change in public policy as a result of this transfer of power." There was almost never any response or questions from the high rolling group of financial kingpins. However, for this call, several members did ask about the cause of President Harrison's death. Charlotte responded, "His cause of death has not yet been revealed but I will call and share that information as soon as I am able to find out." Those that asked replied that would not be necessary. They had known the president and were just curious.

Donald Anniston, had made his fortune because of the way he anticipated any problem that might arise and was prepared to pull the trigger on a solution to a situation before it developed. Grilling Charlotte on her newfound information he asked, "I'm concerned there is no cause of death being reported. Can you look into it and call me back as soon as you have something?"

"Yes, I will do that. It is odd there is a declaration of his death, but nothing else. I will continue to see what I can find out," replied Charlotte.

"Good, I will feel better when I know what it was that killed the poor man and whether or not it was from natural causes or an act of violence. I need to have that information, Charlotte," replied the anxious president of the Bible Study. He repeated himself, "I cannot tell you how much I need to know the nature of what caused the president's death. Find out and call me back as soon as you know."

Washington was in turmoil. President Harrison and his family were respected and admired. When there was no announcement of the cause of his death, the swift wind of rumors began to spread like a wildfire in the California foothills. Those who knew employees at Walter Reed Hospital were aware that the floor the president was on was sealed off from the rest of the hospital and that staff attending the president were being quarantined. Some who knew his attending physicians or floor nurses were aware that those attending the president knew they would be isolated for at least two weeks.

Acquaintances and media speculated that the death of the president was either exposure to a highly contagious disease or poisoning. That the president would be assassinated through poisoning was possible but quarantining the hospital floor and attending caregivers did not support that theory. Some close friends of the family knew that the President's wife and family were not allowed to be with the president in the hospital and were not able to see him even after he died. The idea that he contracted a contagious illness was illogical because the family was not required to be quarantined like the Walter Reed hospital staff.

Charlotte Hall's job with the members of the King David Bible Study was to be aware of conditions in the federal government days before they were announced to the public. Never were decisions made or even changes considered on capitol hill that were not being discussed by decision makers somewhere in congress several days in advance. Donald Anniston did not expect his smart and attractive personal assistant to be on the front row taking notes at a White House News Conference because hearing the news when it was revealed to all of the other reporters was not soon enough. Through her persuasive ways she was expected to know the score before the game was even played. Being people-savvy was how she got her job and earned her $175,000 salary. As one of the highest paid business confidants in Washington D.C., she knew how to get the information before it became public. That was the skill level Donald Anniston expected from Charlotte Hall.

The payoff from the Stanford Personal Assistant's foreknowledge to King David's Bible Study was incalculable. If a change by the administration to reduce the support of electrical energy production through the traditional means of using coal, natural gas, hydroelectric, and nuclear, the business kingpins needed to know that information before it was released to the world.

The change away from doing business through advocating energy conservation technologies and reduction of carbon dioxide in the atmosphere would affect billions of dollars invested by Bible Study members. As government leadership and policies change, so do investments made by high income managers. Information provided by Charlotte Hall was financial insurance for King David's Bible Study. Her vital news would allow the biggest spenders in the country to hedge their bets and come out winners. Advance warning of coming changes was worth millions, and probably more.

The uproar in Washington was that full disclosure regarding the death of President Harrison was purposefully being withheld. That was a problem for many of the representatives and senators not only because of their personal safety, but also for their party's position on national issues. Many had friends and supporters who had major investments based on the financial direction the President of the United States had adopted.

Members of Congress have significant power on how money is allocated and spent on specific projects they support. Oftentimes, earmarked money will also support related projects of city mayors and county supervisors. It can also provide for their travel to different destinations in the country and world as long as that travel is somehow related to the funded project. State and local politicians were waiting for an assurance that the transfer of power would not change the status quo of their local projects and travel plans. Besides their investments in the current Administration's projects, the members of King David's Bible Study were expecting to recover a boatload of cash spent directly to cover needs of the President and Vice President during the first election. All of these groups had a major interest in maintaining the status quo of President Jim Harrison's administration!

President Harrison had firmly established a direction the country would follow. Now, all of the agreements between government leaders and the future direction of projects were potentially up in the air. It was time for the new president to speak to the nation to demonstrate the transfer of leadership and power and to stabilize the financial markets through committing to the programs and direction already established by President Harrison. Investors were anxious to hear that pledge.

Like many others, Bible Study members expected the newly sworn in president to talk to the nation about continuing to support and fund existing programs. It was now payback time. However, if there were going to be any differences from the original administration's programs, President Steve Hardy was obligated to inform the Bible Study group before the rest of the country was made aware of the changes being considered. What this new president had to say would influence their investments, and for sure, would impact the financial markets.

Mississippi Boiled Shrimp Dinner

CHAPTER 25

The Last Supper

After the group's forty-five-minute comforting pause on the balcony enjoying small talk, the call to dinner was sounded. Chef Tony had been up to the balcony twice to top off the exotic tropical island drinks and timed their last refills with dinner. Hungry as they were it was hard for the family to leave the friendship and one-on-one conversation with one another. The exploration of the island brought them all closer together and the balcony chatter was all about each other's impressions of the different landscapes they had experienced and what they would like to do when they came back for another Cat Island visit.

Their idyllic vista overlooking Jean Lafitte Bayou and the bright green salt marshes bordering both sides of the long but narrow marsh pool they had kayaked ten hours ago also prevented the dog-tired group of travelers from abandoning their cushioned club chairs and chaise lounges. But the fatigue of kayaking and hiking for eight hours boosted their need for sustenance and finally drew them inside to air conditioning and a sumptuous dinner around the long pine table now covered with a festive red checkered tablecloth.

Chef Tony had prepared what he called a Barrier Island dinner of boiled shrimp, and deep-fried speckled trout and mullet. That was complimented with a freshly made tangy and sweet tasting slaw, mashed potatoes, butter beans, and cucumber slices immersed in vinegar and sugar. Dessert was lemon pie whose meringue was three inches high! Just the sight of that sitting at the end of the table drew some "ah-ha's," "wows," and "I can't waits!" For the chocolate lovers, Chef Tony had baked "The Help Pie" made famous in the book and movie The Help which was filmed in Greenwood just four hours away in the Mississippi Delta. It was very similar to a chocolate chess pie which was a Chatham family favorite. They had all seen the movie and looked forward to having a slice of the lemon pie and a thin slice of the Help Pie without that one special ingredient featured in the movie.

Before digging into the beautiful looking meal, Pop asked Andrew Reardon if he would return thanks. The boy's eyes cut over to Hannah Thomas and smiled like he was teased. She returned a very reassuring and loving look of encouragement for carrying out an important family tradition.

"Ok, y'all, bow your heads," Andrew Reardon said, spoken with authority from having done this many times before. "Thank you, God, for the food on this table, and for Hannah the River Keeper. She is a pretty-cool lady. Thanks for my mom and dad and help my sisters to realize I am getting to be bigger, and as such I do not need as much looking after as they think I might." His mom, head still bowed, cut her eyes over to her first son. Andrew, with his eyes open to see if anyone else was looking caught the look and quickly continued, "Thanks for Chef Tony's cooking abilities, and thanks for the rabbits along the front entry from the pier. They were fun to play with. This has been a great time, God, thanks for that too. Amen."

There was a little sigh of relief from Pop and he followed with an amen himself. He looked over at his oldest son and whispered, "Good job, Handsome." Andrew Reardon, growing a little bigger and more confident each day, whispered back to his daddy but loud enough so his sisters could also hear, "Be sure to keep your elbows off the table." Dinner that evening was a celebration of an outstanding family trip where each day included an adventure. It was just what the United States Speaker of the House of Representatives had challenged Jake Ingram to plan.

Later that evening, the family sat alone in the two-story living room with big windows overlooking the salt marshes through the old Long Leaf pine trees as the June sun was setting. Hannah Thomas had excused herself and retired to the second bedroom on the main floor for the evening. She thanked the family for their friendship and the fine meal, "Dinner was outstanding and preceded by an awesome blessing. Thanks for including me in your prayer, Andrew Reardon, and thanks, Chathams for including me with your family. Good night, I will make sure y'all get back to Long Beach at the marina in time to fly back to Washington tomorrow morning."

While lounging on the large sectional sofa, Penny asked each member of the family to write a note to Jake Ingram thanking him for planning a trip that was so diverse and meaningful. She asked each of her family members to tell him what their favorite experience was. Sister Leah asked, "Can we list more than one favorite experience? I mean there was the bonfire on the beach and the train ride over from New Orleans where we drew ecology things that Dr. Delgado was telling us about. There was something big we did each day. I don't want to leave out any favorites!"

Andrew Reardon quickly added, "And what about where the train stopped in the middle of the swamp! We can't leave that out! Whoever heard of a train that stopped in the middle of a swamp so someone could get out and throw a cast net to see what kind of critters were in the water?"

"Yes, yes, and yes, my Little Fireflies." Energetically replied their mother. "Be sure to include all of those experiences. If it is your favorite, include it. It does not matter if you have more than one favorite experience." Penny Chatham had quite a few names for her children and when energy was surging through two or more of them at once, to her they were like the luminous insects that light up the landscape after dusk. Creativity and the enjoyment of talking was unrestrained in her children, as in their mother.

They were asked to also write the River Keeper a note thanking her for the expert guidance she provided on Cat Island. Their mother suggested including one personal encounter with Hannah Thomas that had a special meaning. She said she and Pop would write to Jake and Miss Hannah as well.

Shortly after the summer sun set in the northwestern sky, Jake Ingram came into the cavernous living room to tell Speaker Chatham she had gotten a call from her Chief of Staff Craig Gill. She was also to expect a phone call from Secret Service agent Charles Parks at 8:30 pm. "Ok, Jake, thank you. I will go and call your boss. You keep me straight on these calls. We've had a big day, like you did, and are pretty tired. Do you have time to sit with us and enjoy the last bit of twilight in the western sky?

"Of course, Madame Speaker. I would love to." And with that he picked a spot facing due west on the sprawling sofa. "What a picture," he said softly. Sister Leah quickly made conversation with her friend Jake. "What a picture, and what a trip, Mr. Jake! You did good." Fishing for what her mom asked her to write about she asked, "What is the most favorite thing you did on this trip?"

Andrew Reardon abruptly cut in, "I liked the train ride the best. Stopping on the tracks in the middle of the Honey Island Swamp was pretty awesome. What if the train had a broken wheel and they had made all of us get out and walk down the tracks to where there was a road for somebody to come get us?"

"Is your name Mr. Jake Ingram?" quipped back Sister Leah, unhappy that her older brother had cut in on her conversation. "I have never even heard about a train having a broken wheel. That probably never happens, but if it did you would fall asleep on the walk out of the swamp toward some godforsaken rural road. And then you would have to be scooped up from the tracks and toted back on Pop's shoulder!"

Andrew just grinned at his feisty little sister. She was both a wonderful sister and tolerant friend. He loved her. If he was ever feeling left out of a conversation, all he had to do was answer one of her general questions directed to someone else and he would quickly be included into the group conversation! His little sister was like a new kitten and he was the family dog. Her energy was boundless, and she thrived on pestering anyone around, but was focused on the omnipresent, mildly tempered family canine companion disguised as Andrew Reardon.

Mr. Jake interrupted the emerging family squabble, "My favorite part of your family's adventure was being with you all and seeing your reactions to the different places we went to."

This response irritated Sister Leah and in her opinion did not even answer the question. "Mr. Jake, that's a terrible answer. In fact, it did not even answer my question. Andrew Reardon answered better than you did!" As her face reddened, tears of exhaustion welled up in her eyes and she got up and went inside with her forearm over her face shielding her flow of tears.

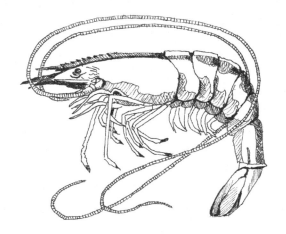

Mississippi Gulf Coast Shrimp

CHAPTER 26

Astonishment

The door to Penny Chatham's bedroom was closed. The family knew to respect that privacy; however, Sister Leah ran in, flopped down, and cried on her mother's made-up queen bed.

Directly, her momma came in to call Craig Gill, her chief of staff. Opening her bedroom door and seeing her youngest child crying she quietly said, "I'll be a few minutes, Baby, and then we can talk. You are just tired, Sister. Everything is going to be all right. The first phone call was to her chief of staff Craig Gill. "Hello, Craig, this is Penny Chatham."

"Hello, Madam Speaker, I wish I had something good to share with you, but I don't. Things are not so good in Washington. As you know, President Steve Hardy has been at Camp David since President Harrison became ill. Now our new president is not doing so well even though he has been sequestered there for two weeks ever since President Harrison came down with whatever it was that killed him."

Penny Chatham, no longer laid back in her family adventure mode, took what her chief of staff said as a matter of national security and quickly snapped back in a pointedly manner, "What does 'not doing well' mean Craig?"

"I have been told he is gravely ill like President Harrison was. I know no more details than that, but his press secretary was very restless when she called me and asked about your whereabouts and were you sick in any way. I tried to get more details about Hardy's condition, but she said she could not share that information with me, yet."

"What information did you tell her about me?" Asked Speaker Chatham emphatically.

Responding slowly with a careful selection of his words Craig said, "Like we have often discussed, in times of a crisis situation, your privacy and whereabouts is confidential. I know that, so I told her you were in Louisiana fishing. I hope you didn't mind me lying a little bit. You are not far from Louisiana and I'm not really good on my geography," he replied hoping he had passed her confidentiality test.

"Good answer, Craig. I don't know what is going on but somewhere off the Louisiana coast fishing for redfish is as specific as we need to be. Steve Hardy's press secretary does not need to be informed of my health and specific whereabouts and no one else does either. For your information only, the Secret Service is going to call me in about thirty minutes. That should be a pretty revealing discussion. When necessary, I will include you in the discussion."

"One last thing Speaker Chatham, it's a rumor but I think you should know what is being said." There was a long pause on both sides of the high-tech satellite connection. "The rumor here is there is an international conspiracy to assassinate the president and vice president which would turn the country on its heels and cause chaos in the financial markets. From what I am seeing, and the calls I am getting, everyone is getting frenzied about leadership in the executive branch. It is creating a crisis atmosphere."

The Speaker of the House of Representatives listened and decided not to ask questions where there would be no concrete answers but only wild-eyed speculation. "Thank you, Craig, keep me up to date. I am due to talk with a Secret Service agent that will call at 8:30 pm. Since we are in the Central Time Zone, he will be calling soon."

Throughout the phone conversation with Washington, Sister Leah had stopped crying and was keenly listening to her mother's reactions and watching a change in her attitude.

"On another note, Craig, my family and Jake Ingram are all fine. I look forward to sharing more details of our trip with you. Be sure to keep my location to yourself. Call me if anyone is persistently asking where we are. We have kept our trip out of the media so those who are aware of where we are is a very limited number. Let's keep it that way. You are an important part of the effectiveness of the Speaker of the House office, Craig. Thank you and stay safe and alert."

"I understand, Madam Speaker, and thank you! I am standing by with the satellite phone if you need me to do anything or make any contacts for you," replied her chief of staff.

Lying on her mother's bed, her youngest daughter began to question in her mind why talking to Washington would make a change in her mother's disposition. Why is talking to the Secret Service such a big deal? Brent and his guys are doing a good job, why is there a need for more Brents who are with another agency in Washington. The phone call to Craig sounded threatening in some way and made her momma's attitude stiffen. As a result, Sister Leah got up, ran through the closed bedroom door and up the stairs to her bed in the loft, where she began to cry again. She was sad, and she sensed fear and danger. The phone call was a warning, of that, she was sure. Her only recourse was to cry and think of her mother.

The association to the pulse of the fast-paced life in Washington, D.C., was quickly being reconnected, and it was adversely affecting Penny Chatham. However, something was different this time. Sister Leah picked up on it immediately. After such a wonderful family time experiencing true wilderness in one of the most remote places in Mississippi, something her momma lived for, returning to the epicenter of creating compassionate change for people was not going to be the same. Leah felt it was different; she could see that in her momma. Like the young kitten that did not walk in the open but stayed in the shadows and beside brushy borders for fear of carnivorous hoot owls or the wily red fox, Sister Leah also sensed fear. It was part of the survival mode for her and for the kitten.

Her brilliant momma was sensing a change that might bring a threat to her and her family. Having this kind of perception was one of the reasons Penny Chatham enjoyed visiting the wilderness. All alone and without the protection of people all around her, it was where she sharpened her skills of being aware of risks and danger. Sister Leah had figured it out.

She had been crying because she was physically exhausted from the day's hiking adventure. Now, she would cry for her mother because of the hurt and fear on her face. Nothing could happen to her dear momma! She was too precious, and Andrew Reardon and Sarah Jane needed her too. They could not lose their mother and retain their own sense of safety. Sister needed her for consolation.

Penny Chatham was coming down to earth from her fabulous deep south coastal adventure and staring straight into the cold reality that as second in line to the presidency, it was now within the realm of possibility that she could be sworn in to the most important office in the land. She did not want that to happen, but if it did, it would be her and her family's patriotic duty to take the job and lead the United States of America the best way she could.

That was a real-life possibility and she needed to share that obligation with her family. An overwhelming responsibility like that could not be sprung on her three children and a loving and supportive husband. It was just too big. Even if it never happened, which she hoped was the case, her family should know the reality and likelihood of the situation.

A feeling of facing harm and the anxiety of change was on her momma's mind as she marched up the stairs. Approaching her youngest child who was sobbing alone on the center single bed in the large sleeping loft, she bent down and hugged the little girl. "Don't cry, Baby, tell your momma what has got you so upset?"

"My heart is hurting," sobbed her youngest daughter. "It is hurting for you, Momma. You were upset by that telephone call and I don't want you to suffer too!"

"Everything is going to be all right, Leah," replied her mother. "The people I work for back home have been thinking we were so successful bringing the Mississippi Sound Estuary back to life that I might need to do the same kind of job with the health of more landscapes in our big, beautiful country."

"Would you like to do that, Momma?" Leah said between sobs.

"If it would mean more adventures like we have just enjoyed, yes, as long as you and your brother and sister and Pop could go as well."

"We would like that. I want you to be happy, Momma, like on this trip."

Her mother softly said, "We can make that happen as long as my family is ok with it and pitches in to help."

Sister Leah reached up and hugged her mom, real tight and said "Ok. I like pitching in, but I am also counting on you to be able to do both your work and help me with my school art projects."

Her mom smiled, wiped away her baby's tears and said, "It's a deal whether or not I get the new job. Let's go and see if the others are ok about me getting a promotion."

With that the two of them walked hand-in-hand back down to the balcony where Pop and Sarah Jane were looking through field glasses and counting the number of great blue herons they saw out on the marsh and along Jean Lafitte bayou. Andrew Reardon and Jake Ingram were off on the north end of the balcony and talking about the cool things Jake did when he was in the Coast Guard. Penny Chatham, clapped her hands loudly to get everyone's attention, "Could I interrupt y'all to have a brief family meeting?" She walked over to the end of the balcony where Andrew Reardon and Jake were seated and pulled more chairs over to that corner.

Sister Leah began the meeting by announcing, "Momma might be up for a job promotion and we all need to decide if that would be a good thing to do, or not to do." Jake raised his hand to say something and the pint-sized orator said, "Its ok, Jake, you are almost like family so you can stay. Anyone that enjoys visiting with Andrew Reardon has a lot of tolerance and would easily get along with the rest of us." Andrew Reardon, still recovering from his all-day exploration experience, didn't say anything, but just smiled at his out-there sister whom he loved.

After returning his smile, she continued, "Momma is going to tell you about the new job which she might be offered. If she gets the job, we all need to support her in order that she could get all of her work done."

Penny Chatham sat up straight like a sixth-grade school girl, and briefly explained the new job obligations, "I have gotten a call from Washington and there is a remote possibility they might need me to do a job other than the one I currently have." Fixed on her every word, all eyes stared back waiting for an explanation of the other job. What could it be? As Speaker of the House, she already had a job where she could become involved in situations and make positive changes happen even when the circumstances were deadlocked among users. She was outstanding at eliminating the logjam by bringing people together and working out problems like she had done with getting more freshwater into the Mississippi Sound.

"The job would be a little bigger that the one I currently have. I found out today when we got back from our island adventure that President Jim died yesterday in the hospital."

Sister Leah with a surprised look, asked, "Why, Momma? What happened? Why, was he sick? Had he been sick?"

"Yes, Darling. He was sick but they did not tell me why," replied her momma. Pop had a shocked look of concern on his face and when his eyes connected with Penny's she said, "I found this out about twenty minutes ago, Jim. I don't know any more than that."

"The bigger issue now is that Steve Hardy," she looked at her children and clarified, "the Vice President, has been sworn in as President." The children knew both President Jim and Steve Hardy. Penny Chatham now calmly looked at each face from those sitting motionlessly around the end of the balcony. Their outdoor room was now a bright yellow color from the sun setting in the northwestern sky. That light which was only a few days away from its summer solstice bathed each anxious face. Penny Chatham briefly thought how powerful that scene would be in a painting. It could be titled Astonishment.

She did not tell them that the vice president who was in confinement at Camp David, was sick and in bed. That would put this new job issue in an entirely different category and the Speaker of the House did not want to go there, or even to acknowledge there was a growing possibility that she would become President if Steve Hardy became really sick or, God forbid, he would die. However, she was taking this first step toward the potential reality that if that happened, her life would dramatically change, forever. Being raised in a small Southern town, playing little league softball, and going to church every Sunday, she had been groomed to be social and a patriot. She appreciated life in the United States, and it was in her blood to protect that at any cost. Not to accept the responsibility of being President was to deny her devotion to country, and that was not even a consideration.

Drawing the family powwow to a close, she said, "I am telling you this because if anything happens to the new President, that responsibility would fall on us. The way it works is there is a line of succession in case the President becomes unable to fulfil the requirements of his job. In that situation, then the vice president gets the job. If the vice president is unable to do his new job, then the Speaker of the House gets to do the job."

Sister Leah and all of her six years of life experiences cut in, "Momma is telling you there is only a possibility that she would get this new job, but if she does, we've got to pull together and help her. It would be a little more work for all of us, but we could do it. However, there would be more hiking adventures and we could be helping more people. If she gets the chance, I think it sounds like a slam dunk."

The end of the Pelican Roost balcony had turned to a pale blue color from its source of light now slipping down below the edge of the earth. Jake Ingram and the rest of the family were still quiet and looking stunned. Staring back at the Speaker of the House, they realized the new job would not be just a step up, it would be a giant leap up the ladder of influence. That was even bigger than taking a giant step in the days of Mother May I!

Catboat – Mississippi Sound Indigenous Sailboat

CHAPTER 27

The Call

It was 8:30 pm and her satellite phone began to ring. Light over the bayou and marsh allowed only the dimmest view of the normally vibrant island landscape as the satellite phone began to ring. Penny Chatham excused herself from the family meeting which was as quiet as researchers in the archival room of a library. It was a good time to excuse herself and tend to another matter. As she answered, expecting Charles Parks who was going to be the head agent of the U.S. Secret Service agents sent to provide additional security for the Speaker of the House of Representatives, a strong female voice responded, "Speaker Chatham?"

"Yes," Penny Chatham responded.

"This is Camille Latady, Director of the Secret Service. Charles Parks will be calling after our conversation. I am sad to inform you that President Steve Hardy is in a coma. He is unresponsive and not expected to regain his abilities to carry out his duties as President."

After a long pause, which Director Latady expected could happen, Penny Chatham responded, "Tell me more, Director."

"I would tell you more, in fact, I would answer any questions you might have, but that is all I know. My agents on the scene and President Hardy's physicians don't know any more than I have told you," replied Director Latady.

This was serious. Penny Chatham kicked into her Washington mode, "Why is this happening? Is there a concerted effort to eliminate the executive branch leaders?" She was communicating with the only one who would give her direct answers, not unsubstantiated scenarios which the Speaker did not want. She either wanted facts or the most feasible presumption from this totally reliable source.

"I can tell you we are probably facing sophisticated assassinations by a foreign group that is payback for punitive international policies implemented by our government." Camille Latady paused, waiting for a response from the Speaker Chatham. The director was not going to speak next. The ball was in the court of the Speaker.

During the long pause, Penny Chatham hung her head and wiped tears from her eyes and moisture from her nose running over her lips. Regaining the short lapse of her stately composure she said, "What do you need me to do?"

The Director now knew Penny Chatham was on board. She was facing up to the daunting role awaiting her physical and mental presence. "You will not be sworn in as president until the Chief Justice of the Supreme Court makes that call, or President Hardy passes. In my opinion it is only a matter of time before one of those probabilities occurs. So, as Director of the United States Secret Service, I have made the call and we are treating you as a sitting president." Director Latady again paused allowing that compelling information to sink in, and then she continued. "We will take you and your family off the island at daybreak."

"The presidential limousine I sent to the Stennis Space Center will pick you up at the marina in Long Beach. Air Force One will be on the ground at the Stennis Space Center airport shortly after midnight tonight. For security reasons, the airport is still closed to all air traffic and Beach Boulevard will be closed to all traffic from the Stennis Space Center to Gulfport at 1300 hours or 1:00 am."

"Charles Parks will call you when we finish visiting. Do you have any questions, Madam Speaker?"

Now fully in the Washington business mode, Penny Chatham responded, "What about my family?"

"They will be escorted off the island with you and accompany you in separate vehicles."

"Why can't they go with me?"

"They will be with you, but they cannot ride with you because of security reasons. They will ride in separate vehicles and will be afforded the usual level of protection from agents provided for families of the president. They will be safe I assure you, Madam Speaker." Penny Chatham knew not to pursue the question. Security measures are inflexible, and it would be useless to badger the Director to change security protocol.

"We have your health and safety under lock and key. You and your family will be protected. I have asked Hannah Thomas to accompany your children and husband along with our agents on the return trip at daybreak. Charles Parks will call you in a few minutes. I will see you tomorrow, Speaker Chatham."

Penny Chatham sat alone in her island bedroom. She thought about the changes that were probably going to affect her and her family's life. Being an optimist though, she thought of the good that would result from her time presiding over the United States. She also thought about the wonderful experiences that would benefit Sarah Jane, Andrew Reardon, and Sister Leah. Her husband Jim would be busier than usual managing the family and helping with her much bigger job and obligations.

Would she rather not have the job of president? Yes, but that was not how inheriting that responsibility goes. As a patriotic person, from a patriotic family she was duty bound to accept that assignment and do it with all the energy and thought she could muster, just like she did her work as Speaker of the House of Representatives. It really wouldn't be that much of a change, or would it? She was unsure of the magnitude of the job but was on solid igneous bedrock she should take the position.

The annoying pinging ring of the restricted satellite phone jarred her from a whirl of speculation about the new position with the federal government. Charles Parks was on the other end of the satellite phone, "Hello, Madam Speaker, this is Charles Parks, I am the division leader of the Secret Service sent to provide protective services for you and your family. Director Latady mentioned to you that I would be calling?"

The Speaker replied, "Of course, she did, Charles, and I am glad to hear from you. Tell me what your plans are?"

He replied, "We have thirty secret service agents in five work boats on their way to Cat Island as we speak. The agents will be dressed in casual, sportsman-like attire and will be stationed around the Pelican Roost home when they get there. My agents will be at all entrances to your home. They will be armed and will provide protection for you and your family. Hannah Thomas, who is there on the island with you, is familiar with the home and its immediate surrounds and will help locate the agents who will provide protection. Will it work for you and your family to leave the island to go to the Long Beach Marina at 6:30 am?"

The Speaker replied, "Yes, 6:30 will be fine. We will be dressed and packed, and ready to go."

Charles Parks continued, "I will be with the agents and will check in with your congressional staff person Jake Ingram when we arrive on the island. He will let you know when our agents are in place and the perimeter of Pelican Roost is fully secured. Once you arrive on the mainland, there will be additional agents for your protection."

"Ok," replied Speaker Chatham.

"We look forward to serving you, Madam Speaker. If you have any further questions, Jake Ingram will be your point person. He will have direct contact with me at all times. Good night, ma'am. You can rest assured you will have the most protected night's sleep you've probably ever had on a deserted island."

The Speaker smiled at the humor, assertiveness, and assuredness of Secret Service Agent Charles Parks. It was comforting to know Camille Latady was on the ball and her employees were meeting the demands of their job. Penny Chatham always noticed when government employees were doing an outstanding job. She reminded herself to remember to write Director Latady a complimentary note on her preparedness.

As she shared the security and departure plans with her husband, Pop said, "That sounds good, although I am concerned about Jim's assassination and Steve's condition. It is terrifying for him to be in the same condition as Jim was."

Penny Chatham looked sad, and distressed. Pop was right, this was not normal times. Would an attempt be made on her life or her entire family's? She told Pop, "The Secret Service Director thinks Steve Hardy will probably die, too."

Pop responded, "This will probably be no picnic getting to the mainland tomorrow. Once we're there, I'm not sure Washington is the place for you to be. It's too dangerous, Penny. I think we would be better off holing up somewhere along the coast until the FBI has determined how Jim was killed and we know more about Steve's condition."

"I think you are right. I should call Camille Latady and discuss the situation and your alternative."

"It's your life, Penny," retorted Pop. "You don't have to recommend anything. Tell her to find a local alternative to returning to Washington. We are not leaving the coast."

Penny Chatham was soundly convinced by her husband's reasoning. The facts were too clear to ignore. She agreed wholeheartedly and would share those feelings with Camille Latady. Continuing to be the mother of three children that were of her and Jim's blood was a powerfully persuasive factor. Even Director Latady had expressed her uncertainty about the situation in Washington and at Camp David.

After a brief early evening call in which Penny shared the thoughts about security, the Director agreed with the Speaker. Nothing further was said about the matter. Penny Chatham was too exhausted by the evening's events to pursue the details. She had communicated her concerns that they were not going to leave the coast and expected they would be fully considered by the head of the most prestigious protection agency in the world.

It was 9:30 pm, central time. The sun was down, the brown rabbits that were always clustered on the pier and boardwalk to Pelican Roost were hidden away in their burrows. The view from the elevated porch was now black dark.

The Secret Service Director who was already on the coast in a command center pulled together for the extraction of the Speaker of the House and her family from Cat Island had a directive from the probable future president of the United States. News from President Steve Hardy's condition was not good. He was in a coma and his heartbeat was slowing. It was expected he would die sometime during the night. Speaker Chatham's near refusal to leave the coast for Washington, D.C., was pretty powerful, but presidents don't always know all of the variables that are considered when plans for their protection are being made. The secret service held the final card in decisions made for protection of their clients including a likely future President. However, Camille Latady was not going to ignore

Penny Chatham's concerns and disobey this first order from the woman who would likely become the president of the United States.

Before the death of Jim Harrison, the Secret Service was forewarned through chatter picked up by the National Security Agency that an attempt would be made on the president's life. It appeared mercenaries from southeast Asia were working with a contact from the People's Republic of China to punish the Harrison administration for its hardline attitude in the two country's trading agreements. Security was immediately increased around the president but was inadequate. From a review of videos of the president's activities they showed he shook hands four different times with visitors to the White House and with foreign members of the international trade agreement. It was concluded a handshake had likely transferred a powerful poison to the president which caused his death.

As a result, any physical contact with Steve Hardy and Penny Chatham was prevented by their security details. Since Speaker Chatham and her family had arrived in New Orleans, that protocol was in place. Since the Vice President and the Speaker of the House were the office holders in immediate succession to the office of president, all attempts to shake hands or touch them in any way were to be prevented and immediately reported to the Secret Service. The Capitol Police reported that the writer of the new book on Jean Lafitte reached out to shake Penny Chatham's hand as did the celebrated chef in Bay St. Louis. In both cases, contact was prevented by their security detail and a thorough follow-up background check was made on both individuals and determined their actions were not hazardous in any way.

On the Director's flight to Long Beach the previous day, unbeknownst to Speaker Chatham who was having a seafood dinner featuring fried and baked oysters they had tonged at St. Stanislaus Reef, she and her team began to seek the possibility of an interim location on the coast for the Chatham family. They were the United States Secret Service and having alternatives was a part of any issue in which they were involved. With both the President being gravely ill and Vice President Hardy showing signs of a rapidly evolving illness, it was determined an interim White House location away from the northeast was a very viable alternative.

Geographer and naturalist Hannah Thomas who provided guidance to the first unit of secret service agents sent to the coast to protect the Speaker, brought to the Director's attention that President Woodrow Wilson's summer home was in Long Beach on Scenic Drive. It was a large home on a picturesque street overlooking the Mississippi Sound. Director Latady said they would check out that possibility.

Pottery Fish Vase Carved by McConnel Anderson

CHAPTER 28

Adventure at Daybreak

The busy mother blessed with the three Chatham children got up a little before daybreak Friday morning. It was still dark at 6:00 am as she walked into the kitchen to get a cup of Community Coffee. One of her professors had introduced her and her classmates to that brand of deep south coffee. She told herself she needed to get a big sack of those coffee beans before leaving the coast as she had looked for that brand but could not find it anywhere in Washington.

Chef Tony was busy frying sausage patties, Tennessee Pride Hot sausage to be exact. The Chatham's preferred their foods with a little heat in them. The aroma was permeating the house and would soon stir the other Chatham's to rise and shine, or at least to rise. Tony had his usual chef's island outfit on which included faded blue jeans and a plaid, long sleeved cotton shirt. Besides the shirt needing ironing and Tony's hair tousled as if he had spent a big night on the town, he was working diligently enjoying making the farewell breakfast for the family. Tony liked that they were not picky eaters. He also liked the happy and expressive attitude of the kids, and the appreciation of his efforts from Penny and Pop.

Taking her coffee to the living room's huge sectional sofa she sat and stared through the two-story windows planning to catch the first glimpse of daylight. The expedition to review conditions on the Gulf Coast had been exceptional. As the low-on-the-totem pole employee on her staff, Jake Ingram had proven himself outstanding at planning an adventurous trip. Thinking about her kid's enjoyment, yesterday evening, choosing what was their favorite part of their vacation, she did the same thing except she was thinking of what her mother might have chosen and what her big sister would choose. She often did this when she was alone and had time for reflecting. Thinking of her extended family members helped her feel a regular part of their lives.

Her mother was a retired court reporter and had led a story-book life raising her family and being a regular part of her town's Methodist church. Even though she was in her 80's, she would have chosen hiking through the slash pine forest, keeping an ear and eye out for either the Ivory Billed Woodpecker or one of the island cougars. She was not worried about encountering the big cats because she always carried a pistol in her purse, or in this case it would have been her hiking bag. A former circuit judge recommended she carry a pistol for security considering the many felons with which they regularly dealt. While having that protection contributed to her sense of being fearless, she was already a pretty hardy lady.

Penny's sister Betty Lou, on the other hand, was soft spoken, gentle, and careful. This was also how Penny Chatham would have described herself. Her big sister would have adored seeing her nieces and nephew pulling up their kayaks to that natural beach and exploring the sand dunes, collecting driftwood, and marveling at the occasional dead fish baking in the sunlight. As her sister's children walked through the shallow salt marsh pools collecting hermit crabs and snails and running up and down the six-foot-high mounds of sand and through the sea oats, she would have been right there with them. However, what she would have enjoyed the most was hiking through the forest, hoping to slip up on the cougars, a bob cat, or even a deer browsing on grass in a clearing or pausing for a drink of water in one of the forest's many ephemeral pools of water that formed after a rainstorm. The element of surprise was always one of her most enjoyable experiences.

Just like her mother and big sister, Penny Chatham reacted the same way to the thrill of hiking through the wilderness island and hoping to see wildlife in their natural habitat. If given the chance by a genie in a washed-up bottle to change her island experience, she would not modify anything about the trip, especially seeing

Pop accommodating lively little Andrew Reardon's eventual state of exhaustion and the boy's dependence on a ride home slung over his father's shoulders. That was sweet. She was hoping someone got a picture of that.

Oyster Schooner Under Sail

CHAPTER 29

Phone Call from Camille Latady - Reality Sweep

As day began to break, the pale light of early morning signaled the beginning of the end of her family's outstanding adventure on Cat Island, Mississippi. Still spellbound by the tranquility of Pelican Roost, she began to make out the forms of the slash pine trees and see their wiggly reflection on the water in the bayou that was beginning to be stirred by the slightest of breezes. When the satellite phone in her housecoat pocket rang, she answered. As expected, reality swept in.

"Hello, Speaker Chatham, this is Camille Latady. I am sad to tell you that President Steve Hardy died early his morning." Not hearing any response, she continued, "As you know, you are the dedicated office holder to assume the office of president." Penny Chatham needed a minute to think. She thought about the safety of her family and the country's need for a fearless leader at this time of uncertainty. Director Latady continued, "I understand your feelings; this is both an unfortunate time for President Hardy's family and an anxious time for you. For your protection, as we speak, we have one-hundred additional secret service agents landing at the Stennis Space Center airport. A local home worthy of the office of president has been secured in which you and your family will reside indefinitely. It will be heavily protected. We are pulling out all the stops to ensure the safety of you and your family, Madam Speaker."

The word about newly sworn President Steve Hardy's death spread quickly, even before his press secretary released the sad and alarming information to the public. His staff was stunned and those attending Steve Hardy were unable to stop the progression of whatever it was that had taken down the former vice president. The rumor was a second assassination. It was speculated that a conspiracy by a foreign entity was hitting back against President Harrison's administration for harsh and debilitating treatment in world markets. The nation was jittery, and the prevailing supposition was, "What next!"

Donald Anniston was on top of Steve Hardy's demise. Charlotte Hall was an ally and friend with Hardy's Press Secretary Rosemary Thomas. Rosemary called Charlotte at 3:00 am and shared the news that Steve Hardy was no longer breathing, but his heart was still beating and it might last thirty to forty-five more minutes before the president would be pronounced dead by his physician Dr. Brunt. His attending physicians were at his bedside and baffled at what else could be done for this celebrated man who had been mercilessly marked for death. Charlotte immediately called her boss to tell him of President Hardy's imminent death.

Their first task would be to inform the Bible Study members of the news of the President's impending death. The world economy would react negatively to the news which would probably be announced at 1:00 pm Eastern Time. This would allow Bible Study members time to move assets around and take advantage of that distressing information. Fortunes are often made and lost based on the time-of-day dreadful information is shared with the public. The situation would require Implementation of plans developed weeks ago when President Harrison first became ill.

Finally, at midday, FBI Director William Adams, in a special news bulletin explained to the public that President Hardy's death was caused by an individual or group who would be identified and held accountable, even if it was a foreign government. It was not yet public knowledge, but the Central Intelligence Agency had been evaluating the situation since President Harrison became ill and a strong case had been built against a government in the far east who was retaliating against trade agreements that had significantly weakened their economy.

The assassinations of President Harrison and Vice President Hardy drove Donald Anniston into immediate action. He was fully aware the individual that was third in line to succeed to the office of the president was the Speaker of the House of Representatives. That individual was Mississippi Representative Penny Chatham who espoused policies of energy use reduction and the dramatic reduction of carbon dioxide in the atmosphere. Those were alternatives that would not work with current policies established by the White

House. In fact, her agenda would be the opposite of what the White House and party had set forth.

While known as a pleasant person who easily worked with both parties, Speaker Chatham had just co-sponsored a sustainability bill to guide the nation gradually to energy efficiency! The innovative bill had been approved by both the House and Senate and was now law. The policies of the Speaker of the House were clearly known and the path and direction she espoused was an affront to the King David Bible Study investor group who were all about depending on fossil fuels and loosening the strings on air and water regulations. The impact on the financial markets because of her positions on energy and the environment would be profound. Through having the power of the office of president she would be able to accelerate the nation's adoption of sustainable ways!

What really shook the leader of King David's Bible Study about Penny Chatham was her dedication to managing and building any and everything sustainably. As President, she would also have executive privilege to bring an immediate stop on the progress for creating a large reservoir through damming the free-flowing Pascagoula River. Her reason would probably be that it was the only free flowing, undammed river in the State of Mississippi and that its freshwater was key to the health and restoration of wild oyster reefs in the eastern part of the Mississippi Sound Estuary. Donald Anniston had amassed huge real estate holdings around the shoreline of the future lake which were estimated to increase in value by 600%. There were many other reasons Bible Study members did not want her to assume the office of president. Billions of dollars in investments by the members would be in jeopardy. As President, her policies could probably bankrupt investments of the members of King David's Bible Study. Donald Anniston could not allow that to happen.

Fourth in line to succeed to the office of president was W. H. Parker, the president pro tempore of the Senate who was an ally of President Harrison and Steve Hardy and a member of the same political party. As vice president, Steve Hardy had presided over the senate. If he was out of town or unable to perform his duty presiding over the senate, through constitutional authority the President Pro Tempore would fill in for him. That was good but not significantly beneficial enough to the Bible Study Group.

When President Harrison became ill, Donald Anniston and Bible Study members unanimously decided it would be advantageous to pass the torch of leadership to someone who believed like they did and would continue support for the Harrison administration's policies and projects. Of course, that was the Vice President Steve Hardy. If there were problems and Steve Hardy could not succeed President Harrison, succession of Penny Chatham to the position of leadership would simply not be allowed to occur. In that scenario, succession to the presidency would go to Speaker Pro Tempore of the Senate W.H. Parker who supported the Harrison Administration's policies.

While it was unfortunate to lose the elected President and Vice President to a probable assassination that had not yet been resolved, the current challenge of successor to the office of president had to be hastily dealt with in order to keep the country moving in a direction that eliminated the risk to the investment strategies of King David's Bible Study. It was imperative to create an opportunity for the Senate's President Pro Tempore Parker to rise to the office of President of the United States.

Speaker Chatham was a looming problem. Days before President Hardy died, alternative plans were being created to ensure the Presidency would pass on to the fourth official in the succession order, Senator Parker from the State of Alabama who would maintain the administration's current policies.

Anniston was outstanding at determining alternatives to achieve a goal, which was usually company takeovers and working with local legislators to establish policies that supported the smooth development of large projects. With the necessity for passing the presidential succession to the fourth person in line, he settled on the need for two alternative ways to prevent the Speaker of the House from succeeding Steve Hardy as president.

In the business world, his knowledge for company takeovers was unbeaten. His strategies were simple and powerfully effective; if something needed to change, always have two ways to achieve your goal. If the first effort fails, then the second must be successful. The wily Anniston was a recognized speaker who shared his knowledge of investing using bold strategies to hit the jackpot consistently. He was a regular lecturer on the Business School circuit and was respected for his roots at his alma mater Harvard University and his acumen for his Double Whammy Business Takeover Strategy.

Using what had become known as The Donald Anniston Double Whammy Strategy, a sharpshooter was engaged to prevent the Speaker of the House from departing Cat Island. The marksman, located 500-600 feet away from the vacation home, would simply shoot the Speaker as she came out from Pelican Roost and walked down the boardwalk toward the pier. The front landscape of the house was open all the way down to the water, thereby providing a clear shot. Through advanced evaluation of the terrain both from satellite imagery from Google Earth and from an onsite evaluation by a business associate disguised as a fisherman, it was determined the strategy would work without any problem. The shooter would then disappear by kayaking through shallow salt marsh pools south of the wooded area to a waiting skiff with a motor on the island's deserted south side. Motoring eastward, the skiff would stop at the public pier at Gulfport's marina and the shooter would depart the coast driving toward Mobile, Alabama, which was only ninety minutes away. With all of the oddly shaped island's inlets and marshes, evading detection through using a water route would be expedient. Depending on conditions, alternative barrier islands and even the Chandeleur Islands of Louisiana were a matter of a few miles away.

If for some reason the initial effort failed or was interrupted by the weather or other conditions, the second part of the never-fail Double Whammy Strategy was to stop the return of the Speaker to the mainland while in transit by water. The Mississippi Sound between Cat Island and the mainland was rich with oyster reefs and was always populated by many different sizes of boats harvesting oysters and seining for shrimp. Sport fishermen were also plentiful fishing the reefs for redfish, speckled trout, and flounder.

Engaging seafood harvesting boats with armed assassins to halt the return of the Speaker to the Long Beach Marina would be simple and effective, not unlike shooting sitting ducks on a pond. Arranging that option would be expensive and complicated; however, with billions of dollars at risk, it was a viable alternative and one that would be fail-proof.

Donald Anniston began working out details for eliminating the Speaker of the House without the help of his personal assistant Charlotte Hall. The specifics of both the first and second alternative of the Double Whammy strategy would not be known to anyone but him and those engaged to carry out his sinister plans. Bible study members were counting on him to protect their investments using any effective manner.

He felt patriotic about his plans. As a public speaker, from whom many students' received inspiration, a strong sense of altruism came over Donald Anniston. In his mind, he was a guardian for the health of the country and those who put their assets at risk for the betterment of the United States of America. Sure, there was payback to the Bible Study group, and it needed to be substantial for the risk's they took. "God Bless America," Donald Anniston and his bible study members often said at the conclusion of their periodic planning sessions.

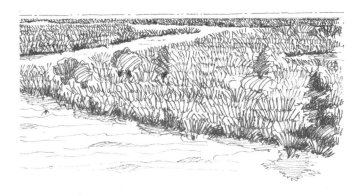

Estuary and Tidal Inlet

CHAPTER 30

Just Across the Estuary

"Charles Parks will be meeting you and your family at 6:30 am in the living room of Pelican Roost for preparation and departure to the mainland. It is important to be on time as preparing to embark by watercraft will take time to acquaint you and your family with our security procedures," explained Director Latady. She continued with a more serious tone, "Under no circumstances are you or your family to leave the building on your own. You will be under our care and are obligated to follow our safety precautions. Beginning now, you personally are not allowed to go out to the front of the building without Agent Charles Parks who will arrange at least four other agents to go with you. We don't want to create a fearful situation for you, Speaker

Chatham, but this is protocol. You have become a very valuable asset and I plan to keep you healthy and able."

"We will be ready. Thank you for your concern and preparedness." Penny Chatham was impressed with the office of the Secret Service. They appeared to be on top of things and to have arranged for a smooth and probably overly secure departure to the mainland. Jim would surely be proud of that effort.

By 6:00 am, the Friday morning of the Chatham's departure back to Mainland Mississippi, the four-lane highway along the beach was closed to all traffic from the Bridge arching over St. Louis Bay to where U.S. Highway 49 intersected with Highway 90 in Gulfport, Mississippi. Armed troops from the Camp Shelby Army base near Hattiesburg were manning roadblocks in Humvees and jeeps at every road that led to the beach along Highway 90. Soldiers had AK 47's strapped across their chest in a combat ready position. Because of the road closures and shutting down of the Stennis Space Center Airport to all incoming air traffic, an eerie quiet settled along the secured section of the Mississippi Gulf Coast.

Camille Latady declared that she was going to do everything possible to ensure the protection of Speaker Penny Chatham who would become the next President of the United States. After her two previous clients had been assassinated with poisonous chemicals, which as yet, had not been fully defined, the Director's actions thus far were commendable toward meeting that promise.

Charles Parks and five workboats each with a capacity for transporting twelve people were lined up in front of Pelican Roost by 6:30 in the morning. These durable steel-hulled watercraft with dual Evenrude 150 hp outboard engines were used for hauling a full load of workers in the worst of weather conditions. They were supplied by the Fred Davis Construction Company in Long Beach and were docked in berths at the Long Beach Marina. Besides a local driver, six secret service agents were assigned to each boat for the extraction of the Chatham family from Pelican Roost and Cat Island.

When the family arose to the smell of country sausage patties, the boats were in place and the newly arrived agents were spaced around the grounds of Pelican Roost. There were also snipers dressed in all black located on all of the sides and on the roof of the elaborate retreat. The number of agents on the ground was a spectacle for the Chatham children who were used to three or four bodyguards on most outings they took with their mom. Looking down from the balcony Sister Leah exclaimed to Pop, "They had better not mess with our rabbits!" He laughed and told his youngest their presence was just part of the security for their mother's new job.

Andrew Reardon had taken his breakfast out to the balcony and was intensely enjoying a sausage and biscuit with the muscadine grape jelly that Chef Tony's mom had made for the Chatham's. "Pop, this is pretty cool. Can you believe the guns those guys have on their belts? Will they be part of mom's new job?"

"I imagine so, Little Man." However, Jim Chatham was beginning to have his doubts about a smooth ride to the mainland because of the number of agents and the firepower they were carrying. He had been with Penny around the President on many occasions and never noticed the overt presence of so many agents and rarely did he see any firearms.

Things were moving rapidly as though the whole scene had been rehearsed many times before. Sister Leah said to a female agent who was standing just inside the front door, "Y'all don't forget my luggage. I have it all lined up at the bottom of the stairs that lead to the loft. Excuse me, but I'm going to go and tell my rabbits goodbye."

The agent sweetly said to her new client, "Don't worry about your luggage, Doll-Baby, we will get it on the next trip. And there is so much going on out front I would rather you wait to tell your rabbit friends goodbye."

"Ok, I can wait. I've got some really good things I found on the island that I'm going to make necklaces with for presents and for sure, don't want them to get lost along the way," said doll-baby. That was a term Sister Leah wasn't sure she was ok with. She did not even know the lady standing inside her front door with a gun on her hip. No, she would not have minded Brent calling her that name or any other friendly name, but not a gun-toting bossy lady she didn't even know!

"We will get it, Hot-Shot. Go on and get your breakfast. Your boat will be leaving for the mainland soon", replied the Secret Service Agent who was one of six agents assigned to guard Speaker Chatham's children.

During breakfast, Penny Chatham and Pop had shared with the kids that they would be extending their coast adventure by staying at a home along the coast instead of returning to Washington. "But why, Momma," queried Sister Leah. "I'm ready to go back home and tell my friends all about our adventures!"

"This is part of my new job, Baby. We will go back to Washington, but not today. We will just have to see how my responsibilities play out. I think you will like this. Where we are going will be a home in a neighborhood, and it will have a view to the Mississippi Sound. I think you will enjoy where we are going." The other two kids were not so sure about what was happening, but they sensed a big change was in store for the whole family.

By 6:30 am, the family had gathered in the living room with their luggage and personal effects including shopping bags of shells and driftwood collected by the Chatham children. To ensure an orderly departure, they lined up together along the back wall of the spacious living room. Charles Parks, the Secret Service Agent in charge came just before their departure and introduced himself to Speaker Chatham and her family. He told them he too was from Mississippi and had grown up in Charleston which is in the Mississippi Delta and the home town of actor Morgan Freeman. He even went to the same church as Mr. Morgan. Agent Parks was in his 50's, very fit and trim looking. He chose his words carefully but his demeanor and body language expressed a sense of urgency about the upcoming move from the island back to the mainland. Attempting to convey a feeling of well-being, he asked if they were ready to load up into the boats that were lined up outside ready for their departure.

As Penny nodded their readiness to Agent Parks, a loud crack rang out! The glass panel above the front door shattered and a large caliber bullet slammed into the thick wood paneling on the wall just above where Speaker Chatham was standing, showering her and the family with splinters of wood and shards of glass.

Parks, and three other agents including the one who called Sister Leah Doll Baby instinctively shielded the Speaker with their bodies and shoved her over to a hallway behind the kitchen that led to the bedrooms. Three other agents came through the front door and rushed the children and Pop into the pantry at the end of the kitchen.

Charles Parks was in animated conversation with others through his coiled ear piece. Within ten seconds of the initial blast that shattered the glass above the front door, three shots rang out from the marksmen positioned on the rooftop of Pelican Roost. Penny jumped at the surprise of the bright, nearby pops of the long-range sniper rifles. No sounds whatsoever were being made from those inside the big house. All of the Secret Service Agents and members of the Chatham family were motionless, partly because of fear and more because of not knowing what was going to happen next.

Charles Parks was so close to Penny Chatham that she could hear his increased breathing when his agents' returned shots from their sniper rifles toward danger that came from the marsh. He was in a hushed conversation with someone, hastily giving orders to his agents on the island on his closed-circuit coiled ear piece. After two minutes, Agent Parks, turning, softly said to Speaker Chatham, "There was a shooter in the marsh, and he is down. Our agents are working their way over to the pine forest where he was located to evaluate conditions. We will sit tight until we hear back from them."

Within a matter of seconds, three other agents dressed in black fatigues came through the front door and over shattered glass on the floor with automatic weapons embraced in their arms to strengthen the Chatham family's protection. After checking with Agent Parks on the security of their clients, they stationed themselves outside across the front of the house and stood by, ready for any threatening disturbance.

After five minutes, as Agent Parks was continuously talking back and forth with someone through his one ear coiled headphone, he quietly told the Speaker the shot fired was from an individual in the pine forest about 600 feet west of the front of the house. He continued with more detail, "His location was picked up as a heat signature by our surveillance drone. With coordinates from the drone, our marksmen on the roof were able to spot his exact location and reduced the target. There were two other heat signatures about 200 feet further west of the shooter that were moving together toward him. After the shots from our snipers, the two other heat signatures split up and quickly retreated westward. It is likely there were two additional shooters."

Speaker Chatham listened and nodded her head up and down, but mostly she just paid attention to the evolving situation. Hannah Thomas, who was on the Secret Service communication circuit reported to Agent Parks that two mature cougars had been spotted on the island and the additional heat signatures might have been them. Agent Parks said his agents were at the location of the downed shooter and would move westward to see if there were tracks of other assassins or large cat tracks. They would report back their findings. Only after the Secret Service announced the immediate area around Pelican Roost to be all clear would the family and backup begin their journey toward the Mississippi Sound and ultimately the Long Beach Marina.

Once again Agent Parks was engaged in a rapid conversation with his agents and what sounded like someone acting as an overall coordinator. The agents in the field found the marsh shooter in an elevated shooting stand about twelve feet up into a longleaf pine tree.

He had been shot three times. Walking westward, agents did not find any evidence of other shooters but did find large paw prints of what appeared to be several large animals. They took pictures of the tracks for future reference. There were no other disturbances in the immediate area and the reconnaissance drone did not show any more heat signatures indicating other possible intruders.

Since the field appeared clear and safe, Agent Charles Parks gave the ok to depart. "It is time to travel, Madam Speaker," he said simply. "Before we depart, we have some body armor for you and your family and your staff member to wear." An agent brought in two tote sacks and kneeled down on the hardwood floor to spread out the body armor. "These are Kevlar upper body vests which will protect you all from harm. We will help you get these on before we go. There are three smaller torso vests for the children."

Agents helped the family into their protective vests and secured them so they would stay in place. There was no discussion from the children. They were both afraid and interested in what was going on, and did exactly as the secret service agents directed. The lady agent who told Sister Leah they would come back for her belongings said, as she was wrestling with the vests to make sure they fit snugly, "You will also be required to wear life preservers which will be provided when we get into the boats." Leah listened to the bossy lady whose breath smelled of Juicy Fruit gum and nodded her head up and down indicating she was going to follow her directions carefully.

Once everyone was suited up, they were prepared to move outside. Charles Parks continued speaking softly into a small microphone connected to his communication system. Penny Chatham overheard him say, "We are ready to go. White Lily is on the move."

Penny Chatham thought to herself, "White Lily, the only White Lily I know of is the self-rising flour my grandmother and mother used to make biscuits." She now had a code name. Being aware that it was not the time to object to her code name, she said nothing. Penny Chatham was aware that all presidents had a code name for security reasons, and it was known only by their secret service security detail.

With bodyguards on either side of her and one in the front, along with three behind her, they were ready to go. The men in their thirties and forties on either side of her put their forearms under hers and grabbed her securely giving them complete control over where she was walking. Penny Chatham was quickly ushered into the closest of the workboats. She could tell the agents had practiced this maneuver before. Their regard of her physical self was a whole lot more protection than that ever provided by her capitol police detail.

Once the Speaker was fitted into her life vest, her family was hastily moved into a different boat. She objected that her family was not with her. Agent Parks, the agent in charge of extracting the future president from Pelican Roost on this remote island looked at her, his face was maybe eight inches away from hers, and said, "It is protocol in hazardous conditions for the President to ride alone or with a spouse, but never with other family members and especially children. Speaker Chatham, we are in a risky situation." His closeness was uncomfortable and maybe even stifling to her. He was consistently three hands away from her at all times. Not only was she able to feel his breath tinged with a peppermint mouthwash when he answered her questions, but she could also smell his soap-like cleanliness and the cologne he was wearing. She knew that fragrance.

Jim had received Versace, the same Italian cologne from her as a Christmas present.

That was the first time the title of president had been used about her in her presence. She had wondered if the threat from the marsh and all of the extra security was because she was next in line to succeed President Hardy who was now deceased. While being President sounded good, all of the challenges that came with the job were not so good. Penny Chatham got settled in the boat with agents on either side and two in the front and two behind. Besides being big guys, they also had on body armor and life preservers. She briefly imagined being in a locker room on a bench at halftime surrounded by football players and being lectured by the coach on how to pull out a win from a very challenging situation.

Once the family was loaded in their separate watercraft and fitted with life preservers, the flotilla of five workboats and four DMR skiffs began their journey up Jean Lafitte bayou toward the open water of the Mississippi Sound. Their destination was north-ward to the Long Beach Marina. As they were about to enter into the Mississippi Sound, sniper agents settled in along the outside gun-wales of the workboats with automatic rifles positioned on the edge of the boat's roofline ready for use in case problems were to arise. Nothing was being left to chance. A surveillance drone flew high overhead scanning the open water of the Mississippi Sound for any-thing that might indicate the presence of additional problems.

Speaker Chatham asked Agent Parks if someone in her family's boat had a satellite phone so that she could talk with her husband. He replied, "Yes, Jake Ingram has one, go ahead and make that call as we move up the bayou. Once we get in open water you will not be able to use the phone."

Penny Chatham thought about how organized the Secret Service was. She also liked how their conversation with her was clear, reasonable, and direct. There was no time wasted discussing alternatives. There was one way and that was the way it was going to be carried out.

Hannah Thomas was in the boat with Pop taking care of the children along with six agents. She was wearing an ear bud like the other agents which kept them in constant communication with Chief Agent Parks and someone in a land-based command center. Jake handed the phone to Pop. "It's Speaker Chatham," he said.

An agent told Pop as he was answering the satellite phone, "You will be able to talk only until the boat reaches open water and then we will be traveling in silence. You and your family will be repositioned to be at a lower profile as well, once we get into open water."

Pop was anxious to be able to talk to Penny. He assumed she was overwhelmed with the forest shooter and the immediate response from the Secret Service sniper agents on the roof of Pelican Roost which were successful in subduing the shooter. Pop could not bring himself to use the word assassin, shooter was bad enough. That Penny Chatham was the target of an assassination attempt reinforced the reality of the predicament she was in. He was overwhelmed himself. That her level of security had jumped ten-fold no doubt was making her uncomfortable. Her Capitol Police detail was a Sunday School picnic compared to the Secret Service protection she was experiencing. "Hello, Penny?"

"Pop, are the kids, ok?"

"They are huddled together on the bench in front of me. Hannah Thomas and Jake are in front of them."

"So, are they ok?"

"They are in a tight sandwich between the River Keeper who is now armed, Jake Ingram, and their daddy."

"Are they saying much?"

"Not a lot, in fact not at all. They are wide-eyed and taking it all in. I think they feel pretty good. Getting ready to leave Pelican Roost shook them up a bit, but they are tough. This experience will be like one of those adventurous hikes we have taken," replied Pop. He was an optimist and always looked at the positive side of things. This experience was not anything like any hiking experience they had ever taken, and both he and Penny Chatham knew it.

Speaker Chatham was cut from different cloth. While confident and gifted with working with people, she was currently experiencing feelings like she never had before. She began to believe what lay ahead between them and Long Beach Harbor was not going to be pretty. And she was right.

Donald Anniston had thought ahead and clearly planned for worst case scenarios. That is what made him wealthy. He always had a solution for whatever situation evolved before it developed and had not based his attempt on Penny's life on one lone shooter.

Penny Chatham was presidential material and she knew it, even before this whole succession situation evolved. But, this was not how she had hoped to move into the office of president. "You are full of it, Jim," replied Penny Chatham. "Tell the kids we will go get lunch when we get to Long Beach. Ask them if they are up for shrimp and oyster po-boys and maybe pralines or Mississippi Mud Cake for dessert."

He laughed out loud. That was a reassuring bit of normalcy his children needed to hear. "Mom said to say hey and that she was going to take us out for lunch when we get to Long Beach." They looked at Pop and grinned.

Andrew Reardon asked, "Can we get dessert, too?"

Brown Pelican Over the Mississippi Sound

CHAPTER 31

The Sound

The workboat that normally carried fifteen-dollars an hour day-la-borers to locations where the shoreline was experiencing erosion was now carrying the imminent President of the United States. As fleet occupants entered into the open waters of the Mississippi Sound Estuary, Agent John Ryan said, "Hang it up, Mr. Chatham, we are now traveling in silence. We all need to be as quiet as we can. For this leg of the trip, I am going to ask all of you to sit on the floor of the boat. You may use the seat cushions. Just pull them off from where you were sitting and put them on the floor. Miss Thomas, would you make sure their life vests are on tight?"

Andrew Reardon asked, "What benefit is there to sit on the floor? Is this like a tornado drill?"

The no nonsense Secret Service agent laughed and said, "No, Tough Guy, sitting lower in the boat will enable the boat to go faster and the faster we get there the sooner you will get to have lunch like your momma promised." Pop smiled, he figured his conversation with his wife was probably broadcast to all of the agents on operation Pelican Emancipation.

Director Camille Latady had been briefed not to expect a smooth exit from the island to the mainland. The shallow depth of the estuary prevented the use of larger Coast Guard watercraft to extract the Chatham family from Cat Island. However, she was confident they were as prepared as possible. Her finest agents had been transferred to the coast for this operation. Charles Parks was top notch and very familiar with working Presidential security details. He was probably her most experienced and dependable agent for the Penny Chatham job.

Like the Secret Service, Donald Anniston was smart and driven toward excellence. He had engaged a former Special Operations army sharpshooter to deliver the country from the policies of a potential Penny Chatham administration. The Bible Study leader had no personal problem with the lady and even thought she was an effective Speaker of the House of Representatives. However, he could not allow her environmental-based thoughts and policies to run the country. He could not let that happen. It was his personal position as leader of the King David Bible Study to ensure the promises President Jim Harrison had made were carried out by the forthcoming administration. He had named his plan to maintain the status quo in government Lady Liberty Keeps Her Promises. He believed in what he was doing.

In case the first alternative to protect the promises made by the Harrison Administration was unsuccessful, the second alternative, which was grander and more costly, would accomplish their objective. Costs were always a consideration, but in this situation, whatever the cost was, it had to be carried out. Eight fishing boats that had the appearance of either shrimp boats or oyster dredges had been deployed on the west side of the route from Pelican Roost to the Long Beach Harbor and marina. They would intercept and prevent the succession of Penny Chatham to the Office of President.

Since the water along the way was four to six feet deep, Anniston knew vessels used to extract Speaker Penny Chatham from Cat Island would be skiffs or, at most, twenty-four-foot-long work boats like those used in marine projects by workers building boat launches, breakwaters, and piers. Those types of boats had a draft of three feet at most. Larger boats could not be used even to protect a president because of the shallow water in the Mississippi Sound Estuary.

When the workboats emerged from the mouth of Jean Lafitte Bayou, a call from the lead covert shrimping boat out in the Sound told Donald Anniston of the emerging watercraft with the Chatham family and security agents. He calmly replied, "Implement Lady Liberty Keeps Her Promises." Those were the code words to begin the second option of the Double Whammy Strategy. Mercenaries in the eight undercover fishing boats prepared to execute the water-based lethal operation.

The presence of eight to ten fishing boats in the general area of the Mississippi Sound Estuary was already known by Camille Latady. At first the fishing boats were scattered around in key fishing areas and everything appeared normal. As their scattered location in the big estuary began to change, and eight of the boats began moving eastward toward the water route from Cat Island to Long Beach Marina, a red flag came up. The change in the scattered arrangement of the boats into a pattern perpendicular with the Long Beach Marina route was abnormal and set off all kind of alarms in the Director's mind.

After the Pelican Emancipation operation began at 2400 hours, the Director placed a late-night emergency call to the Naval Institute at the Stennis Space Center for help with reconnaissance. The Mississippi Sound Estuary was a very big area. Early that morning Commander Bradley Stuart sent over two crackerjack professionals experienced with using drones to provide aerial reconnaissance for the Secret Service. One drone was to scan Cat Island continuously until the Chatham Party departed. It was able to sense any heat sources that would indicate human intrusion. A larger drone was to locate and identify any boats approaching the overall area and specific route where Pelican Emancipation was to take place. Being Naval officers, they were ok with not knowing all the details. It was explained that any vessel in the Sound within twenty miles on either side of the return route of boats departing Jean Lafitte Bayou on Cat Island with a destination of Long Beach Marina could be hazardous to a clandestine government operation.

To cover all her bases, the Director also contracted with Commander Stuart for two attack drones with trained pilots to control those drones that could accurately fire multiple explosives at rogue vessels if necessary. A Reaper and a Global Hawk were provided. While the Global Hawk drone weighs one ton and could deliver explosive weapons, the Reaper weighs one-and-one-half tons and was equipped to fire a modified Hellfire weapon that does not explode but brandishes knives to shred a target. This unique weapon had been designed in the President Obama era to limit collateral damage and focus on a more condensed target. The drones were launched from the Stennis Space Center, a closed military base with heavy security. The combat drones would fly out of the range of small arms fire and were accurate with the delivery of their payloads to dangerous watercraft.

Coordinating allied government security forces as needed was a sizeable part of the Secret Service Director's job. Her greatest skill was to outthink those that had sinister plans for the President of the United States. Being prepared to combat any and all attacks toward the future President was the key to keeping her client alive and capable of meeting the demands of the job. A second set of naval employees to navigate the lethal drones was engaged to operate within her operations center which also happened to be located in the foyer of a large house next door to the Dixie White House. The current owners had nobly given up their homes for the accommodation of President Chatham and her family, and their security team.

As the flotilla progressed northward across the Mississippi Sound Estuary, Penny Chatham could see out of the windows from her seat on the floor of the workboat. The seas that Friday morning were calm and she was feeling good about getting to the mainland, which was safe and had lots of people. While Cat Island was an outstanding adventure, mainland Mississippi was predictable and dependable. She smiled as she thought of her promise to take Andrew Reardon and his sisters to get dressed po boys at Lil' Rays in Long Beach. They were going to love it, and dessert would somehow be included in that meal.

While Charles Parks was talking under his breath through the closed-circuit telecommunication system with Director Latady, Speaker Chatham picked up a look of concern on his face. After a short pause, he turned and gave directions, again barely audible to her but no doubt clearly received by his agents. Penny Chatham watched as the agents within the boat took automatic rifles out of the life preserver benches along the inside edge of the boat. Not being knowledgeable about the levels of firearms used for protection of a president, she asked Agent Parks was there going to be trouble.

"Yes, Madam President, I don't think it is anything we can't handle. I want you to know my agents and I are the most equipped and highly trained security force in the world. You will be fully protected Madam President. Secret Service Director Camille Latady is managing this operation from the mainland near the marina and she is always prepared for any and all incidents. In fact, she is usually overprepared!"

"When I ask, I want you to lie flat on the floor of the boat. There will be agents near you, sometimes very near you, but don't become alarmed. This is just business for us, and you will be protected. You have on a Kevlar vest and a presidential level life preserver. Are you afraid?" Speaker Chatham did not respond. "It's ok if you are because it will make you sharper. I want you to know that if you go, I do too. If I go, you might not, so hold me tight, stay with me, Sister."

Penny Chatham was scared, even though she uttered a short laugh about the idea of a presidential level life preserver. Charles Parks was a good salesman and had a sense of humor. However, from a distance of 600 feet out a shrimp lugger was running at full speed toward Workboat One. Marksmen from the other covert fishing boats began to shoot volleys of rounds toward Speaker Chatham's workboat. Shots were peppering the side of the heavy metal boat and shattered the windows that protected bridge and pier building crews from rain and near freezing temperatures in the wintertime. Nearby, a Secret Service Agent took a rifle shot in the chest. She saw him take a deep breath that sounded like a gasp and fall onto her as she crouched on the deck of the boat.

Agent Parks was now very close to Penny Chatham. In fact, his torso was covering her head and chest. She heard him say to Director Latady. "Two agents are down. White Lily is secured on the cabin floor." With all of the gun fire and shouting he was now speaking loudly to the director. "A shrimp boat is progressing toward our vessel at a high rate of speed from the north west, we are unable to slow it down with our fire power." The shrimping vessel was equipped with a powerful diesel engine probably more powerful than would be necessary for pulling bottom nets to catch the wily shrimp at night. Parks continued, "Our engines are malfunctioning, probably hit, and we are about to be dead in the water. White Lily is vulnerable."

Penny Chatham had never experienced or fathomed anything like this. As the well-coordinated and rapidly paced attempt on her life progressed, she said factually, "Agent Parks, the boat is leaking. I am laying in about six inches of water and it is coming in fast."

Parks continued swiftly communicating back to Director Latady and the rest of the agents. "We are now dead in the water. Engines have failed, one is smoking, and we are sinking, fast. White Lily is challenged. Mayday, Mayday, Mayday."

Camille Latady did not want to hear that. She was not going to lose this president like she had lost her two previous clients.

Three of the four other workboats with agents had created a shield along the west side of Speaker Chatham's escape vessel to block the shrimp boat heading toward the presidential Work Boat One. The boat with Pop Chatham and the children in it had pulled back from the other boats engaged in the deadly firefight in order to protect the president's family. The opposition knew Penny Chatham was in the helpless, sinking work boat.

Agents on the four workboats serving as a barrier between the charging shrimp attack lugger and the sinking watercraft with the imminent president were at a loss on how to protect Workboat One which was now taking on water at a rapid rate. However, they continued to fire at the oncoming shrimp lugger that was on a collision course to ram the president's boat which was now half filled with estuary water. Rounds of shots fired by the Presidential Security team continued to be ineffective and deflected by the steel superstructure of the charging shrimp boat as its crew of armed mercenaries continued to fire back.

Now within 200 feet of the ill-fated workboat containing the President and her body guards, the fast-moving floating torpedo would ram the utility grade steel workboats shielding the President and roll over Workboat One which was now close to sinking below the water's surface. Agent Parks now clutching Penny Chatham like a child might hold a teddy bear gave the order, "Abandon ship. Let us move her as far southeast of our location as we possibly can to get away from the collision zone. Move it guys, currently we are not visible behind the shield of the other workboats. Switch to small arms for security." Moving Penny Chatham out of the back end of the workboat and now swimming as best they could, the agents worked her away from the scene of where the collision would likely occur within the next minute or less.

Hearing the disaster with Work Boat One and with no more local options, Director Latady instructed her attack Reaper Drone pilot to be ready to hit the charging steel shrimp boat with a non-explosive weapon. The specialized impact warhead called a modified Hellfighter would carry a deadly impact on a very localized target. It was not an explosive device because the presidential boat was too close to hit the attack shrimper with explosives for fear it would catch fire and its forward motion would continue toward the president.

Drone operator Loy Allen informed Director Latady, "We have a lock on the charging lugger."

Latady said, "Fire the weapon!"

With a powerful whoosh sound from launching the Hellfighter weapon, its steel blades hit the charging boat's wheelhouse shearing everything in its path. The wrenching sound of steel being torn by a stronger force was awful to hear. The hit pushed the big boat down into the water causing it to list heavily from one side to the next as it bobbed up and down in the water. The damaged boat began turning in tight circles. Its forward action was stopped. The sophisticated nonexplosive attack killed its operator, damaged the operating system, and stopped the forward action of the attack lugger.

With the effectiveness of the charging attack boat destroyed, surviving crewmembers from the remaining assault boats waved a makeshift white flag in surrender. Secret service agents instructed them to throw their weapons overboard, take their shirts off, and stand together in a group with their hands up high in the air. Anyone that did not follow those instructions would be immediately shot. Those instructions were given in English, Spanish, and Chinese to insure communication with the unidentified mercenaries. The communication was effective as the remaining gorilla soldiers did what was demanded.

Only one of the evacuation work boats was still under power and it carried the family along with Hannah Thomas, Jake Ingram, and six secret service agents. The outboard motors of the three other workboats shielding the sinking workboat had been hit by rifle fire and disabled. As they eased toward the battle scene, agents in the Chatham family boat were perched along the edge of both sides of the boat with automatic rifles scanning the subdued wreckage for potential trouble.

It was Sarah Jane that first saw her mother in the water surrounded by Secret Service Agents. They were in a tight cluster around Penny Chatham. Following Director Latady's directive, they were not going to lose this client. Hannah Thomas carefully edged the family workboat closer to the floating agents and Penny. "Everybody all right?" asked the River Keeper.

Penny Chatham, who should have been in shock from such an extremely violent attack quickly responded, "We have two injured agents. Can you get these guys up on deck first? How's my family?"

Andrew Reardon shouted back, "We are still here, and we are still floating. I'm thinking we are doing better than you," he said with tears rolling down his cheeks trying to make light of a very dire situation.

The forthcoming president responded, "The water feels fine, it's you who is missing out." Her eager son grinned back but became very serious at the challenging situation he was witnessing.

After lifting the two injured agents up on the boat deck, Agent Charles Parks gave the order to pull the president up to the deck of the family workboat. Penny Chatham, Speaker of the House was dragged over the gunwales and onto the deck. She sighed and hugged Andrew Reardon and Sister Leah. Sarah Jane put her arms around all three of them. Pop stood by, still cautious about his family. Next, agents pulled up Charles Parks and two other agents including the female agent who had jumped into the water to help the president and other exhausted agents out of the water. Once pulled up onto the deck, the lady agent told Sister Leah, "Don't worry, Baby, we are still going to get that luggage. It will probably be tomorrow."

Penny Chatham heard Charles Parks quietly say in his closed-circuit telephone system, "White Lily is in dry hands united with her family and is healthy. Workboat One has sunk. Two agents are injured and will require medical care from gunshot impacts to their vests."

Director Latady responded, "Three-armed, shallow draft Coast Guard boats have left the Long Beach Marina with officers who will help assist in the relocation of White Lily and secure the assault scene." Because of the water depth between Cat Island and the mainland, inflatable Coast Guard craft had been brought in to the marina to help with Pelican Emancipation. "The presidential limousine will be there to transfer her and her family to Scenic Drive where she will be evaluated by Service Medics. Ambulances for injured agents will take them to the local hospital. White Lily is not to be touched by anyone except your immediate agents. Upload the president first into the Beast to take her to the White House. If there are complications, we have alternatives for secure accommodations. You travel with her all the way. Do you read me, Agent Parks?"

"I do, Director Latady. I fully comprehend," replied Secret Service Agent Charles Parks. He knew the situation. Inside of a week's time there will have been three living presidents and two had been assassinated. The third to succeed to the office of president had survived two extreme attempts on her life and it was not yet 12 noon. Failure was not an alternative. The third living president was alive but had probably suffered some injuries and was possibly experiencing shock at some level.

On the way back to the mainland they were accommodated by two of the inflatable Coast Guard boats with armed secret service agents on each. Charles Parks decided to keep the president in the family work boat to limit contact with anyone except her family and five of his agents. Are you comfortable Madam Speaker?" asked the seasoned secret service agent as he sat beside her on one side and another agent sat on the other side. He had regained his composure and was now more formal with his interaction with his client Penny Chatham.

Feeling relieved the firefight was over, and being surrounded by her family who were safe, she felt good. All of her life she was taught to recognize challenges and depend on the skill and intellect of others to help get through tough times and solve those problems. She had done just that today and it worked out. Throughout the morning's trauma, she depended on her government detail and Hannah Thomas… and she had prayed to God for protection.

Today, she was given the chance to continue raising her family and helping others. Appreciation was an inadequate description of her feelings. "I think I'm fine Agent Parks, thanks to you and your team for bravery beyond belief. God was with us the whole way."

"Indeed, He was, Speaker Chatham. It won't be long before we will be at the marina and you will get to go to your Mississippi Gulf Coast White House," replied the agent. He had been assigned to breathe every breath with Penny Chatham and if she took her last breath, so would he. His client was not going to die. She was going to be safe and secure. He was surprised at how good he felt!

Spanish Moss on a Longleaf Pine Tree

CHAPTER 32

Hallowed Words

At the same time Penny Chatham was being extracted from Pelican Roost, FBI agents in Detroit arrested Donald Anniston for conspiring to kill the President of the United States. Two days later, the Bureau Director issued warrants for all of the members of King David's Bible Study for being complicit in the attempted assassination of a President. Charlotte Hall was not arrested as there was no link between her and the direct planning of the assassination of President Penny Chatham. However, she was told to keep the FBI appraised of her whereabouts and was placed on their No-Fly List for all international flights.

The Long Beach Marina was closed except to Secret Service Agents and Department of Marine Resources patrol boats and officers. DMR Marine Patrol boats were located out in the water 200 feet around the perimeter of the marina. Only secret service agents were allowed to be on the marina piers and land. When the Chatham family's boat pulled alongside a pier closest to the mainland, agents climbed out of the boat and up onto the wide pier with Uzi submachine guns held across their chests. They were prepared for any aggression toward the third President of the United States in a week's time. After five minutes for observation and coordination, the President's armored vehicle nicknamed the Beast, pulled up to the pier as close as it could get to the family workboat.

Four agents in dark suits got out and stood around the vehicle, scanning the area. After five more minutes the future President emerged out of the lone work boat that still had power and stepped up on the wood pier to a waiting group of five fresh agents in dry clothes. Agent Charles Parks was by Penny Chatham's side at every step she took to the waiting open door of the armored limousine. She had a black blanket over her head and around her body, and she climbed into the limousine followed by Agent Parks who sat beside her. At no time was she visible or even touched by the mix of new agents hovered around her. As the door closed, six agents stood around the vehicle with automatic weapons in stand-by mode. Charles Parks, still communicating through his Secret Service telecommunication system said, "White Lily is ready to roll."

The lady on the other end who was watching a real time video from a surveillance drone commented "The road is yours, Charles. See you at the White House. Have safe travels." The imminent forty-eighth President of the United States was ready to be transported to an interim White House residence located three miles east of the Long Beach Marina.

Charles Parks then said to his waiting team. "White Lily is ready to go home. The road is ours. There will be no lights or sirens." With that the armored car moved up through the Long Beach Marina Parking lot and up and onto Beach Boulevard. Agents walked and then ran along the edge of the vehicle until it picked up three more black SUV's that carried armed secret service agents and the rest of the Chatham family. Speaker Chatham and her family were ferried to 1123 Scenic Drive. Hannah Thomas and Jake Ingram were also taken in another vehicle to the Scenic Drive home.

The new residence for the president was named the Dixie Whitehouse. It had been called that since the 1940's when it became the summer home for President Woodrow Wilson. Located on the most attractive residential lane on the Mississippi Gulf Coast, Scenic Drive is on a natural bluff thirty-five feet above the Mississippi Sound. The Secret Service procured that home and the two mansions on either side for use by the President of the United States. The large residences on either side of the Dixie White House were temporarily taken as a matter of national security.

Once Secret Service medics checked the health of Penny Chatham and her family, they were shown to a section of the large home where the family could rest and bathe. At the direction of Agent Charles Parks, their clothing was washed, dried, and pressed, and the family redressed in the clothes they put on that morning on Cat Island. Penny Chatham's condition and appearance was not going to be compromised in any way. Agent Parks was on top of that!

After the family thought they were reasonably presentable, Agent Parks informed Jake Ingram that Federal Judge Granville Munro from Biloxi would soon arrive to swear in Penelope Chatham as the forty-eighth President of the United States. It was important she be elevated to that office and all of the powers held by the president. The country was without a leader and that needed to be accomplished as soon as possible. However, it was challenging for the magistrate to get to the Gulf Coast White House. After going through two roadblocks along Beach Boulevard and being detained and interviewed by agents at the gate to the new White House, Judge Munro was finally cleared to go into 1123 Scenic Drive.

When Judge Munro arrived, Jake Ingram thanked the judge for coming and asked him to settle into a wing back chair in the entry hall of the Dixie White House while he conferred with the Speaker. After first consulting with his boss Craig Gill, Jake Ingram knocked on the door of Penny Chatham's bedroom suite and asked Pop who answered, "Is the Speaker ready to receive Federal Judge Munro from Biloxi? He is here to swear in our next President."

Pop checked with his wife and said, "She said now will be as good a time as any." Penny Chatham began making last minute changes to make herself as presentable as possible for her swearing in as the forty-eighth President of the United States. When she was ready, or as respectable as she could be on short notice, Pop told Jake Ingram she was ready to be sworn in.

While in the entry foyer, Agent Parks told the judge the Secret Service's ground rules for swearing in Penny Chatham. "Judge Munro, I am Secret Service Agent Charles Parks and am the personal bodyguard for Penny Chatham. My Director of the Secret Service

Camille Latady, has given me the sole authority to set the ground rules for interaction with Speaker Chatham. Because of the assassinations of President Harrison and Vice President Steve Hardy, there will be no touching of the Speaker and she will not touch anything including a Bible that you might have brought you. We will use our own Bible. After the ceremony, there will be no shaking of hands, patting on the back or even a hug. You and Speaker Chatham will have to keep seven feet away from one another. I am sorry for the stringent ground rules Judge Munro, but we have a serious problem keeping our presidents alive. Do you understand our situation and the ground rules?"

The Federal Judge was in his late seventies and dressed in a dark gray suit with a striped red tie. The white-haired jurist was anxious to meet this new president who had experienced a life-threatening morning to stand before him, and to transmit to her the Presidential Oath of Office so she could become president.

"Agent Parks, I understand your restrictions and will fully abide by your directions," responded Judge Munro. "A Bible has always been used in the swearing in of our presidents, and this Bible came from the White House and has been a part of the inauguration of twelve presidents."

"If you will give us a minute Judge Munro, we will find an alternative Bible," replied Agent Parks. The Judge looked surprised but as a smart man who was fully aware of the national crises the assassinations had caused, he knew Agent Parks held the high cards in this initial challenge. Turning to Jake Ingram, the disheveled looking agent who had been through multiple catastrophes that day and was wearing the same clothes he had on in the sinking workboat said,

"We've gotta find a Bible somewhere in this house. Can you help find one?"

Jake Ingram immediately began looking in bookshelves and on tabletops throughout the first floor of the home. Charles Parks stayed with the Judge. While he was a recognized judge, the assassinations were probably caused by some sort of chemical that had not yet been identified. There was no room for error. To Agent Parks, the judge could have alternative reasons for being here in the safe house of the future President of the United States.

After searching all of the obvious locations a Bible might have been placed, staff member Jake Ingram went into the kitchen as a last resort. Amid the three shelves of cookbooks, there was an old King James Bible, with a cover that was torn and verses explained with randomly located notes from having been taken to an unlimited number of church Bible studies. Bursting through the large swinging door from the kitchen with the fragile Bible held high in his hand, the coast guard fellow said, "Here I am to save the day!" He regretted saying something so informal as quoting Mighty Mouse from his cartoon addiction days as a child in such an important situation where his boss was about to become the President of the United States!

"Good Job, Jake," replied the Secret Service Agent who was all business, and was the one individual who was charged with the safety of the diminutive lady politician from Mississippi.

Agent Charles Parks said, "Ok, judge, are you ready?" As if on cue, four additional agents in pressed dark suits walked into the spacious living room along with Penny Chatham's Chief of Staff Craig Gill who had flown in from Washington. The situation was becoming formal looking. The agents who had already been briefed by Charles Parks stood on either side of where the Speaker of the House of Representatives would stand. Judge Munro was now facing a line of five-armed Secret Service Agents who were a foot apart from one another. In a few minutes, the next President of the United States would be standing in their midst.

Secret Service Director Camille Latady was enjoying the approaching historical event. Video cameras had been set up in three locations in the spacious living room to provide live feed of this important event. The United States had been without a conscious and cognizant leader for two days. It was apparent Director Latady was calling the shots for this event. For the impending president's security Secret Service Director Camille Latady and her staff were checking on conditions from her aerial surveillance drone. Before conditions in the area around the Dixie White House had been cleared, she asked all roadblock check points to communicate their conditions. Finally, the agents on the ground in the vicinity of the house and on the roof of the old home gave the "all clear" to Camille Latady.

She communicated to Agent Parks, "We are a go, Agent Parks."

The seasoned bodyguard said to Jake Ingram who was standing behind and to the side of Judge Munro, "Jake, we are ready for House Speaker Penny Chatham and her family."

Jake, proudly walked to the side door of the spacious living room, knocked gently and said, "Speaker Chatham, are you ready for the swearing-in ceremony?"

Pop opened the door and said, "Ok, Jake, we will be just a minute. Sister Leah wanted her hair pulled back and pinned on the side instead of in a ponytail."

Jake heard her call from the bathroom, "Daddy! A ponytail is a little too casual for momma's swearing in ceremony! We need to up the dressiness a bit especially since all we have to wear are the clothes we had on in the boat ride."

As the chaos was dying down in the presidential chambers, Jake Ingram returned to his assigned position for the ceremony. Momentarily, Penny Chatham walked through the seven-and-a-half-foot tall wooden door. She was regal looking with her hair pulled back and pinned on either side of her head. Her swearing in outfit was a pair of blue jeans and a long-sleeved blue shirt with pelican's printed on it. It was not regal looking in any way, but it was clean and ironed, and very regional looking. As she approached the awaiting judge, three of the agents stepped to the side and Agent Parks made room for his client. Penny Chatham stood directly across and facing the judge, seven feet away, while Pop, Sarah Jane, Andrew Reardon, and Sister Leah stood five feet behind her as was directed by one of the agents. Duct Tape was even put on the shiny hardwood floors to mark the social distance required between the Judge and the New President.

A small, waist high Empire style round table was between the federal judge and Speaker Penny Chatham to whom he would give the oath of office. The round table had a water stain ring on its top, probably from a decorative pot from the past. In its place sat the well-used King James version of the Holy Bible. Penny, in no hurry to get to the oath of office and become the President of the United

States, took the Bible in her hands and opened the inside of the cover page to see to whom it belonged and how old it was. A note made from a fountain pen from a long-ago past mom said, "To my little boy whom I love very much. May you grow in the ways of the Lord and provide goodness and kindness to all who surround you." The inscription was dated January 28, 1953." Penny Chatham loved the dedication so much she turned, smiled, and read it to her family and Agent Parks.

That dedication fit her perfectly. She had worked her whole life to provide good for her family and friends, and for the Mississippians and Louisianians with whom she worked. She hoped her own children would do the same. After a pause, where she and the family hugged and kissed, and finally regained their composure from all of their experiences this past week, the agent in charge smiled confidently to Judge Munro and nodded for him to begin the simple but powerful ceremony.

"Penny Chatham, when you put your hand on the Holy Bible, I will administer the oath of office for the Presidency of the United States." Penny Chatham looked carefully at the Judge who looked to be in his seventies. He was a man who was appointed by a previous president somewhere in the past to provide unbiased decisions that contributed to the health and security of the country. Looking calmly but intensely at the slightly bedraggled looking bright eyed and proud thirty-seven-year-old lady from south Mississippi, he said, "Are you ready, Speaker Chatham?"

"Yes," she boldly replied.

Judge Munro began, "Repeat after me."

Speaker of the House Penny Chatham bravely and profoundly repeated Judge Munro's hallowed words for becoming President of the United States of America,

"I do solemnly swear, that I will faithfully execute the Office of President of the United States, and will to the best of my ability, preserve, protect and defend the Constitution of the United States, SO HELP ME GOD."

"Congratulations, Madam President", Judge Munro said, smiling at the diminutive lady from Mississippi.

The new president just smiled, really big, at the Judge and then turned and hugged Pop, Sarah Jane, Andrew Reardon, and Sister Leah for a long time. She then turned to Craig Gill and Jake Ingram and hugged each of them in a more reserved manner, saying, "Ok, men, we've got our work cut out for us." The staff members of the former Speaker of the House of Representatives just smiled as they stood in the presence of the President of the United States.

On that afternoon after Penny Chatham was sworn in as the forty-eighth President of the United States, she and the family were invited by Agent Charles Parks and Secret Service Director Camille Latady to come out on the front porch of the Dixie White House in Long Beach Mississippi joined along with her Chief of Staff Craig Gill and Jake Ingram. They quietly looked over the porch railing to the now choppy waters of the Mississippi Sound. Spanish Moss in the old live oaks shading the home was in constant motion rocking back and forth from the ocean breeze. Change was coming as a Category One tropical storm out in the Gulf of Mexico was expected to make landfall along the coast the following day.

As a present from her military Joint Chiefs of Staff, a fly over out in the Mississippi Sound was a stunning salute to the new President and her family. Three jets flew from Keesler Air Force Base east of Long Beach and when they were in the vicinity of the Dixie White House flying westward, they flew the cross formation where aircraft on either side peeled off to the side and the center jet flew upward emitting red. white, and blue exhaust. The family and guests clapped. Andrew Reardon shouted, "I think you were right Sister Leah; this new job is going to be fun!"

Like the weather, change was always occurring. As president, Penny Chatham would lead the implementation of a new national ethic for respecting the environment and living with its natural cycles.

She and her family would make the Mississippi Gulf Coast their home until the cause of deaths of her friends and fellow politicians Jim Harrison and Steve Hardy had been solved and her security was guaranteed. That would take months.

Penny Chatham would continue taking adventurous trips with her family. Sister Leah's forecast was right, the job would be good for her mom and family. While Andrew Reardon did not get to go to Lil' Rays for dressed po-boys and a special flaming desert at Darwells the evening of the day they left Cat Island, they did enjoy lunch at those Mississippi coast institutions a week later.

Throughout her tenure as President, Penny Chatham never forgot the dedication in the old Bible found in the kitchen among old reliable cookbooks and used for her swearing in ceremony. The instructions of the long-ago mom became her credo as President, "To my little boy whom I love very much. May you grow in the ways of the Lord and provide goodness and kindness to all who surround you. January 28, 1953." She would share that with her family and made a point to continue providing goodness and kindness to all. At the conclusion of her speeches, she would always conclude with "May God Bless you and the good people of the United States of America."

The End